Injured Men

Injured Men

Trauma, Healing, and the Masculine Self

IRA BRENNER, M.D.

JASON ARONSON
Lanham • Boulder • New York • Toronto • Plymouth, UK

Published in the United States of America
by Jason Aronson
An imprint of Rowman & Littlefield Publishers, Inc.

A wholly owned subsidiary of
The Rowman & Littlefield Publishing Group, Inc.
4501 Forbes Boulevard, Suite 200, Lanham, Maryland 20706
www.rowmanlittlefield.com

Estover Road
Plymouth PL6 7PY
United Kingdom

British Library Cataloguing in Publication Information Available

Library of Congress Cataloging-in-Publication Data

Brenner, Ira, 1950-
  Injured men : trauma, healing, and the masculine self / Ira Brenner.
    p. ; cm.
  Includes bibliographical references and index.
  ISBN 978-0-7657-0572-3 (cloth : alk. paper) -- ISBN 978-0-7657-0692-8
(electronic)
  1. Psychic trauma--Case studies. 2. Men--Mental health--Case studies. 3.
Dissociative disorders--Case studies. I. Title.
  [DNLM: 1. Stress Disorders, Post-Traumatic--psychology--Case Reports. 2.
Dissociative Disorders--psychology--Case Reports. 3. Men--psychology--Case
Reports. WM 170 B838i 2009]
  RC552.T7B74 2009
  616.85'21--dc22   2009029264

Printed in the United States of America

♾™ The paper used in this publication meets the minimum requirements of
American National Standard for Information Sciences—Permanence of Paper for
Printed Library Materials, ANSI/NISO Z39.48-1992.

In memory of
Leo Madow, M.D.,
a healer of injured men

Contents

Acknowledgments

This book could not have come to fruition without the support of the staff of Jason Aronson Publishers, especially Julie Kirsch and Jessica Bradfield. In addition, Deborah Szumachowski has worked valiantly to type and organize this manuscript. Many friends and colleagues need to be thanked also, especially George Awad (deceased), Harold Blum, James Chandler, Helen Epstein, Marc Lipschutz, Dominic Mazza, Mike Mccarthy, Henri Parens, Nadia Ramzy, Anita Schmukler, J. Anderson Thomson, and Stuart Twemlow, who were always available to read my papers. My patients, however, remain my most important teachers. An artist has given permission for use of the cover image, and a courageous Vietnam veteran was willing to offer his interview. And my wife, Roberta Brenner, has been there for me through it all. . . .

Introduction

Two psychoanalysts walk into a bar (this is not a joke). Actually, many years ago, a psychoanalytic colleague and I were having a drink late one night during the meetings of the American Psychoanalytic Association. It was one of those rare, unplanned experiences during a conference where something remarkable occurred that was not fully appreciated at the time. This rather tight-lipped, classically trained, older analyst let his hair down a bit and revealed a story to me about his own analysis. I listened with rapt attention, eager to learn the secrets of my new profession. I was a very impressionable young candidate a the time, gawking in awe at the living legends of psychoanalysis, like Charles Brenner, Jacob Arlow, and Heinz Kohut, walking right by me on the way to this lecture or that panel discussion. I had to restrain myself from rushing up to them and asking them to sign my program like a delirious fan begging a movie star to sign an autograph book, which was not befitting the decorum that I wanted to maintain. Sitting in the smoke-filled, "safari" atmosphere of Sir Harry's Bar at the Waldorf Astoria, my colleague then told me that when he first started his analysis many years before that, his analyst asked him what he had hoped for. Taken aback by such a direct inquiry, my friend mumbled something about wanting to become a psychoanalyst himself, to perhaps write a paper or two, maybe even teach at the Psychoanalytic Institute, someday have a family, put on a few pounds and live long enough to have gray hair. His training analyst, also a man and one who was described as occasionally waxing philosophical, perhaps a bit too active for my rather reticent colleague, on this occasion simply said, "So, you want to become a man. . . ."

In that moment, both of these men implicitly understood each other and the profound, developmental importance of their joint venture (Loewald, 1960). Taken aback by the perceptiveness of his analyst, my colleague was surprised at the clarity of this interpretation which then set the tone for his analytic journey. Indeed, he spent the rest of his analysis trying to figure out what it meant to him to become a man, to become a certain kind of man, and why he did not feel like one at the time.

We know that there are many different "kinds" of men and that the revival of interest in male psychology has encouraged psychoanalytic writers to further elaborate the nuances and complexities of masculinity. Recent publications, for example, "endeavor to unravel" (Diamond, 2006) the "riddles" (Fogel, 2006; Brady, 2006) of the "masculinities" (Person, 2006) which may sometimes be seen as a "masquerade" (Moss, 2006). Indeed, the various expressions of the English language connote the myriad ways we think of men: There are men with a "fragile male ego" or those kindler, gentler men who were called "men of the 1990s." Then there are those who are "manly" or "he-men" in contrast to Governor Schwarzenegger's "girly man" and, of course, there is the "man's man" who is not to be confused with the "ladies man." The former might be considered a "man among men" and might even aspire to become the "man of the year." But how far will he get if he "manhandles" people, although by speaking "man to man," he may get away with a lot of it. We know that a "gentleman" may not behave that way although as a "young man" he may have been a little rough around the edges. On the other hand, there may be allowances made for an "old man" as long as he is not a "dirty old man." So, we see that a "manchild" has a lot of possibilities and uncertainties waiting for him along the way to "manhood." After all, if he wants to "be a man," does he have to "take it like a man" and "die like a man"? Do crime, jail, violence, and death have to be the "mark of a man" in certain cultures?

Cultural and religious factors need to be emphasized here also. For example, the hardships and the putative undesirability of being a woman were a subliminal message of my own religious indoctrination when I was initiated into manhood during the Jewish rite of passage known as the Bar Mitzvah, or son of the commandments. At that time, I became familiar with the three-time-a-day prayer services. One of the most puzzling prayers was in the morning service where men recited one prayer while women recited another. As the tradition of keeping things separate is a pervasive ritual in Judaism, the division of men from women is such a well-known example that at first it did not seem totally strange. Indeed, the theme of making things separate is such a persistent theme that it may have influenced Freud's thinking about psychological defenses (Brenner, 2000). The men's prayer translated into "Blessed art Thou, oh Lord our God, king of the Universe, who has not made me a woman." The women's version was "Blessed art Thou, oh Lord our God, King of the Universe, who has made me according to Thy will." So, it appeared that men were to be grateful not to be women because women were created to serve a purpose. I recall feeling very relieved when I first learned of this prayer but was totally bewildered.

During my adolescent growth spurt, I must have had a mental growth spurt also, because I began to question everything. As a result, my period of piety was rather short-lived as I could not get satisfactory answers from my teachers and elders whose inconsistencies or invoking articles of faith when they were stymied fueled my growing doubts about the existence of a deity and "His will." Such questioning—not at all rare during this time of life—is much more eloquently described by Hitchens in his account of his own disillusionment in childhood (Hitchens, 2007). While I do not recall asking specifically about the gender-related prayers, I was already quite aware of the special privileges that men had in traditional Jewish religious hierarchy. For example, only they could be called up to read the sacred scrolls of the Torah and only they could be counted when the requisite quorum of ten were needed before a prayer service could proceed and only they had a special bond with the King of the Universe through the ritual circumcision performed at eight days of age. While much has been written in the analytic literature about the symbolic castration and submission to the "father" through this custom (Freud, 1910, 1913b, 1939), that was not my concern—at least consciously—at the time.[1] Rather, I wondered in some inchoate way back then why we were supposed to give thanks to the almighty, not for what we were but for what we were not.

It seemed like we were supposed to feel relief and gratitude for not having to endure what women do rather than take pride in our manhood. At the time, I was not even dimly aware of the publication of Greenson's analytically secular version of this prayer, formulated by his dis-identification with the mother hypothesis in the development of male identity (Greenson, 1968), which roughly coincided in time with the onset of my own manhood. I suspect I kept such musings to myself for a variety of reasons, not the least of which being that I was unsure I could even articulate it well enough for an inquiry to another and doubted that I could trust any spokesperson about God's will. I suspect an element of embarrassment over the new changes in my body also contributed to my silent meditation on such highly sexually charged, allegedly spiritual, issues.

In recent years, I decided to bring up this issue with a number of learned men and, once again, have been disappointed in the answers. This time, however, I listened to them quite differently and felt quite amused to hear from one expert that one should not take such translations so literally, that there are more contemporary, politically correct versions, etc., etc. The bottom line, however, is that the Jewish God still wants us to sing high praises for the anatomical differences between the sexes and extol the masculine self—but only after his foreskin is cut off.

For me, writing this book *Injured Men* has been a very personal and important experience. My feminine side "conceived" of this idea years before I started putting it together, when I realized that most of the volumes on trauma relied on clinical material almost exclusively about women. Despite the fact that posttraumatic stress disorder is thought to be twice as prevalent in females, the written clinical material has been overrepresented by women cases. In clinical conferences, I had the same observation. In, for example, the discussion group that I chair with Dori Laub at the annual winter meetings of the American Psychoanalytic Association which is devoted to studying the effects of the Holocaust on survivors and their families has had a ratio of female to male cases of about 9 to 1. I have been collecting this data for almost thirty years. My experience with the discussion group on dissociative disorders which I cochair with Richard Kluft is similar.

There was another factor involved. I noticed a gradual shift in my practice in recent years to working with more and more men, many of whom were quite successful in the traditional sense of the word, that is, in the "man's world" but inwardly were in enormous pain. The private suffering of the captain of industry, the high-powered lawyer, the prominent doctor, the crusading politician, or the charismatic religious leader should not surprise us anymore. Even the rough and tough cowboy, that quintessentially American icon of virility, has taken a terrible hit as seen in two recent films, *Brokeback Mountain* and the satire, *Thank You for Not Smoking*. In the former, an anguished love affair between two cowboys shattered the stereotype of the "red-blooded American man." In the latter, the actor who posed for the classic photograph of the "Marlboro Man," that macho outdoorsman with a cigarette permanently implanted between his lips, was mockingly portrayed as a terminally ill lung cancer patient who would threaten the whole tobacco industry if the truth about his health were to be revealed to the public.

Injured Men is a unique casebook of clinical material pertaining to men who have sustained trauma. It is not intended to be a gender studies book per se but rather an effort to remind practitioners to consider that men too can be victims or survivors of trauma and their presentations may be obscured by a masculine overlay. The chapters stand on their own as clinical studies and the reader will not get a sense that I am trying to promulgate a particular theory of masculinity. The following chapters describe manifestations of such phenomena as physical and sexual abuse, unresolved grief, genocidal persecution, intergenerational transmission of trauma and, of course, combat. With a perspective on dissociation and dissociative disorders, I begin by offering a traumatic pathway to the development of a masculine self in those with female bodies. In dealing with the long-term effects of trauma, I advocate a pluralistic approach which is illustrated in the final chapter of this volume.

NOTES

1. The use of humor to mitigate the underlying cultural anxiety over the circumcision, or "Brit Milah," can be gauged by the extent to which such jokes become part of the repertoire of comedians who invoke Jewish themes. Robin Williams, for example, in the movie *Mrs. Doubtfire* digressed for a moment in one of his characteristic tirades and blurts out, "Never buy gribinis from a moyel. It's so chewy!" Gribinis is a term for a very tasty but unhealthy thick spread made with onions, seasoning, chicken fat, and chicken skin. Since the moyel is one who performs the circumcision and removes the infant's foreskin, the joke is that a moyel would make his gribinis with foreskins, not chicken skins. Therefore, the joke on a deeper level also alludes to the taboo over cannibalism.

1

On the Need to Be a Man

While we certainly know that trauma occurs in men, it may not be evident at first or even in our thinking when we evaluate a new patient. The cultural and psychological factors which require men to be "strong" may tend to obscure the contribution of psychic trauma to their clinical picture. They may minimize, deny, or otherwise downplay their overwhelming life events. For example, a man who was the first to discover the blood-spattered remains of a relative who had killed himself with a shotgun just "didn't think" to tell his therapist about it until years later when it was discovered he was having disabling anniversary reactions each year during the same month when the gruesome remains were discovered. The patient became extremely depressed, phobic, agitated, and had nightmares of this horrific scene. It therefore seemed like a good idea to offer a text illustrating a variety of traumatic situations from their perspective.

Where women are included in this volume, it is to offer an exploration of their profound gender identity conflicts to further an understanding of the trauma-based pathway to masculinity. Stoller's (1973a) extremely detailed case report of "female masculinity" is the classic model of this approach. With this idea in mind, it therefore might not seem so odd to you that I begin by describing a rather striking phenomenon seen in a subgroup of severely traumatized females, that is, they "become" men in certain states of mind. It therefore follows that if we could learn more about how a woman might become a man, then maybe more could be better understood about how a man could become a man. The creation of such masculine selves in women supports the contention that at least some of the traits of masculinity that we think of in stereotypical terms are borne of trauma.

1

Yet, as with so much related to the human condition, things are quite complex, multiply determined, and rely on a unique and individual, mutual interaction between development, experience and internal, genetic factors. As Freud pointed out with his concept of the complemental series (Freud, 1905, 1916b), heredity may play a very significant role in some cases more than others. Yet, despite the obvious anatomical differences between males and females, the differential effects of estrogen versus testosterone on both the brain and the body, genetic influences as well as the cultural differences and norms for masculinity, there is little documented difference in behavior and attachment between baby boys and baby girls. Utter helplessness and dependency upon the usually female caregiver is universal so it appears that by using this parameter we begin life more similar than different. Nevertheless, psychoanalytic thinking has been replete with theories of gender, such as primary masculinity and universal bisexuality (Freud, 1905b, 1925), parallel lines of gender development (Horney, 1924, 1926, 1932; Jones, 1927, 1933) and primary femininity (Stoller, 1968, 1976).

Despite differences in underlying theories, many contemporary writers do agree that exquisite narcissistic vulnerability and susceptibility to humiliation in males may lead them to murderous violence in order to purge themselves of such intolerable emotions. The role of destructive aggression in maintaining the cohesion of masculine identity or the masculine self is a question that has implications that go way beyond the consulting room, as the management and prevention of violence is a worldwide social challenge (Twemlow, 1995, 2000, 2003). As John Munder Ross describes it, "Men . . . struggle against two dangers—the danger of succumbing to their feminine nature and the danger of affirming their masculine integrity through repeated acts of aggression" (Ross, 1992, pp. 335–336). It therefore behooves us to further our understanding about the nuances, ambiguities, and paradoxes of masculinity.

In a world of fundamentalist thinking, everything is either black or white. There is only right or wrong, good or bad, day or night, left-handed or right-handed, hot or cold, strong or weak, for or against, liberals or conservatives, dead or alive, love or hate, guilty or innocent, man or woman, and boy or girl. There is no gray, no extenuating circumstances, no mixed blessings, no twilight, no ambidexterity, no lukewarm, no medium, no moderate, no life support, no ambivalence, no transgender, and no tomboys. In this world of certainty, everyone confidently checks off "M" or "F" in the appropriate box on the job application form and uses the men's room or ladies' room without a moment's hesitation or doubt. In the real world, as we know, however, things are different. Although they officially comprise less than 1 percent of the U.S. population, according to the National Center for Transgender Equality (Rosenberg, 2007), those with conflicts over their genital anatomy versus their gender identity are becoming more visible and vocal about their plight.

As though the study of human embryology confirms the Freudian notion of the inherent bisexuality in all of us, the fetus is equipped with the rudimentary structures to form both the male and the female reproductive systems. If the Wolffian Ducts prevail under the influence of the Y chromosome, the testes develop and testosterone triumphs over estrogen. If the X chromosome wins out, the Mullerian Ducts develop into the female organs and the ovaries estrogenize both the body and the brain. Even if genetic glitches do not occur resulting in "ambiguous genitalia," such as clitoral hypertrophy in the adrenogenital syndrome or cryptoorchidism and hypospadias, the embryological vestiges of our bisexual origins can be identified in such obscure structures as the man's prostatic utricle, also known as the vagina masculini. As more and more becomes known about the mutual influences of our myriad psychological, sociological, and cultural factors on our constitutional endowments, gender identity is seen by many as overlapping perhaps or perhaps a "soft assembly" (Harris, 2005). Extreme examples of this position can be seen in such "modern" parents who let their young children direct their preferred gender identity. For example, a kindergarten-aged boy in Northern California, Jonah Rose, convinced his parents he should live as a girl. His mother bought him his first dress at age four and they sent him to a private school where he could dress like a girl, use the girl's bathroom, and hide his penis. Lamenting the situation, the father said: "We wrung our hands about this every night . . . she has been pretty adamant from the get-go: 'I'm a girl'" (Rosenberg, 2007, p. 54).

In another case, a young girl demanded to wear boy's clothing as soon as she could use words. At age two and a half, she reportedly overheard her parents referring to "her" and declared: "No—I'm a him. You need to call me him." This young girl maintained "his" maleness and changed his name while she was only in preschool. Then with the help of a sympathetic psychotherapist, the parents allowed their child to guide them and support their now preadolescent child to live as a boy. Feeling assured in their decision, the mother, Colleen Vincente stated: "The most important thing is to realize this is who your child is" (Rosenberg, 2007, p. 57). Furthermore, some physicians reportedly may forestall puberty through hormone manipulation in an effort to support the child's avowed wish for a different gender.

Although sex reassignment surgery is rather rare in the United States, reportedly between 1,000 and 2,000 cases per year according to the National Center for Transgender Equality, such a solution is growing despite the cost, the medical risks, and the uncertain results especially in female-to-male surgery. As a result, less complete transitions involving hormones and mastectomies without penis construction are more popular. Smith College, an institution of higher learning instrumental in spawning the feminist movement several decades ago, is once again in the vanguard of this latest cycle of the sexual revolution, providing a nurturing environment for college-age "transmen." Out of respect to the growing number of anatomically female transgender students enrolled there, gender-specific pronouns have been deleted from the student government constitution. Such a powerful political statement lends legitimacy and support to those struggling with such fundamental issues who do not think that working toward accepting their biological givens is the ultimate desirable psychological goal. This position would be perhaps the polar opposite of those who maintain that a blurring of the gender and a denial of the anatomical difference between the sexes is at the heart of perversion (McDougall, 1972; Chassaguet-Smirgel, 1974, 1978, 1981). Even if one takes a more "open-minded" approach to the possibility and importance of sexual variations, the problem would argue for a developmentally-informed psychodynamic approach, not simply a hormonal, surgical, or political solution. And, especially where there is an underlying history of early trauma, the accompanying mental torture may be associated with life-threatening symptoms which may warrant extensive and, at times, heroic, psychotherapeutic treatment.

In my work with adults who have been profoundly exploited and misused when they were children, I have had the opportunity to treat a number of them intensively over time. Within this group, the challenge of psychological and, for some, actual physical survival has resulted in a particular adaptation reflected in their personality development. In these patients, the persistence of altered states of consciousness from their earliest years appears to be a basic form of warding off anxiety which is in contrast to the more typical development of repression or splitting and their associated defensive operations (Brenner, 1994, 2001, 2004a). Disturbances in the development of self-constancy are manifested by the presence of seemingly separate selves who at times appear to have the power to take over executive control of the body. These selves may not at first "know" about the existence of the "others" or they may experience intensive struggles over ownership of the body. Seemingly separate autobiographies, memories, funds of knowledge, ego functions, psychophysiological responses and sexual developmental pathways may be present also. This condition, which has been known by many names and will be described in detail in chapter 2, is currently known as dissociative identity disorder (DID), or lower level dissociative character (Brenner, 1994, 2001, 2004a). It offers a rare source of clinical data on the genesis of the "masculine self" or what the DID specialists call "male alters."

It is widely observed by such therapists who see many of these patients that anatomic females often have at least one male alter and that, conversely, anatomic males frequently have at least one female alter. In the former situation, it is often ascertained that the male personification serves

as a "protector" and/or as a "punisher" often based on some internalization of the male/paternal perpetrator, i.e., a form of identification with
the aggressor. Since in-depth psychoanalytic exploration is so rare with
this group, it was not recognized until relatively recently that the presence
of these male selves may also represent a dissociated transsexual conflict
which, in fact, may be a central, underlying dynamic in some of these
individuals (Brenner, 1996a). While the study of transsexuals—currently
known as transgendered people—has been considered in the analytic
literature (Stoller, 1968, 1973a; Volkan, 1979, 2004) and thought to reflect their mothers' wish for a phallus actualized in them, the difficulty
in working with this population analytically may account for the relative
paucity of such publications in comparison to other sexualities, such as
transvestitism, fetishism, bisexuality, homosexuality, and heterosexuality.
Drawing controversial conclusions about normative development of gender
identity from work with transsexuals, Stoller posited the theory of primary
femininity from his research (Stoller, 1976). While generally not accepted,
I find myself in need of carefully reexamining this provocative assertion in
light of my own experience working with dissociated transsexualism. In my
experience, such patients enacted, reported, recalled, and/or reconstructed
memories of severe, chronic, sadistic, incestuous, sexual abuse with a parent
that started in early childhood and persisted into adolescence or adulthood.
The nature of the transference, the emergence of material in dreams, the
quality of their sexual relationships, and the propensity for revictimization
was extremely convincing and consistent with such a history of profound
traumatization. Although three cases were victims of paternal incest, one
women's own mother was the perpetrator, and this relationship continued
into the early years of treatment during which Mary's alcoholism was so
severe that just staying alive was the main goal (see chapter 2). Becoming a
woman and staying a woman was incompatible with their life-threatening
circumstances in these four cases. As Mary will be described in detail in the
next chapter, I will briefly discuss the other three cases here.

CASE 1

In Barbara's case (Brenner, 2001), the recognition and addressing of the
existence of a dissociated, sadistic, masculine self was an extremely dangerous and central part of the treatment. The "Admiral," as he was known
to the other selves who cowered in fear of him, would become physically
violent to staff on the inpatient unit as "he" seemed to be in a chronic state
of intense narcissistic rage. Over a period of many months as I got to know
the patient better in this state of mind, it became clear that "he" was convinced that "he" was a freak of nature, being an adult man in the body of

a female. Profound humiliation, vulnerability, despair, and suspiciousness of paranoid proportions would emerge from this otherwise pleasant and depressive woman. She was totally horrified over discovering self-inflicted wounds perpetrated upon herself during amnestic states and lived in fear that she would kill herself without even knowing it. On one occasion, she had almost bled to death after trying to amputate her breasts in an effort to remove female characteristics from the body. On another occasion, she stabbed herself in the abdomen in a "procedure" to try to remove possible products of conception after reviving the memory of incest with her father. He was a brutally sadistic man who had apparently been sodomized himself as a child and had confided as much to the patient in a moment of "tenderness" when she was much younger. The incestuous relationship continued into the early years of her married life and the Admiral's own biography was remarkably similar to the father's, suggesting an element of intergenerational transmission of trauma in her overidentification with the father in this dissociated masculine self. As a reflection of the patient's deep conflict over the incestuous relationship, the patient "became" a man, as it were, through the creation of the Admiral personification who was organized around an identification with the aggressor; sadomasochistic sexuality associated with intense arousal related to cruelty; homosexual panic, i.e., penetration anxiety; and an impulsive violence in response to humiliation (Brenner, 2001).

CASE 2

Cindy (Brenner, 2004a) was a prim and proper executive who never left her home unless she was impeccably dressed with matching shoes and stylish jewelry to accent her perfectly coordinated outfits. It was quite evident from the first meeting that she paid very much attention to her appearance and was the epitome of being feminine. Working overtime to support her alcoholic, downtrodden family of origin, she was by far the most successful of the lot who seemed to expect that she would take care of all of them. She was an intensely private person with few friends and a brief marriage which ended for uncertain reasons, most likely because she was afraid that her secret would be discovered. Her presenting depressive symptoms were associated with a peculiar type of depersonalization to the point where when she received a top honor at work she insisted that not only did she not deserve it but it was not even she herself who had even done the work. As she deteriorated despite intense psychotherapy and vigorous pharmacological treatment, the threat of suicidality prompted a hospitalization where "switching" in and out of altered states with distinctly different affect and ways of relating to others were noted. When she reconstituted and continued in outpatient treatment four times a week, she then became plagued by a series of disturbing dreams where a clown transformed into a menacing figure in one and in another she observed a young girl standing next to her naked, drunken uncle lying on a mattress on the floor in a dingy room pulling the young girl toward him. Overwhelming fears of having been sexually violated as a child flooded her with guilt and confusion. Over time as the delineation of her internal world became clear, she described periods of unaccountable time where she would find herself in various hotels in different towns. Following an enactment in the transference where she became terrified and switched to a younger female self, a rageful and threatening masculine self named Jack essentially introduced himself in the next session. Jack, replete with black leather jacket, boots, and a baseball cap to conceal Cindy's full head of hair, would swagger around and spoke in a deep, gravelly voice. It was rather eerie to be in the patient's presence in this state. Being her deepest secret and kept most separate from Cindy's consciousness, she had virtually total amnesia during Jack's emergences and would desperately look for clues in her surroundings to piece together what might have happened during her absences. She eventually missed a number of sessions during such fugue states and would "come to" somewhere during the hour and call in terror, being totally lost, hung over, and often in physical pain. Trying to communicate about her problems in this dissociated way, she unconsciously asked for help to reconstruct these dissociated states. It was ultimately possible with her help and with Jack's reluctant participation to learn that, like the Admiral in Case 1, he was convinced that he was a man trapped in the body of a woman. This mistake of nature caused him endless humiliation in the presence of biological men. While trying to find out how to medically correct this problem, Jack would drink heavily in nightclubs and bars in various towns, invariably coming to the aid of a woman who was being sexually pressured by another patron of the bar. Jack would then step in and halt the man's unwanted advances toward the vulnerable woman which would quickly escalate to a physical confrontation. Then the two "men" would typically "step outside" to fight and Jack would get beaten up rather badly, often with bruises and sometimes with fractured ribs, from being repeatedly kicked on the ground. Jack would then retreat to a cheap hotel nearby, sleep off the hangover and Cindy would wake up lost and in a panic.

CASE 3

Hannah (Brenner, 1996a) was referred for pharmacological management of what was thought to be an uncomplicated, recurrent depression. However, her hungry, wide-eyed, childlike demeanor seemed to cry out for much more and she ambivalently engaged in a psychotherapeutic process which evolved over time into five-time-a-week analytic therapy. While she hinted at a history of sexual abuse early on, its persistence into the early years of her marriage, as in Case 1, was a most shameful and deeply defended secret which did not emerge until years later. Hannah dissembled psychologically as treatment progressed and she came to believe that her home was haunted since many items disappeared or were mysteriously moved around. During this time she made a parapraxis and referred to herself as "we" which, when brought to her attention, made her feel embarrassed and "caught."

Self-destructive behavior and suicidality soon followed necessitating a rehospitalization. While this pattern was not new, she rarely saw her previous psychiatrist more than once a month so her periods of amnesia and fluctuating self-states were kept from clinical scrutiny. In the hospital she regressed quickly, manifesting infantile behavior such as thumb sucking, rocking, and clinging to stuffed animals. Then she would quickly revert back to her adult self and act like nothing had happened. An extremely sexually provocative and self-destructive adolescent self emerged who recalled and eventually described extremely cruel self-abuse first by her stepfather and then from many others.

In the midst of her regression from extended hospitalization, she reported an auditory hallucination of a man's voice which she was told by another self belonged to "Marshall." Marshall, like the Admiral in Case 1 and Jack in Case 2, was in a perpetual rage ostensibly because he too believed he was trapped in the body of a woman. "He" was so potentially dangerous to male staff that special precautions needed to be taken when "he" was in control of the body. Suspiciousness to the point of paranoia and terrifying to those in the patient's inner and outer world, an autohypnotic jail was eventually created by Hannah and her inside helpers in order to contain Marshall. At first it took all of the patient's psychic energy, considerable doses of medication and external limit setting to keep everyone safe. Despite these efforts, violence did ensue occasionally and the patient severed an artery in a very serious suicide attempt. Marshall's determination to never be victimized again along with his exquisite sense of vulnerability seemed to encapsulate the patient's deepest fears and her worst memories of repeated gang rapes. In the patient's Marshall state of mind, the only solution was to become the one with the penis, avenge his previous defeats, and correct a grievous error made in being born with a female body.

CONCLUSION

In these three brief vignettes, it appeared that the psychological creation of a masculine self appeared to be in response to overwhelming, repeated, and sadistic violation of the young girl's body. In a multiply determined and complex psychic structure which will be described in more detail in chapter 2, such a masculine self embodied a deeply dissociated transsexual conflict. The Admiral, Jack, and Marshall selves experienced profound mortification and humiliation and narcissistic rage. Deep mistrust and projective tendencies of paranoid proportions were associated with a quasi-delusional belief that "they" were the victims of a cruel mistake at birth in that they were men helplessly trapped in the body of women. In addition to identification with the aggressor, fears of being raped were experienced by "them" as a homosexual threat and the risk of violence was ever present. In addition, an element of being a chivalrous protector of victimized women was also incorporated into Jack's identity.

A deep need to obliterate evidence of the female body through self-mutilation could mask the patient's underlying suicidal tendencies as seen in Barbara's nearly successful self-performed mastectomy. Fear and hatred of "real men," penis envy of legendary intensity, sadomasochistic arousal, identification with the aggressor, and impotent rage, both inwardly and outwardly directed, characterized these traumatically engineered masculine selves.

What implications, if any, might there be from these findings for the development of masculinity under more normative circumstances? Here, under the most extreme conditions of sustained sadistic, penetrating sexual submission of the developing child through the incessant demands of the parents, the young girl's mind finds a perverse solution through the creation of a masculine self whose strength, power, ability to protect, and seek revenge requires his completion through acquiring a penis and eliminating female qualities of the body. In their male states of mind, sexual penetration by an older man was experienced as a passive, homosexual act, tantamount to the actualization of the unconscious negative Oedipal fantasy. Even though Freud abandoned his seduction theory of neurosis in favor of unconscious fantasy and psychosexual development, he never discarded the importance of psychic trauma in causing "alterations of the ego" (Freud, 1937). The interplay between overwhelming life experience, fantasy, and development seemed quite pertinent here. In order to survive, these children needed to accommodate to this relationship through the development of deeply conflicted, sadomasochistic gratification, and most unusual disturbances in their identity to be discussed in detail in the next chapter. It is as though they overcompensated for their utter passive helplessness by "becoming" the only kind of man they could become, one whose sense of self was so utterly fragile that "he" had to maintain cohesion through violence and extreme behavior typically associated with very "insecure" men. The paranoia which Freud describes to an underlying homosexual conflict (Freud, 1922) was pervasive here also.

2

Dissociation and Its Vicissitudes

Depersonalization leads us on to the extraordinary condition of "double conscience" which is more correctly described as "split personality." But all of this is so obscure and been so little mastered scientifically that I must refrain from talking about it any more to you.

—Sigmund Freud, 1936

If the shocks increase in number during the development of the child, the number and the various kinds of splits in the personality increase too, and soon it becomes extremely difficult to maintain contact without confusion with all the fragments, each of which behaves as a separate personality yet does not know of even the existence of the others. . . . I hope even here to be able to find threads that can link up the various parts.

—Sandor Ferenczi, 1933

Freud's last words on the subject of "split personality," written while reflecting upon his visit to the Acropolis, left much doubt about it and its place in psychoanalysis (Freud, 1936). Part of Freud's uncertainty perhaps related to his alienation from Ferenczi and his devaluation of his later work with the dissociated mind (Ferenczi, 1933), which contemporary thinkers are finding to be remarkably prescient (Blum, 1994; Brenner, 2004a). Even though Freud was originally very interested in dreamlike, hypnoid states, hysteria, and sexual trauma before his break with Breuer, he never realized his goal of uniting dream psychology with psychopathology (Freud, 1917b). After he developed his ideas about repression, the structural theory and then ego psychology, he was never able to unify all of these earlier concepts. Freud's unfinished work, coupled with the fact that diagnosis in American psychiatry is essentially based on symptoms and not dynamics, have left analysts with a gap in our deeper understanding of those entities characterized by dreamlike, altered states, such as the realm of what are now referred to dissociative disorders. Dissociative identity disorder, or DID, is probably the most controversial and misunderstood condition in the history of psychology, prompting researchers over sixty years ago to conclude that there were two types of believers: the naïve and those with actual experience with such patients (Taylor and Martin, 1944).

The DSM-IV-TR describes the diagnostic criteria for DID as the following:

(a) The presence of two or more distinct entities or personality states (each with its own relatively enduring pattern of perceiving, relating to, and thinking about the environment itself);

(b) At least two of these entities or personality states recurrently taking control of the person's behavior;

(c) Inability to recall important personal information that is too extensive to be explained by ordinary forgetfulness; and

(d) The disturbance is not due to direct physiological effects of a substance . . . or general medical condition (APA, 2000, pp. 240–241).

In contrast to DSM-IV-TR, which categorizes this entity as an "Axis I" major psychiatric illness, the recently published Psychodynamic Diagnostic Manual (PDM Task Force, 2006) considers a "dissociative personality" and thereby promotes the idea of a spectrum of severity of character pathology. This viewpoint is congruent with, but slightly different from, my own clinical understanding of DID, which is equated with the "lower level dissociative character" (Brenner, 1994) and will be discussed later.

Although there is growing recognition of the value of such a characterological formulation from a psychoanalytic perspective, it is not the prevailing psychiatric attitude and is perhaps the latest source of confusion which has enshrouded this condition since it was first recognized.

As a reflection of this historical confusion, it has been known by an extensive list of names such as split personality, Gmelin's syndrome, exchanged personality, multiplex personality, double existences, double conscience, dual consciousness, dual personality, double personality, plural personality, dissociated personality, alternating personality, multiple personality, multiple personality disorder and now dissociative identity disorder (Ellenberger, 1970; Greaves, 1993). The current nomenclature conveys the idea that the underlying problem is not that there are too many personalities or identities, but not enough of one. It also emphasizes the importance of dissociation, a concept which in itself has long had a troubled history among psychoanalysts. Adding further to its own identity crisis was Bleuler's coining of the term schizophrenia, or split mind, which he applied to the condition originally described by Kraeplin as dementia praecox. Indeed, since the introduction of the term "schizophrenia," the number of published case reports of multiple personality had significantly declined, leading Rosenbaum (1980) to conclude that much diagnostic confusion must have ensued. He has even suggested that some of the highly proclaimed psychotherapeutic cures of schizophrenia may have actually been cases of misdiagnosed, severe dissociative psychopathology instead. There is no doubt that the presence of depersonalization, derealization, emotional withdrawal, bizarre conversion symptoms, auditory hallucinations, and other Schneiderian first-rank symptoms of schizophrenia (Kluft, 1987) have further muddied the waters. In addition, it has been reported that it often takes up to eight years of mental health treatment before DID could be definitively recognized (Coons, Bowen and Milstein, 1988). Furthermore, it has been noted that there is great potential for secondary gain in disowning one's behavior and attributing it to a separate personality especially when criminal behavior and legal charges are involved (Orne, Dinges and Orne, 1984).

It must also be noted that it has long been suspected that iatrogenic influences through hypnosis or other interventions are the cause of such fragmentation in the creation of multiple personality (James, 1890; McDougall, 1926). Significantly, however, there has not been one documented case of manufactured DID reported in the literature. Although it has been claimed that it could be created for the purpose of carrying out top-secret military operations (Estabrooks, 1945), it is no wonder that many clinicians today still question the existence, validity, and pathogenesis of DID. Therefore, the question is raised whether it is a hoax, a missing link between dream psychology and psychopathology (Brenner, 1996b) or a clinical Rosetta Stone, which may "reveal an alphabet and a language, and, when they are deciphered and translated, yield undreamed-of information . . . saxa loquuntur (stones talk!)" (Freud, 1896, p. 192). Thus, the ghost of Anna O., Breuer and Freud's legendary case of hysteria, clearly described in their original work (Breuer and Freud, 1893–1895) and later confirmed in Freud's biography by Ernest Jones (1953) as a case of multiple personality, has continued to lurk in the shadows of psychoanalysis ever since.

EARLY PSYCHOANALYTIC VIEWS

Attempts to understand the pathogenesis of this entity have led writers to consider a range of ideas. Correlated very highly with severe, early, sustained trauma, that is, potentially life-threatening circumstances, including physical and sexual abuse (Kluft, 1984; Ross, 1989; Putnam, 1989), the role of psychic trauma is generally accepted by those who are open to the validity of the diagnosis. Janet's (1889) theory of "disaggregation," or dissociation, posited a split in the psyche of traumatized people with a constitutional susceptibility, a passive disintegration of the mind resulting in the development of autonomous components which could be disowned and treated by hypnosis. This spatial model is very appealing and has not only persisted but has also greatly increased in popularity in recent decades owing to the resurgence of interest in dissociative psychopathology. Jung (1902) also subscribed to a split-psyche model in which "personified autonomous complexes" existed.

Freud himself continuously grappled with a split in the psyche model from his early work with Breuer (Breuer and Freud, 1893–1895) and the "splitting of consciousness" and hysteria, to dissociation and perversion (Freud, 1923), as well as neurosis (Freud, 1940a) and psychosis (Freud, 1940b) in his last writings. Although he accurately recognized an active, defensive, unconscious process which was operative in the service of warding off anxiety in contradistinction to Janet's passive, organic model, Freud's theory of repression could not explain all the data. For example, his method of free association, which was intended to replace hypnosis and "reach" all those areas of the mind, did not fully take into consideration the phenomenon of spontaneous self-hypnosis which he (1891) recognized early on could occur in very suggestible people. This defensive style is, in fact, quite elusive to classical analytic intervention as such. Writers such as Fleiss (1953) subsequently described hypnotic "evasion" while Dickes (1965) redefined the hypnoid state as "protecting the ego against unacceptable instinctual demands" (pp. 400–401) and Shengold (1989) considered both "hypnotic facilitation" and "hypnotic vigilance" in the autohypnotic defense. Even Anna Freud (1954) recognized how a patient could ward off sexual anxiety by a trance-like sleep. However, as Glover (1943) pointed out, the term "dissociation" has a "chequered history" in psychoanalysis so while such phenomena have been described in the literature, few writers until recently have dared to reintroduce this term.

Interestingly, in the same way the notion of a split in the psyche has been invoked to explain many types of psychopathology, so too have many theories been invoked to explain DID. Freud's (1923) theory that different identifications could take over consciousness at any given time was very important but insufficient. This theory relied upon repression but did not take autohypnosis or trauma into consideration. Indeed, Jones's (1953) affirmation of Anna O. being a case of double personality suggested there was much more to be understood about her psychopathology than Freud could have explained at the time. Although Ferenczi's (1933) ideas about early sexual trauma were linked to the child's automaton-like states and her enslavement to the parent, he did not apply his formulation to Freud's famous case.

LATER PSYCHOANALYTIC VIEWS

Fairbairn (1952) attributed the structure of "multiple personality" to simply being another model of the mind, analogous to Freud's tripartite model, noting the importance of layering and fusion of internal objects which varied in complexity in each person. Glover (1943) described early, unintegrated ego nuclei as precursors to dissociation while Federn (1952) hypothesized the reactivation of various different repressed ego states. In their pioneering efforts to integrate clinical experience with theory, Watkins and Watkins (1979–1980, 1997) elaborated upon Federn's ego states conceptualizing a continuum of mental dividedness from an adaptive, normative differentiation to a maladaptive, pathological end characterized by dissociation and ultimately DID. Having done extensive research on hysteria, Abse (1974, 1983) maintained that both splitting of the ego and altered states of consciousness were necessary to explain the dissociation essential to DID. He recognized that this defensive constellation sacrificed repression and a clear, continuous consciousness, which because of the amnestic, dissociated "personalities," reflected identity diffusion also (Akhtar, 1992).

In his review of the subject, Berman (1981) also emphasized the importance of splitting, citing seriously disturbed mother-daughter relationships, followed by the loss of a compensatory, overly intense, eroticized, oedipal relationship with the father. Consequently, the separate "personalities" became the crystallization of "part object representations which evolve into split self representations" (Berman, 1981, p. 298). A developmental arrest (Laskey, 1978) as well as psychotic features may also be seen in such a fragmented self, as per Kernberg's (1973) continuum of dissociative psychopathology. Here, psychosis with poor differentiation of self and object is at one end while hysterical dissociation, mutual amnesia of two personalities and repression is thought to be at the other end. Such a continuum with psychosis is an important idea (Brenner, 2004a) to which I will return later in this paper.

DID has also been considered a subtype of borderline personality (Buck, 1983; Clarey, Burstin, and Carpenter, 1984) and a variant of a narcissistic character (Gruenwald, 1977; Greaves, 1980) which invoked Kohut's (1971) updated version of Erikson and Kubies's (1939) vertical split while Marmer (1980) considered it a type of transitional object. Kluft (1984) viewed DID as a posttraumatic disorder of childhood secondary to overwhelming experience, especially sexual abuse, contingent upon dissociation-proneness and the child's propensity for mental dividedness depending upon the level of development at the time of trauma. Arlow (1992) elaborated upon Freud's idea and explained DID on the basis of "alternating conscious representations of highly organized fantasy systems, each of which coalesces into a particular idiosyncratic entity . . . [which] are not compatible with each other and . . . can dramatize internal conflicts" (p. 1975). Especially significant here is his recognition that "altered ego states . . . may be incorporated, in part, into the *character structure* of the individual" (Arlow, 1992, p. 75). Having said all this, the nature of dissociation and its developmental significance was not well integrated into these theories.

I hypothesize that a pathodevelopmental line may exist from the earliest sleep/wakefulness cycle to altered states in disturbances of attachment to aberrations in the repression barrier to the reliance on dissociation as the central defense in DID. Such a consideration allows for an incorporation of more recent findings from child analysis into my clinical experience with adults (Brenner, 1994, 2001, 2004a).

DISTURBED ATTACHMENT AND DISSOCIATION

It is now recognized that the earliest infant-mother relationship has implications for the development of dissociative symptoms and defenses. Following the discovery of disorganized attachment patterns (Main and Solomon, 1990) and their correlation with behavioral problems in latency-aged children (Main, 1993), Bowlby's (1969) controversial notion of a preadapted behavior system which maintains a feeling of security has been rehabilitated and incorporated by developmental researchers. The signs of disorganized, disoriented, infant attachment behavior include simultaneous or sequential contradictory actions such as efforts at contact and avoidance, freezing or confused activity, stumbling, wandering, postural evidence of fear of the parent and rapid fluctuations of affect. Mistreatment of infants is highly correlated with disorganized patterns that are associated with fear and stress responses involving the HPA axis which can create life-long patterns of neurobiological activity. Primate research (Coplan et al., 1996; Kraemer, 1992) suggests that this system is subject to early influences which may result in "stress inoculation" or exaggerated arousal responses. Attempts to replicate this data in humans are underway and much more work needs to be done (Spangler and Grossman, 1993; DeBellis, 2001). Clinical research, however, has clearly delineated the development of the dynamics of fear in infants within the first year of life (Main, 1993) by observing the alterations in attention and affect in response to attachment cues. As a two-person model of conflict, symptom and defense, such early attachment patterns underlie the "unthought known" (Bollas, 1987), i.e., implicit enactive behavior preceding symbolization and explicit memory (Stern et al.,

1998; Lyons-Ruth, 1999). One could, therefore, conceptualize steps along a pathodevelopmental line to include disorganized attachment leading to "internalized dialogue as defense" to dissociation. It is important to note here that Winnicott (Winnicott, 1960b) considered the earliest changes in mental state from sleep to wakefulness and that all-important twilight state in between which can be so variable in infants (Weil, 1970) to be the origin of dissociation. Pine's caveat about drawing inferences from infant observation to adult psychic structure notwithstanding (Pine, 1992), there is considerable research to support Main and Hesse's (1990) hypothesis that unresolved fear in the parent is transmitted through behavior which conveys that fear or other behavior which frightens the infant (Jacobovitz, Hazen, and Riggs, 1997; Lyons-Ruth, Bronfman, and Parsons, 1999; Schwengel, Bakermans-Kronenberg and Van Ijzendoorn, 1999).

Lyons-Ruth (2003) has compiled the array of parental disturbed communication to include (1) physical or verbal withdrawal; (2) negative-intrusive behavior, such as teasing or pulling the infant; (3) confused role behavior, such as seeking reassurance from the infant instead of vice versa and using sexualized, inappropriate tones of speech; (4) disoriented responses, such as becoming dazed, confused, or disorganized by the infant; and (5) affective miscues, such as giving contradictory messages or failure to respond to an infant in distress. Infant disorganization was highly correlated with maternal behavior characterized as frightening, hostile, and withdrawing. Infants of such mothers had elevated cortisol levels in response to mild stressors, increased hostile tendencies in early school years, excessive controlling attachment behaviors by six years of age and chaotic or inhibited use of fantasy and play during preschool (Lyons-Ruth and Jacobovitz, 1999). Not only was a history of maternal trauma associated with their disturbed parenting behaviors and during interviews using the Adult Attachment Interview, these mothers often demonstrated evidence of unintegrated mental processes of their own (Lyons-Ruth and Jacobovitz, 1999; Main, 1993).

Stimulated by Liotti's (1992) observation of the similarities between dissociated mental contents and how disorganized infants behave, this attachment disturbance has garnered much attention. For example, a study (Ogawa et al., 1997) from infancy to nineteen years of age correlated disorganized attachment and the development of dissociative symptoms, which was enhanced by intercurrent trauma. Interestingly, communication errors, role confusion, and sexualized communication by the mother seemed to be more highly correlated than frank hostile or disoriented behavior. Genetic or constitutional factors, such as the proclivity to be hypnotizable (Frischholz et al., 1992), was acknowledged but not considered in this research.

These findings suggest that early interactional or dyadic processes underlie the pathogenesis of dissociative phenomena and lead one to conclude that the clinical treatment which fosters collaboration and healthy dialogue would facilitate an integrated experience for the patient. For example, Bach (2001) has described the importance of the maternal caretaker to provide the infant with an ongoing, relational, intimate experience which enables a continuous sense of self to be experienced. "Knowing and not knowing" (Laub and Auerhahn, 1993) probably begins with a disturbed dissociogenic mother's need not to know about herself which hinders her ability to know her infant who then cannot fully know who she is. Whitmer's (2001) ideas about dissociation are consistent with these views, as he maintains that one cannot find meaning in his experience until it is recognized by the other. Working with adults, clinicians familiar with severe dissociative pathology regularly observe that such patients often have excessive and extensive amnesia for not only their early childhood years but also for events in latency and adolescence, often leaving them with disturbing gaps in memory of continuous self experience. These "holes" in the memory may be embarrassing and be minimized or covered over by confabulation or reports of alcohol or drug abuse which only exacerbates the problem. Once in treatment, it may be revealed that an unusually dense "repression barrier" is present which paradoxically may be easily breached through hypnosis (Brenner, 2001, 2004a).

From the relational perspective, Bromberg (1994) sees dissociation as a ubiquitous, interpersonal defense such that what is not known is unthinkable because it was not properly recognized by the primary caretaker. Whitmer, however, takes a further step, recognizing dissociation as ultimately an intrapsychic defense because finding meaning in experience is blocked by an active decoupling of a natural developmental process. In this vein, Fonagy (1991) explains that a child reacts to the intolerability of knowing her mother's hatred toward her by actively inhibiting the capacity to mentalize. However, since children cannot develop the capacity to integrate mental content unless the maternal object can sustain a "good enough" affective, symbolic and interactive dialogue, dissociation is described as beginning as a two-person, interpersonal experience.

As a result, in those families where a climate of denial accompanies abuse, the absence of acknowledgment in the dyad facilitates a dissociative state of mind, i.e., "conflicted approach avoidance attempts at dialogue of the disorganized child as well as the inability of the abusive mother to help the child integrate the contradictory aspects of her experience through a collaborative dialogue" (Lyons-Ruth, 2003, p. 901). Significantly, however, such dissociative tendencies are thought to come from a continuum of relational disturbances much less severe than frank abuse or the mother's overt dissociative disorder. Essentially, the mother's need not to know that her infant is in distress seems to be a central dynamic factor where facial expressions and behavior show a severely uncoordinated dialogue resulting in "disrupted forms of mother-infant communication [which] are important contributions to the developmental pathways that eventually are culminating in dissociative symptoms" (Lyons-Ruth, 2003, p. 905).

In my own experience with patients with DID, a very disturbed early mother-child relationship is ubiquitous. It seems to set the stage for continued impairment requiring extraordinary measures on the child's part in order to psychically survive. However, we need to be open to additional considerations besides disorganized disoriented attachment, as other pathways may be possible. For example, avoidant attachment disturbances may be implicated also, which I believe is the case in a patient's situation which will be described later. "Mary" seemed totally oblivious, unreactive, and unaffected by my comings and goings for the first several years of treatment. She utilized whatever ego strength she had to create a dissociative defense of not caring and not knowing if I were present or absent. Over time, as her defense became analyzed, we could see that becoming impervious to the object was her only option.

OFF THE ROAD TO SELF-CONSTANCY

Pursuing this line of thought, dissociation has then been described as simultaneously knowing and not knowing due to a persistence of an infantile state of mind where the maternal object failed to ascribe meaning to a sensory experience or mental state (Whitmer, 2001). As a result, one who dissociates presumably cannot know himself except through another's eyes and interpretation. Self-knowledge through introspection is not possible due to a major disturbance in representing one's own experience. There can be no self-constancy because the self-image is always fluctuating due to impaired capacity to represent the self, leaving the individual utterly dependent upon the interaction with others for definition. From a Mahlerian point of view, self-constancy is the reciprocal accompaniment of object constancy, the central acquisition of the separation/individuation process (Mahler and Furer, 1968). More recent developmental research, however, has called some of her major findings into question (Pine, 1992) as there is growing evidence of a differentiated self in infancy which predates object constancy (Stern, 1985).

Therefore, the disturbances seen in DID, according to Stern's (1985) model, would infer major problems in the very early development of the core self, especially in the areas of self-cohesion, self-continuity, and self-agency. Sensory input may be accurately perceived and conscious but its meaning would initially be relegated to the object because the experience is unsymbolized (Ogden, 1986), unformulated (Stern, 1997), and, therefore, unrepresented (Fonagy and Target, 1996). As a result, one would persist in overriding his or her own senses in order to conform to another's reality, leaving him or her unaware and, therefore, protected from knowing very painful somatic and psychological states. This "repression by proxy" (Whitmer, 2001, p. 16) is conceptualized initially as an interpersonal rather than intrapsychic defense that, through another route, keeps the subject from knowing something, not because it is unconscious but because it is unacceptable to others. As such, dissociation is then seen as the quintessential example of the interpersonal nature of the self that must be defined in relation to the object.

Originating in the earliest interactions, "the infant comes to know his own mind by finding an image of himself in his mother's mind. The child sees his fantasy or idea represented in the adult's mind, re-introjects this and uses it as a representation of his own thinking" (Fonagy and Target, 1996, p. 229). Such dependency on the mother's reality, if it persists into adulthood, results in a major impairment of the capacity to mentalize (Fonagy and Target, 1996). It also creates a paradox in that this very inability to think independently may leave the individual impervious to the influence of others. Perhaps this contradiction is an adult manifestation of the gaze aversion in the overstimulated infant who withdraws in order to reregulate himself (Beebe and Lachman, 2002). In so doing, one has to look away from the object in order to compose oneself and, as a result, loses contact. The extreme suggestibility and stubborn negativity in highly hypnotizable people which was observed by Janet a century ago (Janet, 1907) might also be related to this paradox.

This "illusion of an autonomous psyche" (Whitmer, 2001, p. 817) I would contend, is further enhanced, reconfigured, and carried to the extreme in cases of DID where there are seemingly separate selves or personifications which may deny or not know the existence of others or may be engaged in lethal, i.e., suicidal, battles over exclusive control of the body (Brenner, 2001, 2004a). Not only would there be disturbances in the core self but also in the intersubjective self and quite dramatically in the narrative self (Stern, 1985) where the various alter personalities could claim to have different biographies. In order to better integrate these ideas into my preexisting view of DID as a "lower level dissociative character," it seems important to emphasize that it may also be thought of as a disorder of the self characterized by overall lack of self-constancy defended against by a cadre of seemingly separate selves with their own cohesion. The vulnerability to submission and sadomasochistic exploitation is often seen in the scared child selves who cannot say "no" but who also reflect an exceedingly complex, intrapsychic structure which functions as a compromise formation (C. Brenner, 1982). During such times, the patient's intrapsychic conflict over her wishes might be quite evident, as fear, guilt, and self-destructive urges might be deeply felt. However, he/she may employ a unique defense, described as pseudo-externalized displacement, in which her instinctual strivings might be disowned, banished from consciousness and attributed to someone else—in this case, that someone else is not an outside person but rather an "inside" self (Brenner, 2001). Working with this defense as it emerges in the transference is a crucial part of the treatment as it involves altered states, amnesia, traumatic memories, and the pathognomic development of dissociated selves.[1]

Another illusion, that of cohesion of the self, is created by these personifications who may, indeed, have their own biographies, sexual proclivities, relationships, dreams, avocations, and continuous memories. These selves have achieved a degree of secondary autonomy and, as such, may be willed on by the patient in an effort to take flight from an overwhelming situation or be accessible through hypnotic interventions. They also may emerge spontaneously as a result of anxiety in the here and now. This property of "switching" from one self to another in response to anxiety may then occur in the transference, thus providing an opportunity for the analyst to begin to work interpretatively with this seemingly bizarre symptom/defense constellation. However, the patient's overall lack of self-constancy and object constancy may not be generally recognized because the underlying susceptibility to organismic panic (Mahler and Furer, 1968) and separation anxiety is warded off by the various selves who appear to have a narcissistic investment in separateness (Kluft, 1986a). Maintaining this separateness, like with splitting, may reduce anxiety through an illusion of protecting the "good self" or "good object" at the expense of continuity of identity. In addition, the well-known difficulty in symbolic thinking associated with trauma, that is, a quality of concreteness (Grubrich-Simitis, 1984; Ogden, 1986; Bollas, 1989; Levine, 1990; Bass, 1997), may be encapsulated by some selves in DID allowing others to develop extraordinary creativity and high-level abstract thought. A recent memoir by an internationally renowned expert in Asian affairs illustrates such high level capabilities (Oxnam, 2005). These personifications are defensively shielded from one another's traumatic affects and memories, apparently protected by a psychical barrier reinforced by autohypnotic amnesia and analgesia. It seems as though this type of encapsulating organization may allow more normative development to occur in some regions of the psyche (Wholley, 1925) and may even protect from frank psychosis (Kramer, 1993). This protective barrier appears to function as a very powerful repression barrier, but much more extensive and less amenable to usual interventions because of the alterations in consciousness and the patient's loss of observing ego during these dissociative shifts in identity. It is therefore essential to develop a therapeutic alliance with the patient in all states of mind and be able to empathize with his/her psychic reality.

Data from analytic work with adult patients traumatized in childhood reveals the presence of a unique psychic structure, the "It's not me!" Self (Brenner, 2001). Therefore, in DID, in addition to "knowing and not knowing," the patient may experience "being here and not here" as well as "being me and not me." This structure is thought to be the creative force behind the genesis of these selves, incorporating a number of organizing influences, such as the divisive effect of aggression, perverse sexuality, the dream ego, near-death experiences in childhood, and intergenerational transmission of trauma, which I will elaborate upon. This last influence has also been correlated with disorganized attachment to traumatized mothers.

DISSOCIATION, HYPNOSIS, AND NEUROBIOLOGY

If disorganized attachment is correlated with dissociation and if hypnosis is a form of dissociation (Hilgard, 1986), then it would follow that there would be a much higher degree of hypnotizability in those with disorganized attachment patterns. While I am not aware of any current research in this area, it is expected that such studies will be done in the future. Not surprisingly, the hypnotic induction techniques commonly employed (Watkins, 1992) rely on an interactive paradigm which anticipates and coordinates the subject's inner state with the hypnotist's agenda, not unlike the very subtle interactive processes observed in mother-infant research (Personal Communication, Beebe, 2005). While it has long been thought that the hypnotic interchange harkens back to early dyadic relatedness (Fromm and Nash, 1997), the precursors to the autohypnotic state are probably in the fuzzy borderland of the neonate's wakefulness and sleep, which observation has revealed may vary widely from infant to infant (Weil, 1970). Therefore, what likely occurs in a "dissociation-prone" patient is the activation of presymbolic representations of the disturbed dyad (Beebe and Lachman, 2002) where the overstimulated infant may employ observable defenses, such as gaze aversion and freezing (Fraiberg, 1982). We might presume that in more normative development this activation diminishes over time and evolves into a defensive system in which motivating forgetting, that is, repression, occurs without disruptions in levels of consciousness or disturbances in continuity of self.

From a neurobiological standpoint, this infantile reaction of freezing resembles the "defeat reaction" seen in animals (Blanchard et al., 1993; Henry et al., 1993; Miczeck, Thompson, and Tornatzky, 1990). Here, in addition to an increase in circulating stress hormones like steroids and epinephrine which accompany the brainstem-mediated activation of the central nervous system, there is also an increase in vagal tone. As a result, heart rate and blood pressure decrease sometimes to the point of fainting (Perry, 2001). In this animal model which parallels that seen in humans, both the dopaminergic and the opioid systems are activated in the defeat reaction. Significantly, these "reward system" pathways are also activated by cocaine and narcotics which induce euphoria, reduce sensitivity to pain, and cause distortions of reality. Such alterations in mood, sensory input, and orientation are also seen in dissociative reactions to trauma.

DID—THE CASE OF ROBERT OXNAM

A recent memoir written by an internationally renowned expert in the field of Asian studies is most compelling because the author who reveals his tortured inner life is a very credible, high profile individual. Robert Oxnam, Ph.D., describes in great detail how, from the pinnacle of his career in his field, he became depressed, developed a serious eating disorder, and started drinking very heavily to self-medicate himself from his tortured memories. His nighttime formula was "two packs of cigarettes, Polish sausage, a gallon of ice cream, a two-pound bag of peanuts, a bottle of scotch and a pornographic movie on the VCR" (Oxnam, 2005, p. 30). Weeks after he became sober and started to open up during a therapy session, he blanked out and one of his young alter personalities emerged to introduce himself to the psychiatrist. The patient had amnesia for this time and was utterly bewildered to learn not only that the time was over but also that an unknown part of himself had been talking the whole time he was in an amnestic state.

Dr. Oxnam painstakingly describes his complex "system" of eleven different selves with different ages, different traits, different intellectual capabilities, different genders, and different responsibilities regarding the overall functioning of the human being known to his friends as Bob. His inner people resided in a psychological castle which housed a library in which a book of his childhood existed—the "Baby Book." In this highly symbolized, dream-like way, the memories of his severe early trauma by his grandparents, including anal rape and near death by suffocation, were kept separate and inaccessible until therapy: "And the 'Baby Book' was totally etched in my mind, waiting for me to open it. And as soon as I thought of its possible contents, my smile faded with a shudder . . . " (Oxnam, 2005, p. 38). Amazingly, Dr. Oxnam's selves were so geared toward mastery of knowledge and success that, unlike less gifted individuals with this type of mental organization, "they" achieved great prominence. In one extraordinary passage, he describes his horror at being mercilessly plagued by his voices while hosting a multimillion dollar fund-raiser in which former President George H. Bush was the keynote speaker. "Suddenly, just as President Bush arrived, I felt inner vibrations, like a ringing cell phone. I knew there was an incoming Bobby message. 'The president's not happy. He's sad.' Of course he's happy. He's smiling. Please not now! 'Just look at his face. He's not happy. He's making a hurt smile. Who hurt him?' OK, I see. But we can't talk now. I mean it. We'll talk later. Goodbye!'" (Oxnam, 2005, p. 117).

As a cautionary note about the potential lethality of this misunderstood condition (Brenner, 2006), Dr. Oxnam reports that after the death of his mother, he very nearly killed himself with an overdose. Despite this massive regression, Dr. Oxnam describes having benefited greatly from his treatment, which appeared to be a combination of insight-oriented, supportive, and hypnotherapeutic approaches. However, there did not seem to be any analysis of the transference or methodical analysis of defense. In order to do so, one would need to view DID through a characterological lens.

THE DISSOCIATIVE CHARACTER—RECONCEPTUALIZING DID

In my own experience as an administrator on a dissociative disorders unit and as a private practitioner, I have had the opportunity for clinical contact with hundreds of such patients ranging from admission interviews, consultation, supervision, group therapy, short-term inpatient treatment, long-term inpatient treatment, and five-times-a-week outpatient, analytic therapy lasting well beyond a decade. The model that I have found most useful is that of a continuum of dissociative character pathology in which dissociation, rather than splitting or repression, is the central defensive operation (Brenner, 1994a). Although similar to another theory which recognizes the importance of characterological factors, it is nevertheless in contrast to McWilliams's model of the dissociative personality which posits neurotic level conflicts as core issues in higher functioning DID patients (McWilliams, 1994). Data from analytic work does not support this latter theory because, in my experience, even such high-functioning patients with greater capacities for sublimation show evidence of severe preoedipal problems, including a disturbance in object constancy (Brenner, 2004). In the dissociative character continuum, the most severe end or lower level dissociative character would correspond to DID whereas the intermediate level dissociative character with less cohesive and organized "selves" would be comparable to the so-called attenuated cases of multiple personality (Ellenberger, 1970) currently classified as DD-NOS, or dissociative disorder not otherwise specified (APA, 2000). An upper level dissociative character which has an overreliance on defensive altered states but with more overall self-constancy would also exist.

The different personifications or alter personalities, the hallmark of DID, would be considered as multiply determined compromise formations which encapsulate one's disowned traumatic memories, affects, anxiety, drives, and fantasies. The pathogenesis of these selves would be the responsibility of the so-called Dissociative or "It's not me!" Self who, like the "man behind the curtain," wanted to be ignored while he created the illusion of an omnipotent, frightening Wizard of Oz.[2] As mentioned earlier, the illusion of oneness, or self-constancy, is also created, as each self may be kept ignorant of the presence of others. However, through analytic work with an appreciation of the vicissitudes of dissociation, the reconstruction of a massively traumatic childhood might then be possible through the development of a therapeutic alliance with the patient in the various states of mind, enabling the analysis of the ensuing "mosaic transference." The five previously mentioned "organizing influences" which have been discovered so far are recruited by the "It's not me!" Self in the service of creating these seemingly separate identities that are kept apart by the amnestic, autohypnotic barrier. For example, Oxnam was not aware of his other selves until his decompensation in adulthood. When a child self emerged in therapy, Oxnam had amnesia for this period of time and had to utilize his therapist as an auxiliary memory until he could acquire "coconsciousness" and expand his observing ego to these states.

The first organizing influence is perverse sexuality—aggressively infused sexuality with past objects and body parts—in which the individual seems to traverse multiple sexual developmental pathways in different states of consciousness. A frequently seen triad of personifications is a transsexual self, a homosexual self and a sadomasochistic heterosexual self. Oxnam had a secret obsession with pornography while he was married but does not elaborate on his fantasy life, so we are left to speculate. In a case with which I am familiar, it was eventually discovered that a married man would become utterly overwhelmed with urges to drink other men's urine in an amnestic, altered state of consciousness. He would lure young men to a private apartment and carefully feed them calculated amounts of beer to dilute their urine just enough so he could swallow it while performing fellatio and while he ejaculated. In another state of mind, he was a gourmet cook who prided himself on his special recipes and secret sauces.

Of equal importance is the nature of ego functioning in the dream state, especially regarding the "functional phenomenon" (Silberer, 1909), where the ego may symbolize its own alterations in consciousness not only in dreams, but also in hypnogogic and traumatic states. It appears to be the underlying discovery which was described by Kohut in the self-state dream (Kohut, 1971). Utilizing this mechanism, the patient might anthropomorphize a traumatically induced dissociated state and symbolize it in the form of a young child or an angry teenager, which could be expressed in both recurrent dreams and in subsequent traumatically induced altered states. For example, Oxnam's hermetically sealed castle in his mind might have been a transformation of the refrigerator he was locked into which nearly suffocated him to death. The terror and fluctuating state of consciousness he experienced at the time may have been represented and crystallized into this imagery.

A third influence is the role of intergenerational transmission in which the perpetrator's own trauma history may become bizarrely incorporated

into the "biography" of a given personification, usually one based on identification with the aggressor. Originally described in children of Holocaust
survivors (Bergmann and Jucovy, 1983) and as mentioned earlier, currently
recognized in disturbances of attachment with traumatized mothers, this
phenomenon here may be overshadowed by other factors. For example,
a woman with a destructive masculine self who wanted to "take over" at-
tempted a crude mastectomy leading to severe bleeding manifested not
only a dissociated transsexual conflict but also occult transmission of her
father's own trauma (chapter 1). This masculine self insisted he was a military man who was sodomized as a young boy (Brenner, 2001).

The divisive effects of aggression, originally described by Freud (1920),
and the unusual manifestations of near-death experiences (Gabbard and
Twemlow, 1984), such as autoscopic and even psi phenomena, may also
factor into the creation of these selves (Brenner, 2001, 2004a). In one such
case, it appeared that a patient who sustained a near-death experience in
childhood by almost drowning had encapsulated that experience in the
form of a "dead child" self who had uncanny powers of perception and
perhaps extrasensory perception (Brenner, 2001).

While dissociation itself is a compromise formation, the defensive aspects
of it are emphasized here, enabling the analytic clinician to conceptualize a
way to work with it interpretively. Psychodynamically, it has been defined as
"a defensive, altered state of consciousness due to autohypnosis augmenting
repression or splitting. It develops as a primitive, adaptive response of the
ego to the overstimulation and pain of external trauma which, depending
upon its degree of integration, may result in a broad range of disturbances
of alertness, awareness, memory, and identity. Dissociation apparently may
change in its function and may be employed later on as a defense against
the perceived internal dangers of the intolerable affects and instinctual
strivings. Thus, it may be a transient, neurotic defense or become characterological and may even be the predominant defense" (Brenner, 2001, p.
36). In the former, the analyst may see the quality of what is commonly
referred to as "spaciness" in higher-level patients where conflicts are more
oedipally based. However, dissociation, in my view, typically encompasses
qualities of both repression and splitting, thus perpetuating confusion over
its categorization as a distinct means of dynamically keeping mental contents separate. In her comparison of repression and dissociation, Howell
points out that while both are motivated and defensive, the latter may occur
spontaneously during acute trauma or hypnosis (Howell, 2005). In addition, the former typically refers to actively forgotten declarative memories
which were once known whereas the latter often refers to unformulated
experiences (Stern, 1997) which are known and not known simultaneously
(Laub and Auerhahn, 1993). Although parapraxes are typically attributed to
repression and fugues attributed to dissociation, it may be that some of the

psychopathology of everyday life (Freud, 1901) is more akin to dissociation (Brenner, 2007). For example, a very self-destructive patient who repeatedly and intentionally cut herself in dissociated amnestic states became "accident prone" and prone to unconscious "bungled actions" (Freud, 1901) as merging of selves, coconsciousness and neutralization of aggression occurred during treatment (Brenner, 2001).

With regard to splitting as per Kernberg (Kernberg, 1975), the intrapsychic world is divided into aggressively and libidinally self and object representations, that is, "bad" and "good." In dissociation, however, such a division is not as clear cut and amnesia is typically present. And, in an attempt to link the two from a relational perspective, "what we call 'splitting' involves a reenactment of posttraumatic dominant-submissive relational patterns . . . a particular organization of alternating dissociated helpless/victim and abusive/rageful self states . . . [which] may have developmental underpinnings in attachment style and biological states (Howell, 2005, p. 163).

Despite the clinical blurring at times, in extreme situations such as with the changes seen in DID, the underlying mechanism of dissociation seems most distinct. Analyzing not only the timing of such a dissociative defensive switch but also the content of what is being said in that state of mind is of importance. These clinical findings along with the reconstruction of childhood trauma during work with adults dovetail quite well with the data derived from child observation and developmental research. Therefore, it appears that very early developmental disturbance potentiated by sustained, severe trauma in childhood is necessary for DID. Although dissociative symptoms may occur with later onset trauma, it is less disorganizing than in frank DID.

MASSIVE TRAUMA IN ADULTHOOD VERSUS DID—CASE REPORT

The traumatically induced fracture of the already developed adult psyche is poignantly described in the autobiographical writing of an Auschwitz survivor plagued by incessant nightmares of remembered and unremembered horrors. Yehiel De-Nur, the acclaimed Israeli author is better known by his nom-de-plume, Ka-Tzetnik 135633, the number tattooed on his forearm. He laments his psychological paralysis during the Eichmann trial in 1961 when the judge asked him about hiding behind another name in his books. De-Nur writes: "A routine question, ostensibly, but the moment it flashed into my brain all hell broke loose. Not only did they want me to melt the two identities into one, but they wanted a public confession, an open declaration that this was so. Escaping to no man's land was my only solution—becoming a vegetable in a hospital ward" (Ka-Tzetnik, 1989, p. 70).

In this remarkable account written more than forty years after liberation and a decade after LSD therapy with a specialist, De-Nur further elaborates on the dissociation of his personality in Auschwitz and his subsequent attempts at integration. He marvels at finally being able to write in the first person instead of the third person: "All that I have written is in essence a personal journal, testimonial on paper of . . . I, I, I, till halfway through a piece, I suddenly had to transform I into he. I felt the split, the ordeal, the alienation of it . . . I knew unless I hid behind the 3rd person, I wouldn't have been able to write at all. And lo and behold, here I am in the thick of the manuscript and totally unaware of how naturally I am allowing—from the first line onward—the connection with I. How did I miss this until now? . . . Without a shadow of a doubt I can at last acknowledge my identities, co-existing in my body" (1989, p. 71).

During his hallucinogenic treatment, De-Nur revived an intolerable memory of being caught peering through a window of SS barracks where they were raping Jewish women and writes: "I behold 'feld hure' (field whore) branded between my sister's breasts. And I see myself instantly splitting in two. I see how I leave my body, separating into two selves: I stand and stare at my body, in a dead faint on the ground. . . . I couldn't hear the camp commander's order then. I was unconscious. Now that I have left my body, I am also able to see the way Siegfried is dragging me by the feet back to the block; I am my own cortege; I am behind my own bumping head. I see Siegfried spitting in my face because he has to drag a Jew instead of shooting him [he is spared because he is a medic and valued by the commander]."

"I stare at myself, dragged by the feet back to the block and see the key to my nightmare. It's hidden beneath the brand between my sister's breasts. This time I don't fall into a faint, because I've split myself in two. Just as then and now are actually a single unit of time multiplied by two. The I of then and the I of now are a single identity divided by two. I look at my unconscious self, and I look at the self staring at my self; I look and see the key to the split. It stands behind the curtain of the swoon: the secret of the split deciphered. I see a heavy drop-curtain of fire and ash being raised jerkily. In the depths behind it rises the second curtain, blazing red. Just behind the second curtain rises curtain number three, bleeding turquoise within flaming blue. My mother. I see her naked and moving in line, one among them, her face turned to the gas chambers. 'Mama! Mama! Mama!'" (1989, p. 100).

DISCUSSION

The lifting of the amnestic dissociative curtain in De-Nur's mind, evidently aided by the psychodynamic effects of the hallucinatory experience and ten more years of soul-searching, enabled him to decode the nightmare of his life in Auschwitz. While at times in his writing it is difficult for the reader to discern his original horror from the drug psychosis or from his rich literary style, what does come across is his "knowing and not knowing," his "being here and not here" and his experience of self being "me and not me." Although dissociative in nature, his assigning a name to his "traumatized self" (Volkan, 1995b) appears deliberate and conscious as opposed to it being a structured personification which is relatively autonomous, unknown, separated by its own amnestic barrier and capable of taking over behavior as in frank DID as described by Oxnam. In Oxnam's words: "I have come to think that a lot of people, possibly all people, have multiple personae [but] . . . the biggest difference between 'normal multiplicity' and MPD is that most people recall what happens to them and they move through their array of personae. By contrast, MPD is characterized by rigid memory walls that prevent such recall until therapy begins to break down barriers" (Oxnam, 2005, p. 5). Furthermore, we have no evidence of impaired object constancy or of defensive efforts to camouflage a lack of self-constancy or a need to create the illusion of self-cohesion. Instead, De-Nur clings to the Ka-Tzetnik persona intentionally, uses him as a shield and is connected in a manner more consistent with depersonalization. If one were to try to categorize his symptoms, they might fulfill the diagnostic criteria for DD-NOS (APA, 2000) only.

In my experience, even the massive and sustained trauma from genocidal persecution in adulthood would not result in DID because the latter, in my view, is a lower level dissociative character requiring determinants from childhood. However, DID may be confused with schizophrenia which also is thought to have its origin in childhood and be associated with a preponderance of annihilation anxiety.

ANNIHILATION ANXIETY

In his comprehensive view of annihilation anxiety, Hurvich (2003) traces the importance of these "survival related apprehensions" (p. 179) throughout the analytic literature and enumerates the various terms that have been coined. They range from traumatic anxiety (Freud, 1926), aphanisis (Jones, 1929), psychotic anxiety (Klein, 1935), instinctual anxiety (A. Freud, 1936), schizoid anxiety (Fairbairn, 1940), primary anxiety (Fenichel, 1945; Zetzel, 1949; Schur, 1953), and biotrauma (Stern, 1951) in writings through the 1950s. In the latter half of the century, writers have described unthinkable anxiety (Winnicott, 1960a), annihilation anxiety (Little, 1960), background of safety (Sandler, 1960), mega-anxiety (Waelder, 1960), nameless dread (Bion, 1962), basic fault (Balint, 1968), primary unrelatedness (Guntrip,

1969), basic anxiety (Frosch, 1983), organismic distress-panic (Mahler and Furer, 1968; Pao, 1979), adhesive identification (Bick, 1968; Meltzer, 1975), fears of being negated in one's existence (Lichtenstein, 1964), disintegration anxiety (Kohut, 1977), cataclysmic catastrophe (Tustin, 1981), prey-predator anxiety (Grotstein, 1984), doomsday expectation (Krystal, 1988), infinity (Matte-Blanco, 1988), "too muchness" (Shengold, 1989, and dissolution of boundedness (Ogden, 1989).

Defined as "mental content reflecting concerns over survival, preservation of the self and the capacity to function" (Hurvich, 2003, p. 581), this psychophysiological bedrock of the human condition may be intensified as a result of inherent ego weakness, threats to the cohesion of the self, trauma (Hurvich, 1989), and disturbances of attachment, most notably the disorganized and insecure type (Main and Solomon, 1990). This fundamental anxiety may be underlying all of the classic potential dangers of object loss, loss of love, "castration," and retribution of superego (Freud, 1926), or it on its own may be the here-and-now danger of a traumatic moment. As such, it seems that a deeper appreciation of the various ways in which annihilation anxiety may be incorporated and mobilized could serve as a bridge to understanding the vicissitudes of psychic trauma and psychopathology in general. Specifically with regard to psychosis and the realm of dissociative disorders, a comparison of defenses against the manifestations of annihilation anxiety may be a crucial area of inquiry and differentiation.

SCHIZOPHRENIA VERSUS DID

There are times when seemingly autistic preoccupation and hallucinatory experiences quite reminiscent of schizophrenia, associated with the Schneiderian first rank symptoms of schizophrenia, may be present in DID (Kluft, 1987). In such cases, differentiating the two conditions is of considerable clinical importance as the therapeutic approach may be quite different. For example, how one understands these phenomena, such as auditory hallucinations, has technical implications because "talking" to the voices in DID can be shown to further the treatment whereas in schizophrenia, one may be merely colluding with a psychotic process and joining in a delusional world with the patient (Brenner, 2001, 2004a). Many analysts feel very uncomfortable with this approach which may, in fact, be a turning point in the treatment because an empathic appreciation of the dissociated mind's subjective experience facilitates an opening up of the patient's inner life, i.e., a "free dissociation" rather than free association.

These severe regressive states have been a source of confusion and interest to clinicians and warrant a revisiting of the idea of a continuum between the psychoses and the spectrum of dissociative disorders (Brenner, 2004b).

As mentioned earlier, Kramer (1993) has speculated that DID might protect one from frank psychosis and Kernberg (1973) conceptualized such a continuum, from poor differentiation of self and object representations at the psychotic end, to hysterical dissociation with mutual amnesia of personalities and underlying repression at the other end. Abse (1974) likened it to molecular disintegration in the former and molar disintegration in the latter. However, the differentiation between the two is sometimes difficult, as the number of cases of multiple personality reported in the literature were greatly reduced after Bleuler's term "schizophrenia" was introduced. Furthermore, it has been thought that some very highly publicized treatment successes of schizophrenia may have actually been misdiagnosed cases of DID (Rosenbaum, 1980). The diagnostic confusion between schizophrenia and DID has added to the doubt about the validity of the latter, but the resurgence of interest in trauma, advances in the neurosciences, and child studies of attachment styles may enable better distinctions to be made.

Volkan's theory of psychosis offers some very helpful ideas to differentiate the dissociative psychopathology from this most severe realm of psychopathology. In psychotic decompensation, the susceptibility to organismic panic or annihilation anxiety, he felt, could not be explained on the basis of decathexis of objects (Freud, 1924a, 1924b) or regression alone. He postulated the presence of an "infantile psychotic self" (Volkan, 1995a) or "seed of madness" (Volkan and Akhtar, 1997) in those adults susceptible to schizophrenia. The high concordance rate of schizophrenia in monozygotic twins (Gottesman and Shields, 1972), adoption studies (Kendler, Gruenberg, and Strauss, 1982) and neuroimaging studies over the last 25 years (Andreasen, et al., 1982; Lim, 2007; Salisbury et al., 2007) have been very convincing as to the role of biology, genetic vulnerability, and constitutional factors, but the interaction of environmental factors appears essential also (Pollin and Stabenau, 1968). Clearly, the earliest mother-infant environment provides the "channel" through which "disposition and experience" (Freud, 1914c, p. 18) evolve into early psychic structures, about which analytic writers have long been aware (Mahler, 1952; Sullivan, 1962). Therefore, extreme very early trauma, such as severe loss, neglect, and abuse involving sexualized or aggressive misuse of the developing child, may clearly be a factor. In addition, the actualization of the child's unconscious fantasies as a result of trauma interferes with the development of reality testing (Kestenberg and Brenner, 1996; Caper, 1999; Volkan and Ast, 2001, p. 569).

By definition, the "infantile psychotic self" is imbued with aggression and its accompanying affects, has impaired reality testing, and is strained by the tug of war between the forces of maturation and the failure to differentiate self and object representations. In addition, there is a perpetual state of projection and reintrojection of the self-object representations leaving the individual in a chronic state of insatiable hunger for good objects. This disturbance of desire, while not unique to the psychoses, is the subject of renewed psychoanalytic interest and thought by Lacan to be the central issue in the human condition (Kirschner, 2005). Here, however, the only hope for meaningful human contact and reasonable ego functioning would require the later development of an "infantile non-psychotic self" which would be libidinally saturated and capable of self-object differentiation and cohesion.

While an infantile psychotic self may be formed through regression due to later trauma, for example, oedipal or latency, once a child has reached adolescence, maturation of the ego has reached a point that, according to Volkan, protects one from developing frank schizophrenia. Once formed, this infantile psychotic self may theoretically shrink or "calcify" due to successful treatment, mushroom into full-blown childhood schizophrenia, or become encapsulated (H. Rosenfeld, 1965; Volkan, 1976, 1995a; Tustin, 1986; D. Rosenfeld, 1992) by the nonpsychotic self and its more mature functions that attempt to contain this "sick" aspect of the psyche. If this encapsulation is incomplete, one may see a "psychotic personality organization" characterized by a modicum of reality testing and daily functioning but where one may engage in bizarre, idiosyncratic, and private, repetitive activities or fantasies. Perhaps corresponding to the schizotypal personality disorder in the DSM-IV-TR (APA, 2000) there may be a relatively unremarkable social façade which belies such autistic preoccupations which will be recognized by the alert clinician. Another fate is the onset of an acute regression if the protective capsule suddenly cracks due to external factors which replicate the original psychotogenic influence of early childhood.

The last possibility described by Volkan is the onset of frank adult schizophrenia due to overwhelming organismic distress in which the protective, encapsulating structure essentially dissolves and is rapidly replaced by a new outer layer, the "adult psychotic self," which quells the massive pain at the expense of reality testing. This dynamic formulation would explain the sudden onset of a crystallization of "delusional insight" in acute schizophrenia. In contrast to the psychotic personality organization in which the outer layer becomes the "spokesperson" for the infantile psychotic self, here the adult psychotic self almost completely absorbs the infantile psychotic self and becomes the voice of it instead. As a result, this primitive, new self, so unable to handle the vicissitudes of reality, loses the capacity for self-observation and resorts to magical, omnipotent control and hallucinations as well as other oddities of mental functioning.

In this schema, the notions of early traumatic influence, a very damaged young self, a preponderance of aggression, extreme susceptibility to annihilation anxiety, encapsulation by the creation of an outer self, an endless cycle of projection and reintrojection of poorly differentiated self, and object representations and an outer façade which becomes partially or completely nonfunctional under stress are key elements. Thus, the infantile psychotic self would be at the psychotic end of the continuum whereas the "It's not me!" Self of the dissociative character would be at the opposite end, and its fate would be contingent upon later growthful or destructive influences. The following case illustrates the overlap of symptomatology in a patient in the middle of such a continuum.

CASE VIGNETTE

A very masculine woman, Mary, who always dressed in work clothing and was typically confused for being a man, was in treatment for approximately two decades. She was seen up to five times a week, both as an outpatient and through numerous hospitalizations. She was initially presented for treatment with acute suicidality and severe alcoholism. She was in the throes of a homosexual panic as a result of an extramarital affair with a woman and saw killing herself as the only escape from her massive guilt. Severe character pathology with borderline, masochistic and avoidant features was a diagnostic consideration until she eventually became totally abstinent from alcohol at which time her true diagnosis emerged. Her social withdrawal and blunted affect led one psychiatrist who covered for me during my vacation to think she was schizophrenic.

After a particularly self-destructive period of time, I recommended hospitalization and was sitting with her at the admissions office because she had severely cut herself and had planned to cut deeper. Suddenly, she began to look at me strangely and speak with a different cadence and usage of words. She seemed a bit disoriented but calmly told me in the third person that Mary had a blade hidden in her possessions and had full intention of using it if left unattended for any period of time. I commented on how she was speaking to me. The patient told me that Mary was very dangerous to the body and that she, Priscilla, wanted to tell me about it because Mary would not. She said that she herself could only tell someone else but could not stop the cutting on her own. This incident occurred several years into a rather chaotic clinical course of more psychiatric management than psychoanalytic therapy.

Over time, a history of maternal incest persisting into adulthood and even into the early years of treatment was ascertained. This stunning revelation was a turning point in treatment as it signaled a deepening of her trust and her readiness to let go of her sexual relationship with her mother. The patient, through her complex system of seemingly separate selves, revealed dissociated sexuality in the form of transsexualism, bestophilia, homosexuality and sadomasochistic heterosexuality. A literal life-and-death struggle over possession of the body in order to cut off the breasts and perform a sex change operation ensued over the years in which near-fatal overdoses and blood loss due to cutting required extensive hospitalizations.

A typical therapy hour would consist of her staring into space, sitting quietly for several minutes and then describing her suicidal impulses and her constant auditory hallucinations, especially inner voices from a tormented young boy, Thomas, who would scream "God is trying to kill me!" We eventually learned that Mary's mother had told her that if she ever were to reveal the sexual abuse that God would kill her. Thomas apparently represented her dissociated guilt over betraying her secret bond with her mother by telling me. Most significant in Mary's "system" was a series of masculine selves, most prominently and violently represented by Ralph, whose hatred and envy of me and my maleness represented a critical transsexual conflict in the patient's psyche.

In the transference, Mary was prone to intermittent paranoid psychotic regressions that had a "schizophrenic quality" to them. For example, one time Mary's mother told her that she saw me interviewed on TV. Mary was unable to tell me about this incident for several weeks until such time as she finally revealed that she was convinced that my office had a secret device that transmitted our conversations directly to her mother with whom I had had ongoing contact. Mary could not be convinced to the contrary at such times. She also took note of the slightest changes in the placement of the chairs, convinced that there were secret meanings in these deviations and that she was being tested by me to see if she would notice. Able to keep her own secrets inside all of her life, she did not tell me about this referential thinking for almost five years. This delusional thinking eventually resolved and her presentation was much more consistent with DID.

In the mosaic transference, Ralph and his minions expressed the sadism and envy characterized by an erotic fantasy of smashing a window with his fist, removing his bloody hand, taking a shard of glass from the window and cutting my throat as well as mutilating my genitals while he "masturbated." The "children," mostly frightened young girls, sought comfort and protection from me due to Ralph's threats to hurt them, i.e., self-mutilation. "They" eventually began to cry during weekends and breaks, signaling a thaw in Mary's initial stony avoidant relatedness. Mary, as herself, either felt dead or frightened, doubtful that anyone could help her yet remained completely devoted to the therapeutic process. She revealed that she had become mute during first grade after being molested by a female teacher in religious school, quite sure that she would be struck dead if she told. Interestingly, she had periods of silence in the sessions and experienced this conflict over speaking as a menacing, older, female presence—Millie—holding her throat and preventing her from revealing secrets of the incest.

Analysis of her resistance to speak took the form of my interpreting to the patient that she was reliving in the transference fears of retribution from her childhood and that Millie appeared to be an internal representation of her mother. I averred that the injunction against speaking did not apply to treatment as I had no intention of getting her mother into trouble and eventually Mary began to talk more. Her subjective experience was of Millie releasing the grip on her throat and backing off. Once Mary began to speak, she then feared that she would start to cry like "the children" and would never stop. She also sensed that a blood-curdling scream was stuck in her throat which, if released, would also never end. Her deadness and inhibition belied her profound, deep, inner need to finally be "heard." Mary often told a symbolic story about herself and her mother in the form of a puppy stuck in a hedge. Every time it poked its head out, it would get hit with a baseball bat. After a while, the puppy just stayed hidden in the hedge.

Reconstruction of her childhood was extremely painful, fragmented, and without temporal sequence. For example, Mary intermittently reported symptoms of blurred vision and burning in her nose and throat. Despite the disturbing nature of these complaints, they are described with "la belle indifference" and usually during times of anxiety associated with suicidal thoughts. These conversion-like symptoms resolved after an abreactive experience in which the patient recalled in various altered states being held underwater in the bathtub until she choked, started to breathe in the water and subsequently more cooperatively submitted to her mother's sexual demands. Shortness of breath and fears of suffocating were then associated with terrifying memories of her large mother sitting on her face for extended periods of time and forcing her to perform cunnilingus until the mother collapsed with orgiastic exhaustion. Haunted by the contorted expression on her mother's face at a time in her young life when she did not understand the nature of orgasm, Mary could not read her mother's face and subsequently other people's faces and became even more terrified of what was going on especially when she was left with a mouthful of mother's menstrual blood. This extraordinarily painful reconstruction occurred over a period of several years with gradual melting of amnestic states of the children and was punctuated by numerous suicidal crises. Mary's mournful lament was summarized by her cry: "Why did she fuck me? Why did she fuck me?"

The turning of passive sexual victim into active participant seemed to occur during late adolescence and early adulthood when Mary readily identified herself as having been "soul-murdered" and became more masculinized. After a lifetime of having been penetrated with everything from fingers, harsh washcloths with soap, knitting needles and broomsticks, the patient began drinking heavily and using marijuana to further alleviate her awareness of her enslavement to the mother. Ralph became stronger and more defiant, hoping to get revenge one day. What little dating the patient did usually ended in drunken, forced sex and Mary retreated further. Consoled by her writing and growing talent as an artist, she felt safest when alone in her self-created world. Therefore, her opening up in treatment was both desperately longed for and a source of ongoing terror. She had profoundly impaired object constancy, self-constancy, social skills, and consistent capacity for sublimation. To learn how to talk with people and to pay for therapy, she took a counter job in a store and worked overtime six days a week. The owner and his wife became benign, surrogate parents. By creating her own structured day program, as it were, she began to regulate herself in a safe, holding environment and build a semblance of a life.

A crucial junction occurred during an earnest but unsuccessful attempt at a medical sex change replete with bilateral mastectomy and testosterone in preparation for a surgically grafted penis. Overtly due to a lack of funds for the breast removal but owing to profound inner chaos and the realization that such a step would have destroyed her ten-year relationship with her lesbian partner, Mary became severely depressed. Nearly starving to death and ultimately requiring a short course of electroconvulsive therapy (ECT) which restored her mood but did nothing for her incessant voices and warring factions inside, Ralph became even more powerful but also eventually more amenable to talking with me. I explained to "him" that despite his nearly successful attempts to highjack the body and succeed in his plan, there was so much internal conflict that he could not have survived; he would need to compromise and find a way to accept living in the female body.

Originally convinced to the point of delusional thinking that if he killed off everyone inside he would be victorious and become exclusive owner of the body, this dissociated form of suicidal thinking eventually and begrudgingly gave way to a truce and a deeply emotional acknowledgment that maybe I was not Ralph's enemy after all.

Signaling a long-awaited alliance with this most deeply disturbed stratum of Mary's psyche, two significant psychological developments occurred. The first—the dissociated amnestic barrier between Mary and her sadistic, masculine self, Ralph—became quite porous and "coconsciousness" occurred on a more regular basis. Now in a mental state approaching depersonalization, Mary could be present and observe her mental functioning when Ralph was out and vice versa. Secondly, her paranoia and use of projective defenses, an uncommon feature in less disturbed dissociative patients but more evident in schizophrenic states, substantially diminished. As the patient became more able to tolerate and own her psyche, she described how by becoming an active participant in the incest she needed to become a man. Ralph then reported how he began to forcefully "fist-fuck" the mother as he became older, hoping to hurt her and drive her away only to succeed in providing more pleasure for what sounded like an insatiable monster. At a moment when the patient seemed unusually receptive to my own "penetration"—a transference interpretation—I said that I now understood that his wish to smash my window with his fist and stab me in a bloody orgy reflected his wish for deadly, sexual revenge against the mother. Quietly taking in my words, Ralph—for the first time—began to cry and as tears streamed down his face protested all the wrongdoings that they had been subjected to and how they did not deserve any such mistreatment. After the hour, Ralph left me a tender message saying that he actually felt better, had more control, and had never felt so calm. The work continued in this vein as the patient became more integrated over time.

CONCLUSION

The effects of severe early trauma on development may be considered along a continuum from schizophrenia to dissociative psychopathology, which is epitomized by DID. Pending constitutional vulnerability and the level of development at the time of massive interference in the development of the self, such disturbances may result in an "infantile psychotic self" in the schizophrenia and an "It's not me!" Self in DID. The "It's not me!" Self may protect against psychotic disintegration through its ability to manufacture personifications which are compromise formations and may incorporate the dream ego, perverse sexuality, intergenerational transmission of trauma, near death experiences, and the divisive effect of aggression. In Mary's case, the creation of a potentially lethal masculine self may have prevented a frank schizophrenic organization from developing. Therefore, particular attention to the nature of the disturbances of the formation of the self, the role of encapsulation, the reliance upon dissociation, amnestic defenses, and the fate of annihilation anxiety may help in the differentiation of these conditions.

DID, formerly known as multiple personality disorder, multiple personality, double conscience, dual personality, and a host of similar other names, is a disorder of the self characterized by an overall lack of self-constancy and the illusion of cohesion. This illusion is created within the various personifications or dissociated selves which appear to have developed in order to encapsulate traumatic memories, as well as annihilation and separation anxiety. It is probably the most controversial and misunderstood mental condition known at this time. Clinical experience with adults has led to three basic assumptions: (1) that DID is the extreme end of its own continuum of dissociative character pathology, i.e., a lower level dissociative character; and (2) that the central defensive operation is dissociation rather than repression or splitting. Dissociation, rooted in disturbed communication in the mother/infant dialogue, is, to paraphrase Freud, the intrapsychic "precipitate" of these earliest object relations. It may be defined as a "defensive altered state of consciousness due to autohypnosis[3] augmenting repression or splitting. It develops as a primitive, adaptive response of the ego to the overstimulation and pain of external trauma which, depending on its degree of integration, may result in a broad range of disturbances of alertness, awareness, memory, and identity. Dissociation apparently may change in its function and may be employed later as a defense against the perceived internal dangers of intolerable affects and instinctual striving. Thus, it may be a transient, neurotic defense or . . . the predominant defense" (Brenner, 2001, p. 36); and (3) that there is an underlying Dissociative or "It's not me!" Self which disowns mental contents and creates the illusion of separate selves. In contrast to schizophrenia, some of these selves appear to function with rather high levels of ego strength, subliminatory capacities, creativity, empathy, and reality testing. Developmental research and reconstruction from analytic work with adults suggests that these conditions require precursors in childhood even though nonspecific psychotic and dissociative regressions may result from adult trauma alone. A deeper understanding of annihilation anxiety as well as the nature of this putative continuum may provide better insights into resilience, vulnerability, and the refinement of analytic approaches to treatment.

In conclusion, it is my opinion that DID exists. It is not a hoax. In my view, not only is it a clinical missing link but it is truly a clinical Rosetta Stone. The enormous complexity of this entity in response to massive and at times life-threatening, sustained trauma in childhood illustrates the human mind's potential to manifest virtually every type of psychopathological symptom in one individual. Understanding all of these mechanisms will require an integrated, multidisciplinary effort which in turn will help us better understand other conditions and further refine psychoanalytic therapy. Those who survive and benefit from our current treatment present us with an enormous opportunity to rethink our cherished theories and move toward a more encompassing, unifying theory of adaptation and psychopathology.

NOTES

First published in © The Psychoanalytic Quarterly, 2009, *The Psychoanalytic Quarterly*, Volume LXXV, No. 1, pp. 57–105.

1. It should also be pointed out that in those individuals for whom identification with a violent, brutal aggressor vastly predominates over identification with the victim, rescuer or bystander, the prognosis for treatment may be in question as sadism, impulsivity, and severe superego pathology may preclude the development of a therapeutic alliance with such "dissociopaths." A subpopulation of so-called serial hoaxers may be in this category also.

2. Freud's formulation regarding his depersonalization while in Rome (Freud, 1936) is relevant here in that he created an intrapsychic illusion that it was not he who was actually there lest he surpass his father and risk the retribution from his superego.

3. The autohypnotic defense, as described by Shengold (1986), incorporates Freud's early ideas about the hypnoid state and its various functions, including motivated forgetting, enhanced remembering, and increased vigilance.

3

The Enactment-Prone Patient

. . . by the end of the week she decamped from me too.

—Sigmund Freud, 1914

In his second paper on technique, better known to us as "Remembering, Repeating, and Working Through" (Freud, 1914a), Freud describes how the cathartic method of reviving the past was eventually replaced by analytic attention to what was happening in the present moment. Hypnotic retrieval of a traumatic memory at the moment of symptom formation which resulted in an abreaction and a hoped-for cure gave way to analysis of resistance to free association. Introducing the concepts of "acting out" and "compulsion to repeat," he points out how the psychological inability to recover memories, words, and feelings becomes expressed repeatedly in actions, both within and outside of the transference.

Though he confidently asserts that allowing free expression of instinctual strivings in the transference is necessary in order to allow the neurosis to be worked through, he also cautions that the patient must be compliant with the conditions required in analysis. Thus, action-prone patients and those who do not free-associate easily would be very difficult or impossible to treat psychoanalytically. As an example, he cites traumatized women who were subject to sexual aggression in early life as being especially silent at the onset of treatment. In addition, Freud observes that in conversion hysteria the pathogenic experience is usually not remembered, whereas in other conditions one might say: "I have always known it; only I've never thought about it" (Freud, 1914a, p. 148). He comments that such total forgetting is rare except in hysteria, implying but not elaborating any further about the unusual nature of the repression in such cases. He then describes an "extreme example" of untamed instincts and repetitive action in "an elderly woman who had repeatedly fled from her house and her husband in a twilight state and gone no one knew where without ever having become conscious of her motive for decamping in this way. She came to treatment with a marked affectionate transference which grew in intensity within days; by the end of the week she decamped from me too" (Freud, 1914a, p. 154). Perhaps subtly alluding to the disappointment with a much younger hysterical patient (Freud, 1905a), Freud laments that this geriatric incarnation of Dora decamped before he had a chance to say anything which might have prevented this repetition of her tendency toward flight. What if anything Freud could have said to this woman is the essence of this paper as it sounds as though he were describing the prototypical dissociative patient in a fugue. Although the birth of psychoanalysis is inextricably linked with dramatic cases of hysterical conversion and dissociation, the direction of Freud's theorizing and the evolution of analytic technique did not lend itself to deeper understanding of these action-prone patients who, in analysis, may provocatively evoke feelings in the analyst and draw him/her into enactments (Jacobs, 1986; Brenner 2001, 2004a). After a brief review of the "dissociation of everyday life," I will then offer two clinical vignettes to illustrate ends of a possible continuum from benign enactments to malignant enactments in more severely fragmented individuals.

THE DISSOCIATION OF EVERYDAY LIFE

Freud's landmark compendium of the daily eruptions of unconscious mental life is so well detailed and convincing that many feel that the topic is exhausted and requires little more study. In *The Psychopathology of Everyday Life* (Freud, 1901), he describes the forgetting of names, words, and phrases as well as their substitution by other dynamically charged replacements. He describes slips of the tongue, i.e., parapraxes, slips of the pen, and bungled actions to illustrate the endless ways in which secondary process thinking gets interrupted by such internal pressures. It has become so axiomatic that these "errors" are unconscious in origin that it is simply assumed and accepted that repression is the underlying defense mechanism operating here. Surprisingly few articles in the literature have been written which have been focused primarily on parapraxes (Szalai, 1934; Kelman, 1975, Mintz, 1975) and the classic handbooks on psychoanalytic technique certainly mention them but generally add very little to our understanding of them or how to work with them in treatment

(Glover, 1955; Nunberg 1955; Fenichel, 1945; Greenson, 1967). Indeed, Anna Freud advised that trying to interpret a parapraxis may not only be unsuccessful but may derail the patient from the overall thrust of his or her associations at the time (A. Freud, 1936). How is it, therefore, that such a ubiquitous facet of unconscious mental functioning may be both inaccessible yet one of the most convincing evidences of Freud's basic ideas? The reflexive answer would be that, of course, they may be inaccessible because of the "depth" of the repression and the nature of resistance is such that the patient is not "ready" to accept the interpretation without much preparatory work.

In a hierarchy of the "depth of repression," there is the extreme but not unusual situation of the patient who utters a parapraxis and is so completely oblivious to it that even if the analyst were to bring it to his attention, he would have no memory of it, no curiosity about it and maybe even suspect the analyst of having heard him incorrectly. The negation (Freud, 1925b) would be so powerful that the patient would employ all means at his/her psychic disposal to disown intolerable mental content. Over time, however, one would become able to hear the analyst and realize he has made a slip, eventually hear himself without assistance and analyze its meaning. Perhaps one could even assess the progress of an analysis by following the evolution of this aspect of self-analysis. However, in situations where one is extremely resistant to hearing one's own slips, I wonder if what we are dealing with is a process that goes beyond repression and is perhaps more akin to a mini-trance because the patient speaks, albeit briefly, without observing ego and awareness of his vocalization or gesturing. Freud himself observes that in situations where one misplaces an item "it resembles 'somnambulistic certainty'" (Freud, 1901, p. 142).

Interestingly, a suicidal patient with multiple personalities, or DID, reportedly demonstrated a reversal of the usual trend when, after years of treatment resulting in "integration" with more continuous memory and continuity of self, she developed accident-proneness and started making many parapraxes (Brenner, 2001). It appeared that her internalized aggression which had been expressed through dissociated self-destructive behavior of lethal proportion in amnestic, fugue-like states became neutralized and was replaced by a considerably toned-down version associated with repression. It was as though the vestiges of her near-fatal overdose and cutting had been encapsulated into the psychopathology of everyday life where she would trip and fall or bump into things and get bruised. Despite what might appear to be vastly different phenomena, such a clinical report suggests a relationship between dissociation[1] and parapraxes or faulty actions. In this context, a potentially useful psychoanalytic definition of dissociation attempts to reconcile earlier observations of hypnoid states, their relationship to repression, and the role of trauma:

A defensive altered state of consciousness due to autohypnosis, augmenting repression or splitting. It develops as a primitive, adaptive response of the ego to the overstimulation and pain of external trauma which, depending on its degree of integration, may result in a broad range of disturbances of alertness, awareness, memory and identity. Dissociation apparently may change in its function and be employed later on as a defense against the perceived internal danger of intolerable affects and instinctual strivings. Thus, it may be a transient neurotic defense or become characterological, and may even be the predominant defense. The content of associations in dissociation is as important as the defensive purpose it serves and may be accessible through hypnosis, but very resistant to psychoanalysis unless the analyst is aware of its presence (Brenner, 1994, pp. 841–842).

So, if one considers the possibility of a continuum between dissociative phenomena and the prapraxes, then theoretical problems may arise. It is generally accepted that a parapraxis is of very short duration whereas fugue-like states are longer, and if time is a major distinguishing variable between the two, perhaps they have more in common than we generally have considered. If, indeed, there is a connection between these two situations, then perhaps more can be learned about the human mind's active capacity to banish and keep things out of one's awareness through defensive altered states of consciousness which precede the onset of the repression barrier in the young child. The sleepiness of the neonate and the demarcation between wakeful alertness and the sleeping state are the natural origin of dissociation, according to Winnicott (1945), whereas motivated forgetting in a toddler is usually not observed in the child until about age three. Melanie Klein (1921) had suggested that dissociation may trigger repression but perhaps faulty repression triggers dissociation, underlies it, and is the precursor of repression which perhaps never completely is replaced by repression. I will try to illustrate this hypothesis with the following vignette of an enactment during analysis which might generally be thought of as the result of a "neurotic symptom."

CASE REPORT—BENIGN DISSOCIATIVE ENACTMENT

Mr. P. developed a symptom in the second year of his analysis where he would periodically forget to return the men's room key and would drive home with it in his pants pocket. Later on in the day, he would realize it and sheepishly return the key at the next hour of our four-time-a-week schedule. At other times when the key was missing after his appointment and he did not discover it in his clothing, I surmised that he absentmindedly left it in the men's room but it was never found. I, therefore, had to replace the men's room key a number of times. So, I felt both intrigued and a bit annoyed as I wondered about the role of his unconscious hostility in this episodic abscondence of my key. Mr. P. was totally unaware of his behavior and seemed surprised by it each time as if it were for the first time. Efforts at understanding the possible unconscious meaning of this highly symbolic act were met with intellectualized curiosity and anxious laughter. We considered the obvious interpretation of taking my key and enviously wanting to keep it for himself as representing a male version of "penis envy." Indeed, he was plagued by a series of repetitive dreams in which he would be out hunting and would be confronted by a bear or a lion only to find that his own weapons were inadequate to the task. As a young boy, he was terrified of his stern, unavailable father who excelled at everything he did. Although young Mr. P. had many skills himself, he refused to play his father's favorite sport, baseball, with him as he felt perpetually inferior in his presence. In addition, he had a very strong attachment to his mother and felt great rivalry with his father but had to keep his affections quite concealed for fear of punishment. The image of his father swinging his baseball bat in the house was seared in his memory and served as a deterrent to any misbehavior or guilt-laden designs on his mother.

Countertransferentially, I began to feel frustrated at his thoughtlessness which inconvenienced the other male patients who complained and with whom I unconsciously identified. In my self-analytic associations, I recalled growing up in a house with only one bathroom and having to wait for "my turn" at some most inopportune times. My annoyance at family members who, in my view at the time, "took too long" and were inconsiderate was revived. Subsequently, I tried to control his symptom and master my own early dilemma, when I was a young boy, by replacing the tiny, easily pocketed key ring with a much larger plaque which attached to the key. I was sure it would be much more difficult for him to forget about. But, in so doing, I realized that symbolically I was trying to prevent him from taking what was not his by deterring him with a much bigger and imposing paternal phallus. While not as long or as threatening as father's baseball bat, Mr. P. took notice of the change immediately and assumed—correctly—that it had been done with him in mind. I explored his fantasies but neither confirmed nor denied his assumption at that time, aware of my quiet amusement but only dimly aware then that I had also delighted in having outwitted the bathroom culprits of my childhood. My triumph was short-lived because his pocketing of my key continued. This time, however, it was too large to be completely hidden and he would blithely walk into the office with it sticking out of his pocket and the attached key jingling quite noticeably. Mr. P., however, neither felt it in his pocket nor heard it as he walked in; he apparently would unlock the men's room door and in a state of "somnambulistic certainty" (Freud, 1901) put the key in his pocket while he urinated and returned to the office, forgetting to return it to a shelf in the waiting room. The first time it happened I felt amused as I relished the opportunity to finally be able to confront this culprit red-handed! Yet, I marveled at his total obliviousness as the hour progressed even when the subject of the key entered into our dialogue. When he, toward the end of the hour, was dumbfounded to discover that the key was, indeed, in his pocket all along, he reacted with a startle as though some prankster had planted it there.

The turning point occurred many months later when he reported a dream in which he was working on the rehabilitation of an old building. The structure had been stripped down to its girders and all the workmen were on the upper floors secured with harnesses and tethers except for him. He was not attached to any safety rope and he awoke in a panic. Associations to the dream continued for several hours as he recalled in much more depth his early relationship with his mother. Raising him "by the book," she adhered to a strict scheduled feeding routine, determined to raise her firstborn son correctly and to fight her urges to give in to his infantile demands for feeding or holding. Thus, he grew up having to wait for his mother to tend to his needs, an agony to which he unconsciously subjected my other male patients and to which I resonated from my own early experience.

Mr. P. developed into a very controlled, disciplined, and intellectualized man with a sarcastic "biting" sense of humor which sometimes went too far and humiliated friends or coworkers. As a young boy, however, he was extremely sensitive and possessive of his mother. An emblematic screen memory which he felt reflected his basic problem was of him running home during a sudden rainstorm at age eight and being stranded outside because his mother had run out of food and had to go to the store for more. She did not expect it to rain and thought that she would be back in time before young Mr. P. had returned from playing with his neighbor. By the time she did get back home, he was terror stricken and completely panicked. Once again, he had to adhere to mother's schedule for nurturance and wait for her.

Mr. P.'s mother died about ten years prior to treatment and he had not been back to the cemetery since her burial. He did not cry at the funeral and was left in a state of vague ambivalence toward her. His wife had retrieved a necklace of Mr. P.'s mother and gave it to him as a keepsake but he did not know what to do with it. He told me that he kept it on a shelf near the far corner of his desk along with other items that he was equally puzzled over. The first item was an extra-long bolt needed to install a kitchen appliance, a spare phallus just in case. Other items were defective shotgun shells which he could not figure out how to properly dispose of (recall the dreams of his inferior firepower). I inquired about the jewelry and asked him to bring it in as it seemed to have the quality of a linking object (Volkan, 1981) and might be imbued with magical, psychological power, and warded-off affect. Mr. P. was perplexed but dutifully brought it in. He retrieved it from his pocket and handled it like rosary beads throughout the hour. I did not ask him to bring it back but he nevertheless brought it in each day for several weeks and played with it as he associated to his mother. He then recalled that he was told that his mother had abruptly weaned him when he was six months old because she had developed a breast infection. I wondered out loud with Mr. P. if his attachment to my key was not only related to typical phallic oedipal issues that had dominated our conversation so much in the past but also related to a wish to regain his mother's breast and the closeness that he had suddenly lost as an infant. He muttered to himself about being weaned too quickly and then settled into a quiet reverie. The next time Mr. P. walked in with my key he was able to feel it in his pocket, chuckled out loud and returned it. Having found his mother in her necklace, he no longer needed my key and the symptom disappeared.

Discussion

Freud (1901) cited five examples involving unconscious mental errors associated with keys as these regularly used items can quite easily get incorporated into conflicts over leaving, going places, or retrieving things. Interestingly, Freud makes no comment on the obvious symbolism of phallic penetration in these anecdotes. In one example, a patient of Freud's very carefully hid his keys on the last day of his session before the summer break as an unconscious protest against having to interrupt analysis and having to pay his accumulated fee. Freud marveled how, in this altered state of consciousness, the patient managed to very cleverly conceal the keys between two pamphlets in such a way that they would not have been discovered were it not for a thorough search assisted by the patient's servant. Furthermore, Freud noted, not insignificantly, that one of the pamphlets was written by a pupil of his and was intended to be taken along by the patient and read during the long separation. In describing such complex actions, he observed: ". . . the unconscious dexterity with which an object is mislaid on account of hidden but powerful motives is very reminiscent of 'somnambulistic certainty'" (Freud, 1901, p. 142). In his attempt to link psychopathology to the dream states in his "metapsychological supplement to the theory of dreams" (Freud, 1917b), he touches on the "exceptional instances" (p. 227) when, in the somnambulistic state, an unconscious, instinctual demand finds it expression motorically even in such a deep state of hypnosis (Freud, 1905b, p. 295). He notes that this would be especially difficult since "access to motility normally lies yet another step beyond the censorship of consciousness" (Freud, 1917b, p. 227). Apparently content not to speculate further about this anomaly, he concludes: "we do not know what condition makes this possible" (Freud, 1917b, p. 227). It might appear that Freud did not want to venture back into the murky realm of hypnoid states and hypnotic phenomena but, in fact, he noted that patients do appear to be in what resembled an autohypnotic state when they carry out some of the "psychopathology of everyday life."

In Mr. P.'s case, while he has the profile of a "classic neurotic" with a masculine self organized around oedipal conflict, guilt, castration anxiety, and essentially obsessional defenses of isolation of affect and intellectualization, his symptom appeared to be in the realm of what many contemporary writers would label dissociation. His amnesia for his actions of taking the key from my waiting room, using it, inadvertently putting it in his pocket, urinating, leaving the men's room, and realizing much later what he had done suggested a process beyond simple motivated forgetting or repression. However, he had no disturbance of self as seen in more severe dissociative psychopathology and his absentmindedness seemed localized to this behavior. The action and forgetting had the quality of a circumscribed, micro-fugue lasting minutes or hours which was not abated by typical interpretive efforts.

On a deeply unconscious level, we ultimately discovered that he felt entitled to twenty-four-hour access to my bathroom which symbolized his mother. Warded off by a defensive, altered state, a condensation of oedipal and pre-oedipal strivings for her dominated his psyche and, when referring to his wife, he often made slips of the tongue referring to her as "my mother." Since many writers consider that a self-hypnotic state underlies dissociation, it is perhaps significant that Freud ". . . finds a parallel in the way some people sleep, for instance, a mother who is nursing her baby [and the hypnotic state]" (Freud, 1905b, p. 295).

ATTACHMENT AND THE PRECURSORS OF DISSOCIATION

To summarize the findings described in greater detail in chapter 2, it is now believed that the earliest infant-mother caretaker relationship has important implications for the development of dissociative symptoms and defenses. As a defense, dissociation has been previously described as an altered state of consciousness, due to autohypnosis, which develops in response to overstimulation or trauma, but through a change of function, may be redeployed as a defense against perceived inner danger or instinctual strivings or intolerable affect. Depending on the degree of integration of the ego, it may be a transient, neurotic defense or the predominant characterological defense associated with disturbance in identity (Brenner, 1994). Since a recognition of disorganized attachment patterns (Main and Hesse, 1990; Main and Solomon, 1990) and their implications for behavioral problems in school-aged children (Main, 1993), Bowlby's (1969) original idea of a preadapted behavior system to maintain a feeling of security has been enthusiastically embraced by developmental researchers studying the origins of psychopathology. As a two-person model of defense and conflict, such early attachment behaviors form the basis of the "unthought known" (Bollas, 1987), i.e., implicit enactive memories which predate the development of symbolization and explicit memory (Stern et al., 1998; Lyons-Ruth, 1999). As such, there is mounting evidence of a pathodevelopmental line from disorganized infant attachment to "internalized dialogue as defense" to dissociative phenomena.

Since Liotti's (1992) observation of the similarities between dissociation, unintegrated mental contents and the behavior of disorganized infants, this form of attachment has received enormous clinical and research attention. A longitudinal study (Ogawa et al., 1997) from infancy to nineteen years supports the correlation between disorganized attachment and later onset of dissociative symptoms with intercurrent trauma enhancing this link. In particular, maternal communication errors, role confusion, and sexualized communication were thought to be more highly correlated than the more overt hostile or disoriented behavior. Biological or genetic vulnerability, such as perhaps hypnotizability (Frischholz et al., 1992) was acknowledged but not considered in this research. Laub and Auerhahn's (1993) "knowing and not knowing" very likely originates with a disturbed mother with a need not to know something about herself which impairs her ability to know her infant who, in turn, cannot fully know who he or she is. Whitmer's (2001) views on dissociation correspond with these ideas in that he, too, likens it to knowing and not knowing. He asserts that one cannot ascribe meaning to his experience until it is recognized by another.

This idea is not unlike Bromberg's (1994) position who sees dissociation as a ubiquitous, interpersonal defense because what is not known is not unconscious intrapsychically but unthinkable because it was not properly recognized by the primary caretaker. Other writers espousing a relational perspective (Mitchell, 1993; Davies, 1994; D. B. Stern, 1997) emphasized the cocreated nature of what is kept out of awareness in the dyad. Whitmer, however, goes on to define the defensive aspects of dissociation as ultimately an intrapsychic inhibition of finding meaning in experience in that it is an active decoupling of a biologically prepared process as described by Fonagy (1991) who puts forth the idea that a child, in response to the intolerability of knowing his mother's hatred toward him, will actively inhibit the development of his own mentalization. However, since children cannot acquire the capacity to integrate mental contexts unless the caregiver provides a "good enough" affective, symbolic, and interactive dialogue, dissociation originates as a two-person, interpersonal experience.

It, therefore, follows that in families where abuse occurs, a climate of denial of it exists and that absence of acknowledgment in the caretaker/child dyad promotes a dissociative state of mind. There would be "conflicted approach avoidance attempts at dialogue of the disorganized child as well as the inability of the abusive mother to help the child integrate the contradictory aspects of her experience through a collaborative dialogue" (Lyons-Ruth, 2003, p. 901). The caretaker's need not to know that her infant is in distress appears to be a central dynamic from which a host of facial expressions and behavior follows in which a dialogue is severely uncoordinated resulting in "disrupted forms of mother-infant communication [which] are important contributions to the developmental pathways that eventually are culminating in dissociative symptoms" (Lyons-Ruth, 2003, p. 905). In the following case, a very disturbed mother/child relationship as well as paternal trauma created exceedingly unfavorable conditions which the patient repeated in altered states associated with his fragmented self.

CASE REPORT—MALIGNANT DISSOCIATIVE ENACTMENT

Mr. J. was referred for intensive treatment of depression associated with pathological gambling, uncontrollable, violent outbursts, and high-risk homosexual sex. He presented as unobtrusive, mild-mannered, and obsequious; his blasé reporting of his impulse-ridden life belied the profound inner chaos beneath this veneer. From the outset, however, he conveyed such a mistrust of authority and an expectation of being cheated that he had to anticipate all contingencies and take preemptive measures. For example, he asked how he could really know that he was getting his full allotment of time. After all, if our appointment was to be at 1:00 p.m., the clock might say 1:00 p.m. but in fact it could be one second away from 1:01 and he would be cheated. Furthermore, if I ended the session at 1:45 and had someone scheduled immediately afterward, who would pay for the seconds needed for him to exit and for the next person to enter? Or, did the session actually begin when I greeted him in the waiting room, when he entered the office, or when he actually sat down? All these seconds add up in a year. And, for God's sake, if I had the audacity to charge for missed appointments, shouldn't I pay him if I had to cancel? Or, if he were responsible for missed appointments based on the Freudian model of leasing time, if I could fill the hour and charge more for it, shouldn't he be entitled to part of the difference? Or, suppose he couldn't make an appointment; couldn't he send anyone he wanted to in his place to keep an eye on me and make sure that I didn't profit from his absence? And on and on. . . . Though he delighted in demonstrating his cleverness and trying to out-think me, there was a deadly seriousness with which he fought for every penny in every transaction in his life. He would sit in sessions watching the digital clock on his cell phone, often taking calls and welcoming the disruption, but exploding with rage at the stupidity of his employees who would bother him during the sessions. After several weeks of this behavior, I began to have the distinct impression that he was actually cheating me on the time as there were occasional disparities between my timekeeping and his; he refused to leave until he was ready. During this early time when we were meeting only three times a week and, despite his downright provocations, he could be quite engaging with his humor, clever wit, and great range of knowledge. I realized I needed to learn how to "play" with him and join him in the repartee in order to avoid a totally destructive power struggle which could bring therapy to a halt before it began. Therefore, I thought I needed to engage in a certain amount of "kibbitzing" with him which bolstered his manic defense of invulnerability and kept our dialogue on a light plane. Yet, it was clear that he was quite desperate as he was helplessly aware of his utter self-destructiveness and he did show genuine affect around one issue—grief concerning the upcoming anniversary of the death of his beloved sister who died of mysterious circumstances. His eyes would suddenly well up with tears for the briefest moments in the midst of all his bluster. When I pointed out to him that I thought that this was evidence of unresolved grief and seemed like an important point of entry into our therapy, he seemed puzzled but very curious. And, so, our work began amidst this banter as he demonstrated his credo: "If you can't dazzle them with brilliance, baffle them with bullshit."

Mr. J. would become choked up as he recalled losing the only member of his family for whom he felt any love or compassion. The suspicious nature of his sister's one-car accident left him convinced that it was a suicidal escape from the type of pain that he too had been living with. Although unable to tolerate it for more than a few seconds at a time, these momentary flashes of grief gave me hope for his potential to benefit from treatment as I sensed a glimpse of his true self trapped inside, terrified but desperate to make contact with a good object. I did little more at the time than empathically share my observation with him and speak to its vital importance for what he pessimistically expected to be yet another marginally helpful and ultimately disappointing therapy. Not only did Mr. J. seem puzzled but it was also not clear if he were even aware of his tear-filled eyes at the time. Significantly, we recognized a regression during each anniversary of his sister's death, and during the one in his fourth year of treatment he reported a dream in which a young boy witnessed a girl jumping off a cliff to her death. Mr. J. awoke in a dazed state and complained of runny, watery eyes all day long until our appointment. He said he felt numb both physically and emotionally and toward the end of a more serious than usual hour, I offered the interpretation that his watery eyes came from the tears that the boy in his dream could not feel or let himself know about. Having been shaken more than once by his growing recognition of the power of his unconscious mind, he carefully listened to my comment. He then quietly told me the next day that shortly after the session his mysterious symptoms suddenly disappeared, clinical evidence that the inner reaches of his mind were gradually coming forward and being acknowledged. But, until we could proceed with the analysis of his dissociated mind, Mr. J. needed to find words for his enactments which intensified in proportion to the deepening of the transference.

Early on when I suspected the possibility of a dissociative disorder, I asked the patient to take the DES—the self-reporting Dissociative Experiences Scale. However, he was so oblivious to his altered states that he grossly underreported and came out with a score within normal limits. He did, however, endorse those items referable to self-absorption, numbness to pain, and depersonalization. Over time, he revealed in a cryptic, clue-like fashion that he had an uncontrollable compulsion to "suck cock." Despite his overtly heterosexual, married lifestyle, he had a long history of seeking anonymous sex in men's rooms, through "cruising" and, when it first became available, through Internet chat rooms. With no regard for the obvious risks of disease, getting mugged, or worse, Mr. J. thrived on the gamble and prided himself on being shrewd enough to "top from the bottom." He would first delight over haggling incessantly about the price and then carefully script each scenario, warning his pickups that he would go into an uncontrollable rage if they ejaculated while he performed fellatio. He described several occasions where, in a dream-like state, he would become overwhelmed with nausea and gagging and then severely injure those who could not control themselves. He sought out younger, well-built men who did not "look gay" and thrilled at the fantasy of convincing a straight man to submit to his sexual seduction. He emphatically denied that I was his type and sarcastically sexualized all aspects of our arrangement. He also craved anal penetration by especially extra-large dildos, priding himself on being able to take as much pain as anyone could give him. Over time, he seemed to take great delight in describing his ordeals in graphic detail. Knowing he could numb himself to enormous amounts of physical pain (as a defense against his intolerance to emotional pain), he derived a sense of omnipotent control over his paid-for assailants whom he would quickly dismiss so he could rush to the casino slot machines. Then, sitting in a trance for hours, he would often win or lose thousands of dollars at a time. So, while he was trying to "dazzle" and "baffle" me during his daily dance of evasion, he would leave the office and live out his sadomasochistic perversion on a regular basis.

Mr. J. did not like me at first as he was convinced that I came from a privileged, wealthy family that offered me every opportunity that he never had and that I held him in complete contempt for his own background and utterly twisted way of life. He mocked everything he thought I stood for, such as liberalism, materialism, conspicuous consumption, naïve idealism, hypocrisy, and exploitation of the disadvantaged. Yet, to his surprise, not only did I withstand his harangues, provocations, and insults but I even joined in with him on an occasion or two. For example, after several months of his controlling time management of the sessions, I produced a stopwatch one day which I activated as soon as I sat down with him, dismissing him immediately at the appointed time and offering him a view of my watch to "prove" I was not cheating him. He was stunned and amused as I, for the moment, beat him at his own game as I exhibited my own timepiece/phallus which would prevail in this often-contentious duel between us.

I persisted in this daily ritual with him for several more months until he realized that I was watching him watching me and he calmed down thinking that I had become more honest with him. At this point, our intersubjective experience was such that each of us was feeling that he had to watch the other very carefully. Resonating with his constant state of hypervigilance and wariness during this early phase of treatment gave me some insight into both his childhood screen memories and his current behavior. For example, Mr. J. as a very young boy recalled having an itchy rash and a rectal irritation thought to be worms. At age four, he remembered taking a greasy hair preparation belonging to his father, rubbing it around his rectum and not knowing why. At age eight, he recalled being in the men's room of a theater, putting his penis in a cup of warm water and not knowing why. He was afraid of the basement in his house and had recurring images of the burning tip of a cigarette in the darkness. While he always suspected that he had been sexually abused by his uncle who had lived with the family since his parents traveled excessively, he did not have any clear memories and offered no associations at the time. Instead, he raged on about how his self-centered, insatiable, and immature mother interfered every step along the way with his development, especially with his interest in women. He used the most vile and offensive slang when talking about women and their genitals. He was shocked that I was not shocked and became convinced that psychoanalysts are obsessed with theories about sex.

Mr. J. eventually revealed that he had several aliases, i.e., names and personae he had used during his sexual episodes and at other times where he would talk, act, and sometimes dress differently. Although he claimed to have a sense of continuity of memory and of self throughout these charades which he would have me believe were under his complete control, it was becoming more evident that he had periods of amnesia for some of the sexual experiences and their aftermath. His façade of omnipotence and imperviousness was beginning to crack as he opened up more. As perhaps an unconscious illustration of this, not infrequently he would absentmindedly leave important papers behind in my office after a session, minimizing their significance but insisting upon their return.

In the transference, Mr. J. developed an inexhaustible curiosity about me, making Sherlock Holmes-type deductions about every detail pertaining to the office. For example, he counted the ceiling tiles, estimated the square footage of the suite, and called several office buildings in the area to determine the cost of rent per square foot. He would then estimate my income and expenses, offering a number of scenarios based on how many appointments per week he thought I had, etc. Occasionally he would charge his cell phone in the waiting room before his appointment, triumphantly gloating over stealing a penny's worth of electricity from me and tauntingly justifying it based on the fact that he had to sit in a waiting room that was so cramped that he thought it violated the health code, so in return I should be grateful that he did not report me and would allow him to take my electricity. Such "deals" were the substance of his relationships, quid pro quos that he could extract from all of his interactions. Having more than an inkling that he could be a most provocative character and feeling utterly defective and unworthy of feeling better, he could not help but be most suspicious of my motives, ability, and sincerity about continuing to treat him. He needed to find out more about me before he could go any further but I was not forthcoming enough for him.

Unbeknownst to me, Mr. J. discovered my published writing and tried to play a trick on me by reporting as his own dream one that he had read in one of my case reports. Delighted with his devilish cleverness in his endless pursuit to outwit me, he could barely catch his breath before trying to find another ruse both to beat me at my own game and avoid analyzing his own dreams. A crisis and turning point in the treatment occurred when he discovered an institution that I had been affiliated with and acquired very personal information about me by misrepresenting himself to a naïve employee there. Fearing that he had finally gone too far this time, he ultimately confessed this violation of my privacy in a very emotional hour where he tearfully expected to be thrown out of treatment. Initially, I felt astounded, outraged, violated and, indeed, had an urge to throw him out of the office as he fully expected. Mr. J. very perceptively heard the tightening in my voice and became quite anxious as I struggled with the same mélange of feelings he grew up with—a sense of invasion, injustice, and rage. I told him he had precipitated a major crisis of trust, and while he may have felt entitled to violate me because of his own mistrust based on his past, I was now feeling what he feels for what he had done to me in the present. I also said that I believed that it was so phenomenally important that every detail of his thoughts and feelings needed to be analyzed if we were to move forward; at the moment, however, I was not sure I could and I told him so. In his sadomasochistic transference perversion (Purcell, 2006), he was trying to get a rise out of me, both literally and figuratively. Self-analysis of my countertransference was essential at this time.

What he learned about me through his subterfuge and through my restrained reaction set the tone for the duration of our work. He started to use the couch during our five-times-a-week schedule, became more open about his various states of mind, and began to express enormous interest in what was behind the bulging zipper of my briefcase. Through analysis of a very ambivalent paternal transference, his recurrent dreams of broken back doors and the secrets of his trance-like aliases, we were able to reconstruct the fondling, fellatio, and anal intercourse by his uncle. Eventually when his behavior outside the office was out of control and he "found himself" in a high-risk situation, such as in a gambling casino or about to pick up a young man, he would call me and leave me a message before acting on his impulses. He knew he would go so deeply into his trance that he might "forget" to tell me unless he informed me at the time. He was also asking for help to keep him from descending into a self-destructive cascade of traumatic repetition and suicidal despair. That these calls came before his action were highly significant and reflected his growing observing ego acquired through internalization of our therapeutic relationship.

Discussion

Mr. J's need to re-create his family constellation wherever he went became recognized over time. Eventually, he started to take sexual histories of the young men he would pick up, saw that they too were traumatized and felt empathy for them. As he quipped that he was playing the role of psychiatrist with them, he also saw how he identified with the aggressor and scripted his own story each time. The more painfully aware he became of his own past, the more control he acquired over his perversion. One day, he casually mused, "You know, I haven't sucked cock for over a year." However, he lamented that "I still can't come unless I have a dildo stuck up my ass. . . ." His passive longings for his uncle in the transference were poignantly expressed by his first absentmindedly turning over on his stomach while on the couch and eventually being able to articulate both his present wishes and his past trauma.

We eventually recognized that an elderly woman in the neighborhood who provided childcare essentially rescued him as he was welcome to stay at her house, often for days at a time. According to reports from other neighbors when Mr. J. was an adult, she absolutely adored this little boy and her life revolved around him. Unfortunately, her abrupt death when he was eight years old ended his safe haven. As a teenager, he stayed away from home as much as possible and moved out as soon as he graduated high school, arranging for his own college education. His longing and unresolved mourning for this maternal presence lie beneath the unresolved mourning for his sister.

It appeared that Mr. J. had a Type II "It's Not Me!" Self and an Intermediate Dissociative Character (Brenner 2001, 2004a), which would be consistent with the DSM-IV-TR diagnosis of DD-NOS (APA, 2000). In other words, his altered states of consciousness and depersonalization were such that he felt that they were partially owned and partially disowned by him, i.e., "It's me and it's not me!" According to diagnostic criteria, they did not seem to reach the level of two or more organized personifications which could take control of his behavior as seen in full-blown DID. However, Mr. J. had significant amnesia for many of his sexual encounters, was prone to impulse-ridden behavior, and provocatively drew me into enactments with him on a regular basis.

Mr. J.'s quasi-personified states of consciousness appeared to have taken form with the help of the divisive effects of internalized aggression and perverse sexuality, especially sadomasochistic homosexuality, as he maintained a heterosexual life with his wife in another state of mind. Also, there was evidence of the dream ego as an organizing influence (Brenner, 2001), as seen in his dream of watching a young boy watch a young girl jump to her death. That boy, his fragile, young masculine self, seemed to live on past the dream state in the patient's crying without conscious affect during the session and quite possibly was evident in other aspects of his child-like-self states. Over time and after countless repetitions of elements of his childhood horrors in the transference, Mr. J. appeared to acquire self-constancy.

MORE ON SELF-CONSTANCY

Self-constancy is a concept that has been surprisingly underutilized and there are considerably fewer articles written specifically about it than its counterpart, object constancy.

A review of the PEP disk through 2000 reveals that of the seventeen articles on object constancy, four of them are about object constancy and self-constancy but none are specifically about self-constancy. I am not quite sure why but perhaps it has simply been taken for granted to be an obvious counterpart or reciprocal (Parens, 2005) of object constancy. Indeed, Mahler's last stage of development in her separation-individuation model is officially termed "on the road to self- and object constancy" (Mahler et al., 1975). Although many have shortened this wordy title and simply omitted "self- and . . ." another possibility is with the advent of the school of self-psychology such earlier terms have been thought to be subsumed by Kohutian concepts such as cohesion of the self (Bach, 1986). Yet, interestingly enough, self-constancy has been described as "elusive" (White, 1987), which introduces an element of mystery or uncertainty. So, perhaps, a reexamination of the history and application of this notion might be warranted in light of more recent findings about the newborn's emerging self (Stern, 1985; Beebe, Lachman and Jaffe, 1997; Beebe and Lachman, 2002). Such a review might also yield some new insights into another entity that has been elusive and certainly much more controversial, multiple personality or, as it is now known, dissociative identity disorder, or DID. Indeed, the hallmark of this condition is the presence of other seemingly separate personality-like structures often unknown to the other due to dissociative amnesia, which appear to "take over" one's consciousness and control of the body. This phenomenon, in my view, would be the quintessential example of the problem with self-constancy.

Bach identifies three components underlying self-constancy: "(1) A reliable sense of one's continuity in space and time; (2) a reliable sense of emotional homeostasis (self-esteem regulation); and (3) a reliable sense of self-continuity across alternate states of consciousness" (1986, p. 150). This third facet is notoriously absent in one who regularly employs defensive, altered states of consciousness which are amnestically encapsulated, have different biographies and their own sense of continuity over time through what Janet called "reciprocal amnesia." Indeed, their individual senses of identity may be so great, i.e., a narcissistic investment in separateness (Kluft, 1986a) that one may experience a defensive sense of self-cohesion—an illusion, as it were—but overall has not achieved self- or object-constancy. A dramatic example of this phenomenon was seen when I showed a patient with DID videotapes of herself switching from one alter personality to another. After carefully viewing the tapes, she proclaimed with an inappropriately jubilant affect: "That's not me!" She apparently did not even recognize her physical self let alone her psychological selves at that point. Mr. J. experienced this phenomenon, but to a lesser degree. He gave up his aliases eventually and felt elated when he sensed that he was "together" enough to use his real name all the time.

CONCLUSION

In conclusion, the two male clinical cases presented illustrate that vestiges of the early mother-child relationship are represented in both benign and malignant dissociative enactments. Their masculine selves seemed to reflect different levels of development. Even in a patient with a more integrated ego who apparently has self- and object-constancy, such typically "neurotic" behavior can be traced back to its pre-oedipal origins. In the more disturbed patient with dissociated selves and polymorphous perverse sexuality, such action-proneness, until it becomes contained and tamed within the transference, may have life-threatening implications. However, there may be "deterioration during treatment" (Freud, 1914a) which may require more active intervention when such behavior is catalyzed or exacerbated by pressure in the transference. Dissociation seems to predate repression developmentally, and it may be much more ubiquitous than originally thought as it may be operative in the "psychopathology of everyday life."

NOTE

1. A full review of dissociation, a controversial phenomenon with a checkered history (Glover, 1943), in psychoanalysis is beyond the scope of this paper but will be discussed later. Originally associated with hypnosis and hypnoid states (Breuer and Freud, 1893–1895), it more recently has been seen from a relational perspective as an interpersonal defense originating in a disturbed mother-child relationship (D.B. Stern, 1997; Mitchell, 1993; Davies and Frawley, 1994; Bromberg, 1998).

4

September 11 and the Analytic Process

INTRODUCTION

While the ruins of the World Trade Center were still smoldering and the whole area was cordoned off as a crime scene, family members of those missing were permitted to visit the site and see the destruction with their own eyes. They were transported by heavily armed ferry boats, protected by Coast Guard vessels, which were dispatched from the Family Center located uptown along the Hudson River. Accompanying these groups of utterly overwhelmed people were mental health volunteers who offered them flowers, stuffed animals, and hugs. The volunteers were encouraged to "connect" with a family and to be with them during the whole ordeal, which consisted of the boat ride and a walk to an observation area and a memorial garden that had been hastily dedicated. The memorial garden contained photographs, personal effects, flowers, and placards containing vital information about the victims, enshrined in a green space along the way. All the workers, police, and military personnel silently saluted the family members as they made their solemn funeral procession to that great communal cemetery known as Ground Zero.

During one of these surreal trips, I was struck by the sight of a particularly distraught woman who tried to console herself and her family by pointing to the twisted remains of the buildings, muttering repeatedly that "there" was where her husband was, even though he had vaporized. Indeed, it was hoped that giving family members a chance to see the wreckage, to see how nearly complete it was, would help with their grief by showing them the final resting place of the victims. The discovery of tiny fragments of bones and tissue that allowed for DNA testing became further evidence that these people really had died, and it was a very important activity at the Family Center to provide the opportunity for everyone concerned to check the list to see if any of their loved one's pulverized remains were accounted for. It was a grisly and emotional task.

Early on, psychoanalytically informed volunteers could see significant differences in people's reactions, ranging from something approaching a realistic appraisal of the great likelihood of death, to denial of psychotic proportions. While the latter may have been masked by hopefulness and optimism in the initial days following the attack, when it persisted over weeks, it soon became clear to those of us in a helping capacity that mourning would be almost impossible without very active and vigorous efforts to assist those so afflicted. I felt that I was watching the genesis of a mass pathological grief reaction (Volkan, 1981).

This dreadful experience helped me better understand what an analytic patient, Mr. N., must have endured on a personal level many years earlier when his mother died suddenly and unexpectedly. He, too, never saw the dead body of his lost loved one and was left in shock and disbelief for more than twenty years. Mr. N. was in the termination phase of analysis on September 11 and, not surprisingly, his ending treatment was complicated by the events of that day.

In addition to the surveys that documented the extent of psychological stress experienced initially (Schuster, 2001) and within weeks afterward (Galea et al., 2002), reports from psychoanalysts pertaining to September 11 are also appearing in the literature. They describe their personal reactions to the horror, the unconscious motivations of those who volunteered to help in the aftermath, and the shared experience with their patients, as well as crucial technical questions about the analytic situation itself (Boulanger, 2002; Cabaniss, Forand, and Raase, 2004; Frawley-O'Dea, 2003; Gensler et al., 2002; Taxman, 2004).

In this vein, I offer this contribution and will focus on three issues: the revival of trauma, termination issues, and the effects on the patient reading his or her own case report.

CASE REPORT: MR. N.

Mr. N. gave me permission to write and publish this report as long as he could review it and give his input before it was formally presented or published. His involvement became an important step in the very process that is discussed here: the termination of psychoanalysis.[1]

Mr. N., a middle-aged, married man of Irish descent, was referred by his family doctor for psychotherapy a number of years earlier following an event that threatened to bring back bad memories of his childhood. He had attended a special gathering of people from his old neighborhood, the place where he had grown up before leaving for college, but to which he had not returned since. In fact, he had moved away from it as far as possible. During the reunion, he became flooded with paralyzing anxiety and difficulty thinking; he became very worried about his health and feared he was having a stroke. After a medical exam and reassurance that he was physically healthy, he ambivalently called me for an appointment. Although he had never consulted a mental health professional and was rather skeptical and apprehensive, he was somewhat knowledgeable about psychological matters. However, like so much of his life, this area of sophistication was intellectual and disconnected from any emotion.

In fact, there were many things in Mr. N.'s mind that were so disturbing that he could not even allow himself to think about them or to remember them, let alone to feel them. His body language reflected this stance: he appeared rigid and stiff and moved in a very deliberate, almost robotlike way. As his history emerged and our work evolved into five-time-a-week analysis, the following story was slowly pieced together.

Mr. N. was the youngest of three children born to a very sensitive, depression-prone mother and an overpowering, aggressive father. With the exception of a screen memory in which neighborhood boys teased him and broke a special toy when he was about five years old, very little was known about his young life. He could not describe the nature of his relationship with his mother until years into the analysis, when he realized how close he had felt to her, how loved he had felt by her, and how similar their dispositions were. He essentially had amnesia prior to a catastrophic event, which literally changed his life overnight.

When he was a teenager, his mother left to do an errand one evening and never returned. The events of that fateful day were never explained to him and he never asked. All he knew was that she had fallen and died. It was a blur—the police cars, the funeral, the flowers, the people, the snow—flashes in his mind, a dream-like experience which left him in a lifelong trance, as he described it. His father quickly remarried. Mr. N. drifted off to college, and his mother's death was rarely spoken of again. His stepmother, whom he never fully accepted, became the new center of his father's life, which seemed hardly to have been interrupted by the tragedy.

Mr. N.'s strong constitution and his tenacity—qualities not always used in the most adaptive ways—helped him move along through life. He could be quite obstinate, fixed in his ideas, and prone to procrastination to an almost crippling degree. He refused to be rushed about anything, and surprises of any kind threw him into an uncharacteristic rage. With the exception of these outbursts, he expressed very little emotion; it was as though he were living behind a glass wall.

Although he yearned for deeper relationships with people, his involve-
ments were tentative, superficial, and unsatisfying. As a young man, Mr.
N. traveled around the world, vaguely aware that he was searching for
something, not realizing until well into his analysis that he was looking
everywhere for his mother. During a wandering pilgrimage throughout his
ancestral homeland in Ireland, he became disoriented and panic-stricken,
so he sought comfort from a local religious leader, who invited him to
study at his seminary. Mr. N. further deteriorated, feeling helplessly trapped
and a bit paranoid. He eventually "escaped," but only with the help of his
bigger-than-life but usually unavailable father, who feared his son was becoming brainwashed and indoctrinated into a cult.

The theme of Mr. N.'s vulnerability to domination by powerful and
charismatic men figured prominently in the transference, as Mr. N. was
extremely wary and skeptical of my motives, especially as he felt himself
becoming more and more enchanted by the psychoanalytic process. He associated to the mythological figure of Theseus, who, he said, could not get
off the bench on which he was sitting in the anteroom of the underworld
without leaving the skin of his buttocks behind. Mr. N. feared he would
become so attached to the couch that he would not be able to pull himself
away without enormous effort and pain. It did not consciously occur to
him at the time that he was also on a journey to the underworld in search
of his dead mother.[2]

By the time he started analysis, Mr. N. was married, with children, and
was an architect in a large firm. His wife was kind and devoted. Since she
had experienced losses in her own life, issues of intimacy and abandonment
plagued them both. Beneath the surface of his "success" in life, therefore,
the patient felt rather fraudulent as he sensed there was something deeply
wrong inside. Devoted and dutiful himself, he could not feel or express his
love to his wife and lived in abject fear of a catastrophe befalling her or his
young sons. His life was scheduled and structured to the minute. He could
not tolerate anything unexpected or out of place. He needed to anticipate
every detail of his life lest panic and rage overcome him. Spontaneity was an
anathema to him. Though he sought refuge in the perfection of his building plans, many of his best projects never got off the ground, as it were.
He always suspected that his father used his influence to get him his rather
prestigious position in his firm and wondered if he really had the capacity
to achieve success on his own.

In the first years of his analysis, which continued for well more than a
decade, Mr. N. wore a very dark suit and lay perfectly still on the couch with
his hands folded. Between his fear of making a mistake and the stiffness of
his joints, at many times he appeared to be lying in state. He often spoke of
flowers on his mother's coffin and his dread of opening it up. This image
became a metaphor for his resistance to free association and the opening

up of any painful topic. He never saw his mother's dead body at her funeral, deferring to his father, who shielded him from the horror of it all. So,
even after all these years, how could he really know she was actually dead?
Maybe it was all a cruel hoax or a bad dream.

Many years later, during the seventh year of analysis and after much hard
work, I told him one day that, having heard all the evidence, I thought she
was indeed dead.[3] Mr. N. was stunned and he cried, as though hearing this
for the first time. He hated me intensely for being the bearer of such bad
news. But until he could begin to accept this reality, he fought this fact in
analysis with all his psychic might. His associations were sparse. His dream
material was fragmented and was typically about bleak, ice-covered mountains, barren landscapes, or frustrated attempts to obtain a meager meal.
Despite the terseness of his thoughts, his syntax had the quality of a long,
run-on sentence that made it difficult to know when he was finished. As a
result, my interventions often felt to him as though I were interrupting his
reverie. As perhaps an early foreshadowing of his difficulty in terminating,
I sensed this tendency in him most acutely toward the end of each hour,
when it seemed as though he could go on indefinitely. His feelings were
very easily hurt despite his veneer of imperviousness.

Metaphors from the world of athletics entered our discourse as his enormous difficulty in allowing things to come to his mind without censoring
were seen as "running out the clock," in the hopes of tiring me out so that
I would give up on him out of sheer exhaustion. We became rivals in a
competition to see who had greater stamina. As in a daily mental wrestling
match, he created a representation of our bodies twisting, turning, and lying
on top of one another in an effort to gain an advantage over the other. Unspoken fears and wishes to sexualize our imagined body contact increased
his anxiety, as he felt under the spell of a deepening transference with no way
out. When he discovered that I had done work related to the Holocaust and
correctly suspected that I, too, had a personal connection to an enormous
tragedy, he felt momentarily relieved. As though he could now rationalize
his feeling so close, he allowed himself a fantasy of us hugging each other
and crying in each other's arms. It was striking to me how only through grief
could the two of us—two men—become emotionally intimate.

Mr. N. had few friends, and his feelings of being separated from people
by transparent barriers, his "trance," came to be ever so slowly challenged
by our daily meetings. The opportunity to really be known by another terrified him most of the time, and I was very aware of his quiet panic. Much
later, in the eighth year of analysis, he attended a talk I gave on the Holocaust. We analyzed how his curiosity, envy, admiration, and secret pleasure
at having a relationship with the speaker enabled him to overcome his
embarrassment about his increasingly deep feelings in the transference and
permitted him to attend. I felt pleased that he found out about this talk and

came to see me there. I was aware of how intensely he was watching me as I spoke, and that I became more of a flesh-and-blood being for him. As I became more fleshed out, so, too, did his mother become more of a three-dimensional being, not just an apparition from decades earlier. Yet such ideas terrified Mr. N. most of the time.

Attempts in the first year to have his father rescue him yet again from another cult-like figure were unsuccessful, as I politely refused to accede to his father's demands to talk to me about his son's latest misguided adventure—psychoanalysis. To his credit and as an example of his scrupulous intellectual honesty, Mr. N. ambivalently acknowledged such a desperate wish for rescue as he vehemently protested the man's controlling nature.

The sad truth was that Mr. N. really did not know that his mother had actually died, and much of his work in treatment was about coming to terms with this incalculable loss. In fact, the construction of the sequence of events from the last time he saw her until the end of the funeral, a period of fewer than four days, was one of the central topics of our work. He came to realize that this hole in his memory, much like a mysterious black hole in outer space, exerted such a gravitational pull on his psyche that it almost sucked the life out of him. It became a touchstone to which all of his associations could be linked. Each day of the week took on a special significance in his temporal connection to the actual day she died.

On the anniversary of her death,[4] we began to commemorate the tragic events that the patient slowly constructed from documents that, despite being easily obtained, took him years to prepare himself to acquire. He planned to visit her grave but would get lost. He also "practiced" by visiting another cemetery and finding a headstone with the same last name; he could then pretend that this was *her* grave, but knew that it really was not. In so doing, he could "prove" to himself that she really was not dead, since he knew that her remains most certainly would not have been actually buried there.

Terrified of making a trivial mistake for fear that another calamity would occur, Mr. N. found any changes of his schedule a source of enormous anxiety and confusion. He had great difficulty remembering any changes and on occasion showed up at the wrong time, being unsure what to expect. Such events took on an almost mystical significance as he eventually associated to the fantasy that his mother might be there at such times—either she was secretly coming to see me then, or he would find her in the waiting room. In a sense, *he* would be the one surprising *her*. Terrified of what she would say to him and how she would look, he tortured himself with fantasies of her deteriorated body rising from the grave, and of her being very angry with him for not having done more with his life. He reported a dream of being in a desert and coming upon dried bones. These daytime and nighttime preoccupations seemed to reflect his blocked mourning process and concretized what he was determined to do—to find his mother once again—through analysis.

In the third year of treatment, Mr. N.'s young son had a potentially life-threatening experience, which revived the past and eerily foreshadowed the events of September 11 years earlier. The young boy witnessed a freak accident in which debris falling from a building fell to the ground and crushed two passersby to death. He was just yards away with a group of classmates on a school trip. At first, Mr. N. seemed unfazed by this tragedy, but it actually triggered his sinking deeper into his self-hypnotic reverie. He became fixated on this event, despite his best efforts to banish it from consciousness, as his worst fears were almost realized by this senseless, random loss of life. The falling down of parts of the building reactivated the mental fog associated with his mother's death, so he wordlessly anguished on the couch for many weeks before he could verbalize this most recent tragedy. He had all-consuming fantasies about digging up dead birds and reburying them. The birds were symbolic of both him and his mother, as he sensed that his emotional self had died, too, and was buried with her. He developed other obsessional symptoms, such as a long-standing preoccupation with water filling up his basement. Over time, he came to realize that these reflected his unconscious wish to exhume his mother's body—both to make sure she was really dead and to see her one more time, to say good-bye—as well as his dread of being overwhelmed with grief. He feared that, were he to start crying, he would never stop and would flood his whole house with his tears.

Gradually, over the years, the patient's dream life also reflected a thaw in his emotions. The ice mountains gave way to greenery and water in the seventh year of treatment. And Mr. N. brought in personal items associated with his mother, such as a blanket and an alabaster egg; he identified with the egg, as it was impenetrable, rock-hard, and yet quite breakable. Like Mr. N., it sat silently and enigmatically for a long period of time, hardly being noticed while it, too, longed for new life to develop inside and burst forth—to hatch a new bird to replace the dead birds of his obsession.

Mr. N. eventually remembered an incident with his mother that illustrated his profound guilt over her death. Several years prior to her death, she nearly lost her balance walking down some steps while arguing with Mr. N. over a curfew issue. He felt blamed for her misstep, and this insight into his guilt helped him understand why he was so plagued over what had been her last thoughts during her fatal accident. Indeed, he had been tortured over whether it was a concealed suicide, simple clumsiness, or just a random twist of fate. Over the course of analysis, a new possibility emerged: that she had been distracted by an unconscious conflict, perhaps about him.

Oedipal longings for his mother emerged powerfully in a cross-gender transference, as Mr. N. experienced jealousy over my family and other

patients who might take up my time. The revival of his mother in the transference facilitated memories of his early life with her, as he eventually discovered that his mother and he had in fact been very close; indeed, she had
loved him dearly, and her sudden death had profoundly altered the course
of his life. The paradox in his analysis was that she needed to be resurrected
in the transference in order for him to truly know that she had died in the
first place (Brenner, 1988). Then, having worked so hard to find her again
in the transference, he could only be rewarded by having to give her up once
again through termination, to permit his taking a huge step forward in the
mourning process. Recognizing his own internalization of her and knowing
that she was always inside of him consoled him.

Mr. N. agonized over termination and envisioned it for several years,
postponing it numerous times before setting a date in the autumn of 2001.
I believe that he would have terminated at that time, but the events of September 11 affected him so deeply that our work continued for another two
and one-half years. His professional activities frequently took him to the
World Trade Center area, and he was very familiar with a number of firms
that were greatly affected by the destruction. On September 12, when he
entered my office, he was pale, tentative, and almost devoid of emotion.
Here is an excerpt from that hour:

Patient: When I heard about the World Trade Center, I got very concerned
about you.

Analyst: And I got very concerned about you . . .

Patient: It's more than I can feel. I am stunned and numb and sick. I have
an urge to sit. All the losses, and to think that I was here crying at just that
time yesterday. Then, I went by [the location where his son almost got killed
by debris falling from a building]. I feel that sensation in my groin again [a
recurrent, somatic manifestation of strong affect]. [Silence.] I was sitting with
my friend and talking. [Very long silence.] I have a big wish to have a beautiful
young wife like him because she reminds me of my mother. [Silence.] How do
I live my life after a catastrophe? [Silence.] It's decades later and there's still
cloudiness. [Silence.] I'm pulling out my hair. It's too hot to tell you about.
[Silence.] I had such a strong relationship with her and I tricked myself into
telling you about her in this transference. [Silence.] But she was very controlling and I think she felt suicidal when I tried to date a girl. [Silence.] The night
she died I was home watching TV. She should have been home by 5 p.m. I
got very anxious. My mother never came home again. [Silence.] But I had to
leave for a meeting and didn't wait, and then never even thought of calling my
father to find out where she was. [Silence. When the patient came home from
the meeting much later and had seen the police cars, he had known something
was terribly wrong, and at that point his father had told him the bad news.] My
wife called my father and told him about the World Trade Center, and then I

spoke to him, so this time I told *him* the bad news. A reversal. Perverse satisfaction. [Silence.] Like Pearl Harbor. [Silence.][5]

Mr. N. was reluctant to talk much more about September 11, and shortly afterward he reported two dreams. In the first dream, a huge crane was suspending a car, which was being repeatedly smashed against a building. The building was insulated with very thick Styrofoam. The Styrofoam insulation was like his self-induced trances, which insulated him from both outer dangers and inner anxieties. He could not acknowledge the reality of September 11, which, like the car in his dream, repeatedly bombarded him and everyone else at that time. In the second dream, the patient went to his doctor and received two (twin) injections of a vaccine. His associations to this material led him to the realization that he had hoped analysis would not only cure him of the complications of his first catastrophe, but would also inoculate him against any future calamities, such as the death and destruction of the Twin Towers. The near death of his son years ago and the massive destruction on September 11 shattered any such illusion.

The recurrent images of the jets smashing into the Twin Towers, the falling debris, and people falling out of the buildings overwhelmed him. The falling death of his mother and the near death of his son telescoped into the horror of September 11, and he became frozen once again. Learning of memorial services with flowers and large crowds for victims who were never seen again induced a regression in him. Thus, the building insulated with Styrofoam in his dream seemed to represent his mind's wish to insulate itself from this terror that he could not escape as reality kept hitting him in the face.

However, Mr. N. experienced not only regressive but also progressive trends. While unresolved grief over his mother and great worry about his family's safety consumed him, he was able to construct more details of his childhood, as well as to further emancipate himself from his father. Termination was a daily topic and, now more than ever, the idea of abruptly breaking off contact with me, despite years of anticipation of exactly this, was an intolerable enactment of his mother's sudden disappearance from life. Mr. N. insisted upon a "weaning," allowing himself the option to increase the frequency of visits if he felt too anxious. We talked extensively about this idea, which to him seemed the only way he could muster up the courage and strength to get off the couch. Once more, he associated to his mythological alter ego, Theseus, whose skin was torn off when he got up.

I felt that the patient's profound attachment to me, coupled with his passivity and penchant for procrastination, was such that respecting his initiative in this matter was vital.

I was, therefore, ultimately agreeable, and we maintained our five-times-a-week schedule for the next year. In September 2002, Mr. N. decided that it was time to cut back to once a week. Each time he wanted to make a change, we analyzed his feelings and the importance of his feeling himself to be in control of his fate. Though he initially denied the significance of the anniversary of September 11 as having any influence on the timing of his plan, he easily recognized that his internal calendar was always quite reactive to dates and times. He quickly felt that the transition was too drastic and opted for twice-a-week meetings, continuing to use the couch. Knowing he could find me if he needed to was very reassuring, and we continued with this pattern for the next several months.

By the time we reached the anniversary of his mother's death during the winter, Mr. N. was once again determined to cut back to once a week, and he did so. Significantly, at his request, we met each week on the day of the week that she had died. The poignancy of this weekly commemoration intensified our sessions and the imminent loss of his analyst. He tried sitting up at that time, and reported a dream: He was riding on an empty bus with only the driver. They drove through a new development and he could not get off when he wanted to. It was unclear if there really was a stop at this point. However, he eventually did get off and walked back home. A woman was there and he realized that he had left a package behind on the bus. Once again, knowing that he could control our meetings and emotional distance, he was quite content with this "new development" and was not quite ready to leave. He still had some unfinished business, represented by the package left behind on the bus. That unfinished business consisted of a further reworking of his oedipal longings for his mother and a reduction of his fear and defensive idealization of his father.

Mr. N. then decreased his visits to twice a month throughout the spring and summer of 2003, prior to my break. He then wanted to reconsider the situation in September. Around this time, Mr. N. read an article that I had written in a medical journal about September 11, in which I described my volunteer work in New York at Ground Zero and at the Family Center (Brenner, 2002). Earlier he had accused me of pushing my own agenda with him about the significance of the events on that day; now he had "proof" of this, but was still not inclined to elaborate.

In fact, I *was* deeply affected and his supposition was not a complete projection. I acknowledged as much to him, but also pointed out that he would have avoided the issue without some inquiry on my part. He sheepishly agreed and associated further to his father's perennial avoidance of his mother's death. He cited his recent break with a long-standing family Christmas tradition, which silently colluded with that denial. During the first Christmas after his mother's death, his father was already remarried, and his stepmother literally stepped in and occupied the mother's seat at the dinner table. Mr. N. had not missed a Christmas dinner with them since, although he was unable to speak up and say anything about his missing his mother. It was a triumph for him to confront his father and to start a new tradition with his own nuclear family after September 11.

He finally disclosed that each time he went to New York, he actively avoided the "hole," which was a condensation of Ground Zero, his mother's grave, and a cesspool. This "hole" also alluded to his old obsession about dead birds in a hole and his wife's/mother's genitals. He so regularly referred to his wife as his mother that these parapraxes became somewhat of a standing joke that made him very sad. Further "digging" enabled him to more deeply address his buried longings for his mother and his dissociated rage at his father, which were symbolized by the birds. He also recognized an increased aversion to visiting his mother's grave, even though he had managed to go there a number of times in recent years. As the fantasies of her physical appearance and his sexual wishes for her became more conscious, it was too painful to visit again.

Mr. N. continued to imagine resuming a full schedule on the couch—essentially having analysis for life, which would ensure him meaningful human contact and a forum in which to address the next catastrophe, whenever it might occur. I was flexible with his plans and went along with whatever he wanted, maintaining an analytic stance and expressing curiosity along the way. We recognized that a variety of familiar internal factors conspired to make Mr. N. want to continue on the twice-a-month schedule, and at that time, he opted to sit up in a chair across from me for part of the sessions. He had sat up several times during the previous winter, and in retrospect felt that he had rushed things by doing so. We continued with this protocol during the fall and winter, through February 2004, noting a milestone anniversary of his mother's death.

Mr. N. was intrigued when I asked if I could talk to colleagues about our work, as he hoped he would finally learn what I *really* thought about him. However, he did not want to feel pushed by this request, as was his attitude about most requests or demands made of him in his adult life. The fantasy of being the subject of one of my papers had come up a number of times over the years, and now his opportunity to achieve "special" status had arrived. I did not know what he would do, and had other ideas in mind for my talk should he be unable to give his consent. However, I did not try to conceal my interest in wanting to discuss *him*. Knowing his propensity to postpone a decision indefinitely if possible, I realized that by telling him when the presentation would be, I was essentially giving him some sort of a deadline. He then agreed and began to pressure *me* to get on with it and show him the report at once! I was impressed by his disappointment the week before I handed it to him, and sensed how important this activity might be. Perhaps it had the quality of a final exam, a rite of passage, or some other concrete document verifying an individual's status. But unlike his mother's death certificate, this report would certify the patient's life. He waited with uncharacteristic impatience for me to give him the report, as though I were suddenly holding him back from leaving.

ON READING HIS CASE REPORT

Mr. N. seemed triumphant when I handed him the report (a version of the previous section of this article), but suppressed his curiosity to read it until after the session. He expressed envy over my ability to write, but also took stock of his own abilities. With this document now in hand, he felt he could finally go forward, although he wondered if he could truly continue analysis on his own, i.e., do self-analysis. In response to his own question, he described a shelf on which he assembled a collection of photos and mementos, a concretization of the construction of his life through analysis. This chronology of his life was very reassuring and organizing for him, since he had not been able to see the unfolding of his life before analysis. Like child survivors of the Holocaust whose lives were massively interrupted and who did not experience a sense of continuity of the self into adulthood (Kestenberg and Brenner, 1996), Mr. N. now felt that he knew who he was.

Mr. N. then told me he wanted to meet me the following week instead of at our prearranged appointment for the week after. I knew he would be eager to discuss the report and chose not to inquire any further about this change; I simply complied with his request because I did not want to inhibit his enthusiasm, as he remained quite prone to shame and embarrassment. In the next session, he quickly handed me a two-page response to my report. We decided, since he was eager for me to read it, that I would do so silently while he read it to me aloud. Here are excerpts from Mr. N.'s response, written in the third person:

> Very strong—almost overwhelming. Almost enchanting. Exhausting. He had feelings of sadness and joy—evidenced by his tears and smiles . . . the story of his falling down and his rising up. . . . The case study was a descriptive review and the analyst's eulogy [bereavement]. This concrete document was reminiscent of the unveiling of the headstone of a grave. . . . It was a documentation of Mr. N.'s life and hard work in analysis. Documentation has been an important tool to combat Mr. N.'s skepticism and disbelief. That this documentation came to be a means for termination is an interesting occurrence. . . . He, too, fell and died. . . . Individually and together, analyst and analysand interpret and craft this story . . . [and] the analyst assists Mr. N. to thaw, resuscitate, and revitalize. . . . Both analyst and analysand work and grow (mature) together. . . . Sharing stories was instrumental and helpful to his process of termination. . . . His journal writing appears to mirror and concur with the case study description. In fact, his activity of reading the case study and writing this response was a literal

step forward ([but] he experienced a physical stiffness reminiscent of his initial visit while typing. . . . Evidences of avoidance; intellectualization). He better realizes that much of his visions of perfection—both good and bad—are pipe dreams, defenses and distortions. . . . The remainder of his life waits for him to love and work. . . . He is somewhat fearful, anxious, and at times still despairing. Alone, daunted, and not good enough. This termination is a powerful occurrence. . . . Yes, September 11 was a calamity for him. . . . He notes in his journal that the trauma of his mother's death is being brought to the forefront of his mind. . . . He did his best to mourn and grow confident and embracing in the last decade. . . . Termination is/has been intolerable to Mr. N. He has resisted with all of his might. . . . He dreams and uses the metaphor of vehicle and vessels. . . . He has stepped off the train . . . hung around the station . . . but for now, Mr. N. desires to leave the station and begin his life (love his wife?). . . . This particular journey now has increased integrity and coherence. . . .

Mr. N. was pleased with himself and his ending with "feelings," he said, as tears welled up in his eyes. He was deeply appreciative that he never felt pushed to leave before being ready. He was now more ready to give up his fantasy of perfection (Gaskill, 1980) and to accept the limitations of life and of his own life in particular (Ticho, 1972). Although he had wished for a never-ending analysis and certainly wondered about his capacity to terminate (Dewald, 1982; Firestein, 1978; Freud, 1937; Klauber, 1972), Mr. N. found a way out.[6]

At this point, Mr. N. said this would be his last session, and I quietly said, "Okay." At the time, I felt that acceptance, rather than further analytic inquiry, was appropriate. My response, I imagined, was much the way child analysts might behave when they are loath to interpret a recently acquired sublimation in their young analysands. While I realized that how much to have analyzed his *apparently* sudden wish to end analysis is an arguable issue, I was concerned that with his propensity for procrastination and obsessional paralysis, I might be feeding into his symptomatology by too actively inquiring about and analyzing this wish.

After a bit more talk about his feelings, the report, and some photos he had brought in, we ended the session. Mr. N. told me he would mail me copies of the photos if I wished. As he exited, he smiled, shook my hand firmly, and said, "Be well." After he left, it felt to me like things were truly "okay." I was happy for him and felt quite peaceful. Ironically, this date was the anniversary of the death of one of my parents, and I was very aware of feeling quiet and reflective, a state that would allow me to further mourn my personal loss as well as the fact of losing my patient. The extent to which my own sense of the inevitability of object loss colored my clinical judgment that day needs to be considered also, as this sad coincidence seemed to punctuate our ongoing intersubjectivity of intimacy, made possible because of shared mourning.

Mr. N.'s photos arrived about a week later. In one, he stood under an interstate highway sign pointing both north and south, looking rather uncertain. In a later one, he was looking through binoculars into the distance. In another photo, he displayed his shelf of memories, which included pictures of his mother. And, finally, there were happy photos with his family.

About a week after that, he left me a telephone message telling me he was doing all right and feeling more hopeful about his decision. He knew that he was welcome back any time, but I got the distinct impression that he was determined to go it on his own for the foreseeable future.

Discussion

To paraphrase Ferenczi (1927), who described analyses as terminating when the analytic dyad gives up out of exhaustion, I decided to let Mr. N.'s analysis "die of natural causes." I use this expression metaphorically to emphasize the importance to Mr. N. that he have control over the formal ending of our relationship, in sharp contrast to the ending of his relationship with his mother, who had died so prematurely and "unnaturally." In so doing, I was as flexible as I could be in order to allow for what Goldberg and Marcus (1985) refer to as a *natural termination*. I had to be aware of pressures related to my potentially keeping his hours available to him throughout this process, a practice that would have been masochistic (and could result in financial strain for us analysts who need to keep their schedules full). Furthermore, consideration needed to be given to the possibility that such an approach would have actually delayed his leaving, giving credence to his periodic charges of being financially exploited.

In addition, I needed to be aware of whether I was treating Mr. N. specially—i.e., as an exception (Freud, 1916; Jacobson, 1959; Kris, 1976)—due to his terrible loss and defensive, compensating sense of entitlement. However, Kramer (1987) points out that under certain conditions, it may be appropriate not to interdict the patient's wish for something a bit out of the ordinary, as it may reflect a developmental achievement to be able to ask and feel worthy of this.

With these factors in mind, I sensed that it would be most therapeutic for Mr. N.—that is, a *corrective emotional experience* (Alexander, 1946), in the broadest sense of the term—if he were in as much control as possible of this termination (given that his life-altering trauma was his mother's sudden death, over which he had had no control whatsoever). It has been suggested (Miller, 1990) that Alexander's relegation of genetic construction to second-class status and his emphasis on role-playing have tainted the concept of corrective emotional experience so permanently that the overall value of it may be lost. Indeed, Wallerstein's (1990) scholarly historical overview of this notion leaves the reader in no doubt that he believes that it has no place in psychoanalysis. Alexander's experimental approaches belong to the realm of time-limited psychotherapy, as he espouses ideas about manipulation of the transference by, for example, a series of progressively longer interruptions, in order to assess the patient's readiness for termination, or by intentionally reducing the frequency of visits at just the right time, in order to increase the emotional intensity of the transference.

In this case, I did not orchestrate any of the usual changes in frequency, use of the couch, or ending date; Mr. N. took the initiative. If the central event in analysis is indeed a change in the patient due to an integration of the transference neurosis, the patient's past life, his or her current life, and the intersubjective matrix, then it truly *is* a corrective emotional experience (Miller, 1990). However, less historically encumbered terms (Jacobs, 1990) that describe the essence of the therapeutic experience—like, for example, the analysand's relationship with the analyst as a "new object" (Loewald, 1960)—engender much less controversy.

In retrospect, I may have been unconsciously influenced by Freud's (1918) use of a deadline in his analysis of the Wolf Man, because I, too, gave Mr. N. a bit of a nudge due to a deadline for obtaining his permission to present at a meeting. However, it was not clear to me—consciously — if he would even agree, let alone want to collaborate.

That this activity or parameter (Eissler, 1953) helped Mr. N. out the door is noteworthy. Stein (1988) has suggested that if the analyst has good intentions and respect for the patient, then the patient's reading of his or her own report may facilitate the work, as Mr. N's termination was facilitated. Stoller (1988), in a provocative way, actually recommended that analysts invite their analysands to collaborate this way on a regular basis; but to my knowledge, few have taken up this challenge. Aron (2000) also suggested that there could be a beneficial effect to such a practice, citing ethical considerations over not getting consent to write about patients. However, he questions whether some writers (e.g., Lipton, 1991) fully consider the issue that the analyst's authority and transference factors may make it doubtful as to whether consent can truly be given. Nevertheless, the dialectic between confidentiality and the need for accurate scientific reporting of our clinical work continues (Goldberg, 1997), and, unless analysts feel free to write and to be innovative, within reason, concern about stagnation in the field may be warranted.

Kantrowitz (2004a, 2004b), based on data collected from a subgroup of analysts who have published clinical material, offers us an idea of how today's analysts contend with these issues. In her interviews of thirty analysts who have published clinical reports, only eight regularly asked for consent, fifteen chose only to disguise the patient's identity, and seven varied their strategies depending on the individual situation. Overall, twelve patients were shown their reports, and there was concern in six of these cases about the adequacy of disguise. Of the five analysts who asked permission during the termination phase, one patient was shown the report—and responded by returning it with many editorial changes marked in red! While the analyst was not aware of any harmful effects and noted the healthy expression of the patient's competitive urges, he did wonder if the patient was masochistically submitting to his request. Also, this analyst chose not to write about his countertransference for fear of disturbing the termination process, illustrating the point that what we choose to write is affected if we anticipate its being read by the patient.

In the case of Mr. N., my asking for his consent enabled him to invite himself to collaborate with me, and this initiative was certainly a step forward, as he himself commented. That the report itself became so catalytic in his finally terminating is striking, and, though not premeditated on my part, the timing of my request was no doubt a factor in its effect. I suspect that by introducing a third influence into the analysis—the analyst's professional self, as described by Crastnopol (1999)—I was including Mr. N. in the larger academic analytic community, which appealed to maturing ego and sublimatory capabilities.

Interestingly, Mr. N. brought in his own "third" also—i.e., describing himself in the third person. By acknowledging *I* but using *he*, Mr. N. emulated my writing style, a choice that carried with it the cost of emotional distance. This intellectual veneer, a reflection of his usual defensive style, softly gave way to tears in the last session, as this episode seemed to recapitulate the course of his entire analysis. Identifying with his analyst, Mr. N. wanted to make a contribution, and by being able to share his experience in order to help others, Mr. N. also memorialized his mother.

Kantrowitz (2004b) points out that, in clinical writing, both analyst and analysand are connected by the written words on the page "in perpetuity." Mr. N. had never been able to make any public acknowledgement—e.g., a donation, plaque, etc.—in his mother's memory. His need to document both her death and his own life were crucial to the success of his analysis and his readiness to terminate. The report therefore served to provide an ongoing bond between us, which paradoxically enabled him to leave.

In another article of her very important series on writing, Kantrowitz (2005a) described a trend in recent years for analysts to seek permission from their patients in order to publish clinical material, and to analyze the impact of both the request and the reading of it. Seeing written case reports as a stimulus rather than an imposition of the analyst's agenda, she published data obtained from nine analysts who had published clinical papers between 1995 and 2003 in *Psychoanalytic Dialogues*. According to her survey, 77 percent of these authors asked permission some of the time, as opposed to 50 percent of those who published in the *Journal of the American Psychoanalytic Association* (Kantrowitz, 2004a), versus 42 percent of those who published in the *International Journal of Psychoanalysis* (Kantrowitz, 2005b). Acknowledging the debate between those who insist upon informed consent (especially in this era of the Internet), versus those who maintain that a patient in the throes of transference neurosis cannot truly give informed consent, and material must, therefore, be disguised (Gabbard, 2000), Kantrowitz (2005a) studied this technical innovation. In speaking of the former of these two groups of analysts, she noted that from a relational perspective, their "conscious rationale in this practice is that the therapeutic action of psychoanalysis occurs in the context of conscious and unconscious engagement of the patient and analyst where the meaning that occurs is coconstructed. As such, these analysts welcome, and may even create, through the introduction of their papers, heightened transference-contertransference interactions" (p. 371).

La Farge (2000) found that reading clinical material helped her patients deidealize her, whereas Crastnopol (1999) observed that the patient's wish to be a larger part of the analyst's life motivate him or her to agree. She was emphatic about the importance of the writing being part of the intersubjective experience that helped each member of the dyad become more understanding of the other. Similarly, Pizer (2000) maintains that writing brings into focus recurring patterns that are clinically useful, and that the patient's permission can further "a loving bond that opens further potential space in the treatment relationship" (p. 250).

In her sample, Kantrowitz determined that in most cases, the conscious motivation was *not* to further the analysis, but positive effects were noted nonetheless. She identified three categories of effects: (1) countertransference recognition by the analyst with the patient's help; (2) enabling the patient to experience the analyst as a separate other, and thereby facilitating maintenance of boundaries; and (3) highlighting ongoing issues that became more central in the analysis over time. She concluded that "some patients may benefit from the concrete experience of writing . . . perhaps because they can hold the ideas constant by reintroducing them into awareness when they begin to slip away . . . a kind of transitional object, creating an object constancy. . . . But not every patient needs this particular approach" (2005a, p. 385).

Kantrowitz (2005a, 2005b, 2005c, 2005d) concluded that this technical innovation may be helpful, but should be used judiciously. She cited a number of potential pitfalls for the analyst, such as excessive censoring of analytic literature out of consideration of the patient's feelings, undue intellectualization when affect is needed, erosion of boundaries due to explicit revelation of erotic countertransference feelings, and aggressive turning against the self due to the revelation of strong negative countertransference feelings. Nevertheless, it seems to me that Mr. N. was one of those patients who benefited from this particular approach.

Mr. N., like his mythological alter ego, Theseus, was trapped in his own underworld, but his was an intrapsychic one of pathological grief and characterological paralysis. As a result, the further maturation of his masculine self could not occur without analysis. By necessity, his analysis was protracted, but it enabled him to participate in the form of his termination and take an active role in his emancipation from death in life. It appeared that reading his own case report and writing his response to it concretized and catalyzed his ability to get up from his own metaphorical "Chair of Forgetfulness." This written material ultimately functioned as his ticket to freedom.[7]

CONCLUSION

The events of September 11 could not help but become incorporated into Mr. N.'s psyche and into his analysis. While the revival of earlier trauma by more recent events is axiomatic in psychoanalysis, it seemed as though Mr. N. was especially susceptible, even though he was not directly affected by the new tragedy. The totally unexpected nature of his mother's fatal collapse and all its concomitants—the police involvement, uncertainty over the facts, his never seeing her dead body, the large funeral, the flowers, and his father's getting back to business as soon as possible—did not allow him the chance to metabolize this catastrophe; as a result, he had experienced his own personal September 11 three decades previously.

Mr. N.'s character had thus solidified along rather rigid obsessional lines, and his own "homeland security" system had had him on twenty-four-hour alert for the next disaster ever since. Every detail of his existence had to be planned, and no surprises could be tolerated. When his son narrowly missed a fatal accident, Mr. N.'s philosophy of life was only further vindicated, and, had he not been in analysis at the time, he perhaps would have become even more difficult to engage subsequently. That he already had begun a dialogue with me about his ever-present dread was essential, in that we were involved in the process of finding words for the ineffable, and the foundation for the symbolization of his trauma was gradually being built.

It cannot be known for sure that Mr. N. would have indeed kept his termination date in the autumn of 2001 had the September 11 attacks not occurred. However, we can note that, by his continuing and by my permitting and perhaps even encouraging him to associate to this national tragedy, he could not avoid the issue in a way that would have enacted his father's avoidance of his mother's death. Instead, Mr. N. could begin to learn that, while psychoanalysis cannot bestow immunity from future tragedy and loss, he was not alone, and was better equipped than ever to deal with the human condition.

NOTES

First published in © The Psychoanalytic Quarterly 2006, *The Psychoanalytic Quarterly*, Volume LXVV, No. 3, pp. 753–781.

1. For the sake of confidentiality, the patient's identity and certain historical details have been disguised.

2. According to legend, brave Theseus was persuaded by his friend Pirithous to retrieve his beloved Persephone, who had been kidnapped by Hades. The two men were tricked by Hades into sitting on the "Chair of Forgetfulness," where they were held securely by coils of snakes. Interestingly, Theseus would have languished there forever, even though it was before his time to die, had he not been rescued by Heracles. Theseus was one of the few characters who traveled to the land of the dead and returned, but part of his bottom was ripped off when pulled from the chair. The transference implications of this myth were prophetic in this case.

3. It has been noted that, in situations of "pathological hope," it may indeed be necessary for the analyst to be the one to dispel the analysand of unrealistic hopes and wishes (Akhtar 1999; Amati-Mehler and Argentieri, 1989).

4. The dynamic significance of anniversary reactions is well known by psychoanalysts (Engel, 1975; Mintz, 1971; Pollock, 1970), and they, too, are susceptible to such recurrent upheaval. Engel's (1975) account of his annual regression on the date of his twin brother's death is a powerful illustration of this phenomenon.

5. The theme of being the bearer of bad news and the power associated with it was also experienced by another patient, whose appointment preceded Mr. N.'s on September 11. She was the one who first informed me about the horrors occurring that morning, and immediately became wracked by guilt over having been the one to tell me.

6. Indeed, my experience with severely traumatized individuals has taught me that their analyses take a long time, and that it is counterproductive to worry early on about terminability in such cases, as we might never offer them an analytic opportunity in the first place (Brenner, 2001).

7. About nine months later, a serious family crisis occurred for Mr. N., and he was able to take appropriate initiative, discovering a newfound resilience in himself.

5

A Time-Traveling Man

Ideas came forth that had a strange reality value. They could be best understood in terms of the "time tunnel" into which present day people are
able to descend to change the course of history. . . .

—Judith Kestenberg, 1980

A number of years ago Orville consulted me because of marital problems.
The fact that his parents were Holocaust survivors was incidental and part
of their past, he insisted—not his. Sure, they had problems, he cheerfully
added, but didn't everyone? This man exuded so much thoughtfulness
and compassion that even considering the possibility that he might be angry about anything was totally shocking to him. His martyr-like capacity
to endure his young wife's inability to function due to her drug problem
was because he understood how much of a troubled background she had,
so he quietly waited and hoped that she would "grow out of it." He had a
long history of trying to save very troubled women who would inevitably
abuse and betray him. His tolerance started to wear thin when his young
daughter developed a potentially life-threatening condition which required careful monitoring and daily medication. In order for him to get to
work since his wife was incapable of child care, the toddler was entrusted
to various members of the wife's family who neglected her medical problems. As a result, the child's health often deteriorated by the end of the
day and he would spend many evenings on the phone with doctors or taking her to the emergency room. His identification with the rescuer (Blum,
1987) was so great that he could not see himself as a victim or, worse
yet, the aggressor. His sense of masculinity was organized around being

a heroic helper who could save people, especially women in distress. He had great difficulty talking about his feelings regarding his dead father, a man of contradiction, who was quite quick with his hands to punish him but who was also deeply religious and prayed daily. As a tribute to the survivor father's strict devotion, when he died, his little prayer book was buried with him. It was the only tangible relic of his earlier life and was with him throughout his entire ordeal in the concentration camp. There he met a few men and prayed secretly with them every day. He hid the tiny book in his pants and would have been shot on the spot if it were discovered by the Nazi guards. My patient's intellectually sophisticated alienation from organized religion belied a claustrophobic panic whenever he was in a synagogue. However, he had no curiosity and saw little connection to anything in his family. The father hid the prayer book in a special drawer that was off-limits to everyone. As a child, my patient was terrified to even think about snooping around for it; as a grown man he was relieved to have it buried forever with his father. When it was becoming clear to him that elements of his parents' legacy were being enacted in his own life, he fled from the psychoanalytic shovel that I offered him in order to dig deeper. The horror written on the pages of that tiny prayer book would have propelled him back in time and he was afraid of getting stuck in the past, not realizing he was already living in two time zones, unconsciously.

TIME

Psychoanalysis is very much about time. From the initial encounter to the last minute of the last hour (Lipton, 1961), from the well-timed interpretation to the premature interpretation (Strachey, 1934) and from the missing appointments to the nuances of starting and stopping on time (Freud, 1913a; Kurtz, 1988) as well as "the decline and fall of the fifty-minute hour" (Greenson, 1974), we analyze and are analyzing time, all the time. Similarly, we are very concerned with the subjective variations in the sense of the passage of time as well as being very interested in developmental aspects of the capacity to comprehend it (Orgel, 1965; Hartocollis, 1972; Kafka, 1972; Yates, 1935; Gifford, 1960; Colarusso, 1979, 1998). In particular, we study those agencies of the mind which concern themselves with the past, the present and the future, recognizing the roles of id, ego functioning and the superego, respectively (Loewald, 1962).[1] In addition, the sense of timelessness associated with unconscious processes such as defense, punishment, and wish fulfillment (Arlow, 1986) provide a dynamic tension unique which we believe to be unique to the human mind and very much in the realm of psychoanalysis. This realm, as Loewald summarizes it, includes

"Memory, forgetting, regression, repetition, anticipation, presentation; and representation; the influence of the past on the present in thought, feeling and behavior; delay of gratification and action; sleep-wakefulness and other rhythmicities in mental life; variations in abnormalities in the subjective sense of elapsed time; the so-called timelessness of the id; the role of imagination and fantasy in structuring the future; values, standards, ideals as future-oriented categories; concepts such as object constancy and self-identity; not to mention the important factors of time in the psycho-analytic situation itself in technical aspects, appointments, length of hours, etc." (Loewald, 1972, p. 402).

SPACE

Psychoanalysis is also about mental space, a seemingly unrelated phenomenon. It is not to be confused with a literal interpretation of the structural model actually occupying certain loci in the brain (Freud, 1922). Seen as a "potential space," this metaphorical area of the psyche where cognition, creativity, play, and the analytic encounter may take place, is a concept put forth by Winnicott (1971) and richly elaborated upon by others (Ogden, 1985, 1986; Resnik, 1995). Potential space is seen as a representation of the developing autonomy of the infant who begins to recognize his separateness from his mother. This "me-not-me gap," a transitional space which allows for paradox and dialectic, may be externally represented by the well-known inanimate objects such as teddy bears and security blankets which are imbued with elements of the mother. A derivative of this space is the analytic space (Poland, 1992), that realm in which the analytic dyad resides. Accordingly, a healthy potential space permits the development and differentiation of the symbol, the symbolized, and the thinker, a necessary threesome for mature cognition and empathy (Ogden, 1985).

TRAUMA

Psychic trauma and its myriad repercussions appear to have effects on both time and potential space. From the frequently reported sense of a slowing of time in the acute state to the disorientation to time in the subacute and chronic traumatic states, the overwhelmed and helpless ego undergoes a regression associated with neurophysiological changes and cerebral blood flow and stress regulating hormones (Yehuda, 1999). Kitty Hart, a survivor of Auschwitz who was deported there from her ghetto at age fifteen, described it this way: "Keeping track of time was impossible. One hour of the morning was memorable: 4 o'clock, when the whistles screeched and there was shouting and bullying and you turned out for roll call but soon you lost track of the days and months. The seasons ran into one another . . . there was no way of working things out from the vegetation—there was not a blade of grass, only vast tracts of mud." (Hart, 1981, p. 96).

Terr (1984) points out that since the perception of time is a recent acquisition evolutionarily, it is especially susceptible to distortions in psychic trauma. Seen as a defensive and restitutive attempt to regain a sense of control, the victim may, for example, look for evidence of omens which, if only they had been recognized in time, could have prevented the disaster. She emphasizes alterations in "rhythm, duration, simultaneity and sequence, and temporal perspective" (Terr, 1984, p. 662). Rather than a stimulus barrier per se (Freud, 1920), she sees the perceptual apparatus serving more as a filter than as an actual barrier to be breached by sensory input. As though the psychic apparatus becomes frozen in time, one may experience a reliving of trauma in dreams, flashbacks, and fantasies, and in unconscious behavior. Recognized by Freud over eighty years ago as contradictory to the pleasure principle, this compulsion to repeat (Freud, 1920) and its vicissitudes may occupy a central role in one's mental functioning. So, when the offspring of such massively traumatized individuals manifest the stigmata of the scars of their parents, a number of explanatory mechanisms may be invoked, from strain trauma (Kris, 1956) or cumulative trauma (Khan, 1963) to intergenerational transmission of trauma (Kestenberg, 1980, 1982; Kogan, 1995; Brenner, 2002). For the purpose of this chapter, I will consider how the potential space of the young child may become suffused with the parent's traumatically induced disturbances of time and affect his masculine self. To put this mental space-time problem in perspective, I will cite a vignette from the literature and then make a brief detour around a major development in physics this past century which may offer an analogy for psychoanalysis. I will then present a clinical case to illustrate my hypothesis.

Arlow, whose study of time includes déjà vu (1959), depersonalization (1966) and timelessness (1984), described a woman prone to dissociative trance-like states whose fantasies were visualized with such intensity that she would lose track of time and space. Although he, in my view, mistakenly described such cases as "rarely seen these days" (Arlow, 1986, p. 509), he astutely points out that her absorption was inversely related to her awareness of both herself and her surroundings. The patient had safely walked about eight very busy blocks in her fugue-like state before becoming aware of this lapse. Reportedly, the intrusion of unpleasant, anxiety-laden imagery burst her bubble and she was abruptly redirected to reality where she felt disoriented, especially to time. Consistent with long-held observation that "Time flies when you're having a good time," her reverie was disrupted by painful affects which were intense enough to slow down her subjective sense of the passage of time.

The role of unconscious fantasy and wish fulfillment as well as defenses and self-punishment are clearly in the domain of the psychoanalytic study of time. In addition, the progressive awareness of the inevitability of death and all of its psychical repercussions might have at least as much of an influence on the adult mind as have our early gratifications and frustrations during the time when our brains were immature and unable to even conceptualize the dimension of time (Piaget, 1955). Arlow, who concludes that the experience of time is a compromise formation which incorporates unconscious fantasy and conscious elements such as perception, memory, self-awareness and awareness of death, agrees with other writers (Gifford, 1960; Yates, 1935) that we rebel against time all throughout life. As Schiffer observes, "time moves more slowly for the young, holding a promise of great things to come. As a potential healer of the sick, time may hang heavy. For the imprisoned, it is a stretch to be served just as for the bored it is something to kill. For those maturing into adulthood, time may be a trustworthy guide but for those who are well beyond childhood, it is an enemy to be thwarted, an unwelcome agent of transience taking us on all too swift a journey. Indeed, for those of us over forty, it is enemy number one—a target for assassination" (Schiffer, 1978, p. 13).

THE SPACE-TIME CONTINUUM

Arlow also introduces a term from physics without fully elaborating upon it and perhaps not even realizing its implications. In his description of the woman in the fugue, he offhandedly states: "So absorbed had she been in her fantasies that she had no awareness of herself as an independent entity operating in a space-time continuum" (Arlow, 1986, p. 510). This term "space-time" is defined by Greene, a renowned physicist, as "A union of time and space originally emerging from special relativity. It can be viewed as the 'fabric' out of which the universe is fashioned; it constitutes the dynamic area within which the events of the universe take place" (Greene, 1999, p. 421). Theoretically, tears in this fabric could result in openings which could bridge one remote region of the universe to another. Such hypothetical bridges or tunnels, known as wormholes, have fueled the imagination of science fiction writers who have sought modern explanations for the ancient fantasy of traveling through time. Thus, the notion of the space-time continuum provides such a rationale and perhaps such a metaphor for certain psychological processes.

Using analogies from this complex field is not new. Freud's psychodynamic theory itself with its emphasis on forces, energy, and counterforces is modeled after the hydraulic physics of his day. More recently, numerous writers have cited various facets of the wave versus particle theories of electromagnetic radiation as a metaphor for the need to reconcile disparate theories of the mind, and for other purposes too (Alexander, 1940; Arlow, 1988; Brenner, 1980; Edelson, 1983; Glick, 1966; Meissner, 1985; Spruiell, 1989). Furthermore, Bion (1970), Tustin (1972), Grotstein (1990), and Eshel (1998) have referred to the mysterious cosmological entities known as black holes which are thought to be collapsed stars which trap light in their unimaginably strong gravitational fields. Such phenomena are quite evocative and make useful metaphors, too. The space-time continuum is yet another appealing notion, and it is based on Einstein's theory of special relativity which revolutionized how physicists thought about time and space. This theory, published in 1905 during the time Freud's[2] own theories were revolutionizing the psychological world, run counter to our intuitive sense about the absolutism of time and space.

Einstein's theory claims that the objective passage of time and the lengths of distances are literally different for those traveling at different speeds. In other words, clocks run slower as one travels faster and faster. Since, however, such differences are so minute at the velocities we usually travel—be it by foot, automobile or jet—they are virtually (and mercifully) undetectable by the human brain. Nevertheless, precision testing proves that since time does slow down and the distance between two points does shorten as one goes faster and approaches the speed of light, there is no such thing as absolute time and length. It is all relative and depends on one's state of motion and vantage point. For example, a forty-five-minute analytic session conducted on a fast train or even at high altitudes would be shorter than one at sea level in an office. The actual difference is infinitesimally small, but even if it were large, neither analyst or analysand would notice the difference, since they are both moving through the universe together at the same velocity at the same point and it is all relative. Objective time as we know it, therefore, is not as immutable as we think. The only constant is the speed of light which is an inconceivable 670 million miles per hour![3] And, since time and space are intimately linked, that is why they may be referred to as space-time (Hawking, 1988; Greene, 1999). With such a theory about the continuum of space and time, it has been speculated that if one could exceed the speed of light, time would slow down so much that one could travel back and experience events before they happen.

Analogously, Kestenberg, in her description of children of Holocaust survivors who have the uncanny feeling of living in a Holocaust era and unconsciously reliving elements of their parents' lives, has described this phenomenon as a "time tunnel." The term she used for this intergenerational transmission of trauma was "transposition" such that the child seemed to be living in both the present and in the parent's Holocaust past (Kestenberg, 1980, 1982). While much has been written about this phenomenon and a variety of theories have been invoked to explain it, very little, to my knowledge, has been written about the way in which inanimate objects from that period of time facilitate this psychological time travel. In contrast to this dearth, much more has been noted about how the "second generation" might become triggered by such things as uniforms, prisons, trains, large smokestacks, and even the sound of German language rather than the actual relics their parents may have been able to retain. For example, a photograph of a dead child, the lost older sibling of the second-generation replacement child (Volkan, 1981; Levine, 1982), who grows up in the shadow of an unspoken ghost from another era, may be a prototype of this phenomenon.

In the following case, a male child of survivors who had incorporated an inanimate object into his developing masculine self had remembered it during analysis at an important time in the evolution of the transference.

CASE REPORT

Mendel, a man in his late twenties, was referred for treatment of anxiety and depression after a deteriorating situation at work threatened his job. An aspiring young executive in a company that was on the verge of bankruptcy, Mendel's boss was replaced by an aggressive man with a mandate to reorganize the workforce and make whatever cuts were necessary. A number of his peers were instantly laid off while others quit in order to avoid pay cuts, demotions, humiliations, and the uncertainty that those who stayed were likely to experience. Because of a particular expertise he had in computers, Mendel thought he might be spared and when he was called in for a series of private meetings, his boss seemed to take a peculiar liking to him. He felt he was being evaluated in a strange way by the man who started to confide his contempt for others while at the same time lament how necessary it was to eliminate so many people. He subtly suggested that Mendel could be a special help to him by reporting on the activities of his peers whose knowledge of the company and its product could be used by its competitors and further threaten the company's future. In addition to feeling very uneasy about being asked to spy, certain expressions that the man used revealed him to be extremely prejudiced and anti-Semitic in particular. Apparently not recognizing Mendel's own Hebraic background, the boss's continued attitude made Mendel feel very, very anxious and unable to speak up.

Mendel felt that he was in the presence of a Nazi and experienced a sense of panic. Then, he felt something snap in his mind and a helpless rage consumed him. His choice to betray his friends in order to keep his job filled him with enormous guilt yet he did not want to leave. He had carefully researched the company and its location, deciding it was the ideal arrangement for him. He pushed hard for the job, moving quite a distance for this golden opportunity. In his life plan he had hoped to find a wife and settle down in this new city and climb the proverbial ladder of success. Now he did not want to leave this promised land and felt an eerie sense of having to go into exile. Images of the Holocaust began to plague him and he became quite symptomatic. Faced with this no-win situation, he became paralyzed with anxiety. He could not tolerate being in the same room with his boss and was horrified by murderous thoughts that kept him up at night. When not consumed by a fear of attacking him directly, he would imagine all sorts of ways of making an accident happen that would seriously injure or kill the new boss who would either corrupt him or drive him out of his new homeland. Mendel tried to suppress his fantasies of revenge and started suffering from a variety of somatic symptoms, including headaches, backaches, chest pain, and sweating. After a series of extensive medical tests and trips to specialists, he was ultimately referred to me. At the time, he had little insight or curiosity about his condition except for being puzzled by these recurrent thoughts and thoughts about his father and all he had been through. Compared to his father's suffering, he felt that he had no right to complain. The psychodynamic significance of the presenting events as well as the following early history emerged slowly over time in a treatment that evolved from weekly psychotherapy to five-time-a-week analysis.

The patient was the older of two brothers born about eight years apart to a Holocaust survivor father and a refugee mother whose family fled Hitler Europe on one of the last boats allowed to leave. Though very much from the "old world," she was spared the horrors of genocidal persecution directly, but lost most of her relatives who were not able to leave. At the time, she was a preadolescent and an only child. Mendel grew up in a largely rural area with a considerable survivor population, although his parents tried to distance themselves from the "ghetto mentality" that was prevalent in some parts of this area. Initially he reported very few memories of his life prior to the birth of his brother, insisting that there was nothing either remarkably good or bad about his childhood except for very little money and an oppressive religious atmosphere which resulted in a virtual shutdown of his life during the Sabbath.

Curiously, one of his earliest memories was of running with a group of boys down the street behind the big truck which would regularly spray insecticide to kill the mosquitoes. He recalled feeling the cool mist on his skin and breathing in the moist fog on hot summer nights. He was about five years old at the time. He also recalled briefly living in a dingy apartment between moving from one house to another and being terrified looking under the bed at an infestation of bugs scurrying about. His mother, described as a quiet, dutiful, and nondescript woman, seemed to be overshadowed by his father whose very presence at home changed the atmosphere into one of urgency, intensity, and unpredictability. Although his father rarely spoke of his wartime experience, as Mendel remembered it, it was as though he had always known that the man had been through something terrible. Father was often lost in thought, irritable, brooding, and easily startled. He had visible scars and tattooed numbers on his arm that he joked were his old girlfriend's phone number. This attempt at humor was to cover over the horror that he tried to protect the patient and his family from feeling and knowing about. Yet he would tell stories from time to time. When he was not at work at his factory job where he jumped at the chance for overtime and any opportunity for extra income, he would be at home eating, reading, or watching TV. Though apparently not without some charm and social skills in public, his father's extreme preoccupation made young Mendel feel as though he were unapproachable and formidable. When the lights were turned out at night, his door was shut and he was not permitted out of his bedroom. Any disobedience might be met with a spank or belt. Yet Mendel felt strongly protective and responsible for his father, feeling intuitively that if anything bad were to ever happen to him or his brother, his father would never recover from it. As a result, he was constantly aware of changes in the father's moods and as a young boy tried to be good in order to keep him calm and in control.

There were very few frivolities in his childhood as an atmosphere of austerity and "uncertainty about tomorrow" pervaded the house. Every dinner was an event as his mother rationed the food until the next payday while the father reassured the family that there would always be enough food, that no one would have to eat fast and that no one would starve. Buying clothing was also a special event as much of his "good clothing" came from donations from relatives or "care packages" as he half jokingly called them as he got older. It seemed that the article of clothing that his father took the greatest interest in getting for him were his shoes—they always had to be gotten new, always had to fit well, always had to be durable, always had to be a bargain, and always needed to be shined. Since Mendel craved any attention from his well-intentioned but essentially unavailable father, these rare father-son outings were highlights of his young life. Going into shoe stores was unlike many other purchases that his father made which were often done through his connections with "landsmen" after hours in the backs of stores with men who had tattoos and spoke Yiddish also. Romanticizing these activities, young Mendel felt they were a bit exciting and clandestine until he realized later that Father was destitute and the only way that he could buy, for example, a nice piece of furniture was if it were damaged and at a discount price from one of his survivor friends. So, the expedition to buy shoes for an active, growing boy was filled with great anticipation. It was not until a number of years into analysis when he suddenly remembered a mysterious, old pair of black boots that the father had kept in a dingy storage room that it occurred to me that there might be additional meaning to the footwear beyond the classical psychoanalytic considerations of phallic symbolism of the growing boy.

The timing of his derepression of this memory was significant in that, indeed, phallic-oedipal issues were prominent in the transference. He was feeling very downtrodden and envious of what he perceived as my unattainable, elevated status in the professional world. Any schedule change I made filled him with rage at the control I had over his life and made him feel I were mocking him for being so puny, inept, and at my mercy. He made provocative sexual comments about an attractive woman seen leaving my office intermittently, fantasizing having an affair with her and teasingly trying to get me to confide in him about her. He insisted she would prefer him over me, but fearing a punishing reprimand from me, he would try to be very careful in his taunts until he would get angry, at which time he would criticize my attire, my appearance, my virility, and brag about flirting with her on his way in. Interestingly, it was also during this time of competition for the desired woman that he developed a taste for foot-long hot dogs, frequently stopping at a roadside stand before afternoon sessions to quickly ingest such a weiner in order to have "the strength" for our daily analytic duels.

Around this he also brought in a dream which disturbed him. In the dream he was at a gas station inserting the gasoline hose into his tank and starting to fill it up. The scene then changed abruptly and his uncle, a domineering, arrogant, and powerful man, was leering at him in a peculiar way and was about to make a sexual gesture toward him. The patient then awoke in a confused and agitated state. He associated to his uncle's lecherous tendency toward young girls, his demeaning treatment of others, and how he used to incessantly mock him for having long hair when he was in high school. When Mendel finally cut his hair for some occasion, he defiantly sent the uncle an envelope full of hair which shocked him; the man never said another word to him afterward. In the sessions, he haltingly and bitterly associated to submitting to a powerful man's demands for painful anal intercourse, his curious new penchant for foot-long hot dogs, and his homosexual fears.

Over time his ambivalent wish to please me through fellatio in order to avoid anal rape came to the fore. This transferential material was laced with a very emotional reference to an incident his father had alluded to about the degradation, torture, and murder of a chief rabbi. During one of their endless roll calls in the concentration camp, this elderly man was pulled out of line by the guards while the rest of the prisoners were forced to watch him being spat upon, beaten, kicked, and having his beard cut off. He was then stripped naked and a water hose was inserted in his rectum. The water was then turned on full force and filled his intestines until his emaciated body expanded like a balloon and he ruptured. The prisoners stood at attention at gunpoint until the rabbi stopped writhing around and died as they were given this demonstration of what all the Jews deserved. This material was very difficult to listen to as sadness, despair, and impotent rage filled the room for both of us. It was one of those times that has been described by Grubrich-Simitis (1984) as a joint acceptance of the Holocaust reality in which there is a powerful, affective communication between analyst and analysand.

Much later on in treatment we were able to consider how one of his latency-age "cowboys-and-Indians" games was an attempt through fantasy and play to master the affects associated with such transmitted trauma. In one of his repetitive fantasies, he, a cowboy in a white hat, would be captured by the bad guys and tied up. While at their mercy he imagined they might beat him up and sometimes might even want to take his clothes off. He recalled that this scenario filled him with a mixture of fear and a peculiar sense of excitement which was short-lived because he would always get rescued just in time. Interestingly, he developed a strong attachment to a pair of leather cowboy gloves which he pretended gave him special power and the strength to fight off his would-be attackers so he would not get caught. He ascribed a magical phallic power to the gloves which protected him from the sadomasochistically tinged fantasy of capture and passive surrender to the bad guys. It appeared that the gloves were a symbolic upward displacement of his wish for a mature, idealized super phallus and the boots which were associated with such intense affects that they could not be included in his play.

The boots, as we eventually learned, were a source of pervasive wonder, awe, fear, and dread which preoccupied him throughout his childhood. The earliest and most sanitized version of the story of the boots which he recalled hearing around the time he was in first grade was that a long time ago his father's feet were cold and a soldier gave them to him. However, they were too small for the father but he accepted them anyway because he had no money and squeezed his feet into them until he could get new shoes. Mendel thought that he was told the boots were a size 5½ which was just about the age he was at the time. Due to his age-appropriate concrete thinking and cognitive immaturity, he assumed that a five-and-a-half-year-old boy would wear a five-and-a-half size boot, so perhaps they were for him and was eager to try them on. Much to his dismay, the boots were enormous and so high that they went up above his hips, making it impossible for him to stand; he lost his balance and fell. Furthermore, he sensed a peculiar silence and uneasiness from his father which frightened him. His mother said nothing also. He intuitively knew not to ask any more about them and would forget about the boots except when it snowed and one needed to wear boots.

As he grew, he would secretly venture into the storage room and see if he fit into them, silently waiting for what he was not sure would happen at such a moment. He did imagine acquiring a certain strength and power when he would fit into these mysterious boots which would be just what he would need to stand up to his father and anyone else who might bully him. He was rather small for his age and would get picked on by a boy who lived nearby. His father assured him that one day he would grow bigger than the neighbor and then he could really get him back. In the meantime, his father advised him to kick the boy in the shins and run from his persecutor. Mendel felt ashamed, thinking that he would be behaving like a girl were he to kick his oppressor in the shins. He wanted his father to teach him to box like a real man, not kick like a sissy. Nevertheless, his dream of deeper revenge and vindication seemed unconsciously linked with the feet and boots from another era. He learned a little more about this time as he got older, but as his knowledge of the horrors of that time grew, he could not tolerate that his father had actually endured such atrocities. His father's history, pieced together during analysis, was as follows.

His father, the younger of two children, was born in eastern Europe in the 1920s into a recently urbanized family. During the Nazi invasion, he was a teenager and tried to escape the ghetto in order to join the partisans and fight the Nazis. However, word had gotten to him that his family would be shot if he did not return. He did return and he and his father were arrested, sent to a slave labor camp in 1943 and ultimately to Auschwitz. The father discovered many years later that his mother and sister died of disease and starvation in the ghetto, while his own father died during the evacuation of Auschwitz in January 1945. Mendel was named for this grandfather.

It was not clear exactly what the circumstances were during the chaotic time immediately after liberation but Mendel's father and several other men attacked and subdued a German soldier. They divided up his belongings and, among other things, Mendel's father took the Nazi's black boots. What was clear to Mendel was that the incident, more than any other one that he had heard, was especially vague and told in clipped phrases. Father would seem as though he had forgotten the details and would never elaborate, leaving much to the imagination which the patient could never allow himself to think about consciously. The obvious question of whether the father had participated in a murder of that German soldier was deeply warded off and was not able to be articulated until analysis. All that Mendel knew was that he had a strange attachment to the boots throughout his latency and had forgotten about them by the time he was in his midteens.

The patient did recall a turbulent summer during his teens where he spent much time splitting firewood and guiltily imagining splitting open his father's head each time the axe made contact. He vaguely remembered hearing that one of his elderly male relatives was killed by a Nazi who split his head apart with an axe, but made no conscious connection to it at the time. All he knew was that he was angrily building up his muscles and strength for a long-awaited time of revenge, but it filled him with great anxiety and guilt. At the time he could not understand why he simultaneously felt so entitled yet so awful about wanting to get back at his father whose oppression smothered him. After all his father had been through, the idea of his own son wanting to hurt him made him feel like a Nazi. Indeed, the fact that the patient himself had fantasies of literally filling the boots of a Nazi throughout his childhood was his own repressed, abhorrent secret which did not emerge until he was on the couch.

DISCUSSION

The collapse of time (Volkan et al., 2002) experienced by children of Holocaust survivors has been variously described as both a telescoping of generations (Faimberg, 1988) and a time tunnel (Kestenberg, 1980, 1982). In this fusion and confusion, elements of a parent's "traumatized self" may get deposited (Volkan, 1995b, 1996) into the developing child whose own milestones become saturated with the unresolved grief and struggle for survival during genocidal persecution who serves as a container of the parents' damaged psyche (Kogan, 1995). The child's internalization of the massively traumatized mother and/or father may intensify not only his developmental dangers but also may result in a quasiliving in two time zones. This transposing of the Holocaust era for the mundane realities of the child is multiply determined and puts an enormous burden on the immature ego which may prevent adequate integration of the psyche and appear as a split (Brenner, 2001).

Early on, disturbances in attachment, characterized by a disorganized/ disoriented pattern of reacting, have been described in children whose mothers have been seriously traumatized but have not abused them directly (Hesse and Main, 1999). A young child's psychosexual fantasy world may then become suffused with images of unseen horrors, repetitive survival scenarios of unspoken brushes with death, and transmitted unresolved grief over unknown relatives. It may be that such transmitted trauma accentuates a basic assumption in very young children that they were always part of their parents' lives. For them to conceptualize and comprehend that there was a time in the world before they were born is not only a function of the separation-individuation process (Mahler, Bergman, and Pine, 1975) but also a cognitive milestone. The uncanny, surreal, or dissociative quality that they were there during the Holocaust, a sensation reported by many children of survivors who were by definition born after liberation in 1945, suggests a process beyond identification. The developing ego of such children was challenged not only by the usual task of adaptation but also with the need to integrate the parents' traumatic reliving of the Holocaust as they were frequently preoccupied and emotionally unavailable during their reveries or repetitive enactments. The daily absorption of the parents' living in their two time zones complicated the child's task of learning to distinguish the past from the present. As we see with other universal anxiety-laden issues, this theme is depicted in popular literature and films and is often in the form of time travel. Interestingly, the hero is frequently a child who goes back in time and gets caught up in the dilemma of changing the past in order to avenge a crime, correct an injustice or prevent a tragedy.

The underlying oedipal component to this reparative fantasy was humorously depicted a number of years ago in the very popular film, *Back to the Future*. In it, a young man who is very ashamed of his parents and wants to disown any relationship with them, travels back in time and lives out his prehistory with the help of a wild-eyed scientist. He becomes entangled in a triangular love affair with his parents when they were in high school but they do not know he is to become their son. He anxiously resists his future mother's sexual advances and helps his defenseless, pathetic father stand up to a class bully who humiliates him regularly. In the process, his future father gains strength, respect, pride and, most necessarily, the love of the boy's future mother. The son, the hero, avenges his father's victimization and rehabilitates him. He helps his father become the kind of man that he would want to look up to. In order to do so, however, he must renounce his own oedipal strivings. In return, he builds a strong and successful father with whom he can identify, in order to develop a healthy masculine self. And, as is the case in transposition, there was an ambiguity between the past and the present. This ambiguity can progress to confusion and disorientation, especially when there is blurring among dream, fantasy, memory, and reality which accompanies severe early trauma (Brenner, 1994, 1996a, 1996b).

A related organizing fantasy frequently seen in children of survivors is one of "the selection" (Brenner, 1988). Woven into this Holocaust scenario, both oedipal and preoedipal conflicts may be played out with surprisingly real imagery from the parent's past. Here, too, this theme has emerged in popular literature in William Styron's novel *Sophie's Choice*. In the analytic literature, Kogan (1995) described a woman with a selection fantasy who could neither escape the symbiotic engulfment of her perpetually grieving mother nor could she tolerate the guilt and anxiety of an oedipal victory. Consequently, she found safety in a perverse sexual solution, a phallic woman fantasy (Bak, 1968) in which she became the female Doctor Mengele in an S.S. uniform wielding a deadly phallic baton as she enacted sadomasochistic sexual fantasies. In such a fantasy, she made "selections" on the entry ramp to the death camp, deciding who would live and who would die by a casual wave of her large stick. People in her life were used and discarded at will. Within her inner world, she could therefore maintain omnipotent control over her objects, being the all-powerful Nazi "angel of death" (Lifton, 1986).

Fueled by instinctual pressures and the inevitable frustrations over never truly being able to possess one's parents, the desire to be part of their all-consuming world of trauma may heighten such children's anxiety over primal-scene issues and add another dimension to it. Citing her position as somewhere between McDougall's (1982) and Laplanche's (1976), Davies (2002) postulates that the parent's own unintegrated sexuality is transmitted to the child unconsciously in our Western society's child-rearing practices, which result in an area of dissociated, unarticulated, early somatic experiences of sexual arousal. It may be that in some cases of intergenerational transmission of massive psychic trauma this inchoate sensory experience contains the parental traumatic affects also which contributes to the feeling of living in the parent's past. Such confusion may then be associated with this population's reportedly increased lifetime risks to develop post-traumatic stress disorder, PTSD (Solomon, Kotler, and Mikulincer, 1988; Yehuda, 1999). Children of survivors seeing combat in the Israeli army have been more vulnerable (Solomon et al., 1988) and analytic reports from Israel (Kogan, 1995) as well as our Holocaust discussion group's findings in the aftermath of 9/11 suggest a powerful merging of Holocaust pathology with here-and-now trauma.

It may be that in their metaphorical time travel, as the theory of relativity would predict, a shortening of space-time occurs and is associated with a constriction or collapse of the "potential space" in the psyche of the second generation. Indeed, such a collapse has been postulated in which the capacity for symbolization is either unable to develop or to be maintained. Problems in abstract and metaphorical thinking in severely traumatized people and even in some of their offspring have long been described (Herzog, 1982; Grubrich-Simitis, 1984). In one of the manifestations of this disturbance, the reality of a given experience or situation may be so overwhelming that it confirms in the child's mind that one's worst fears and wishes may indeed come true. This was the Holocaust nightmare in which reality was worse than fantasy. As a defensive solution, the child may then hypercathect elements of this reality as a defense against fantasy and in so doing may become unduly preoccupied with certain details, structure, or functioning of the external world. As a result, "the dialectic resonance of realistic and fantastic meaning is foreclosed, leaving the patient incapable of imagination" (Ogden, 1986, p. 221). Yet, unconscious preoccupation with Holocaust-related themes is quite prevalent.

In Mendel's mind, the symbol and the symbolized were fused such that his aspiring to grow into the boots of a Nazi would have actually made him a Nazi should he experience any aggression or hostility toward his loved ones. Furthermore, the growing but intolerable awareness that his own father may have murdered a murderer may have, on one hand, rehabilitated his image as a helpless victim, but, on the other hand, increased the danger that he posed to the young boy, thus greatly intensifying his castration anxiety. Indeed, the relatively small size of the boat, assuming it was accurately remembered, suggests that a small soldier or even a Hitler youth was attacked by the survivors; the father's potential dangerousness to his small son was never doubted by him but regularly rerepressed. As an adult, the sudden change in his work situation reactivated this dangerous situation, precipitating his neurosis. In Orville's situation, his unusual screen memory of massive extermination of mosquitoes while he inhaled the deadly fog with impunity suggests a deeply embedded unconscious knowledge of the poison gas of the gas chambers and his omnipotent fantasy of survival.

THE BOOTS

While we could only speculate upon the various reasons that the father chose to include these boots among the meager possessions he brought over from Europe during his immigration, we may assume that on one level they served as a trophy and as concrete evidence of his personal triumph over his murderous captors. Laden with conflict, however, they were hidden in a crowded and poorly lit storage room, perhaps symbolizing his unconscious attempt to compartmentalize his own trauma and hide it in some forgotten corner of his psyche in order to make a new life. Inevitably, the past could not be completely encapsulated and it was transmitted, both tangibly and intangibly, to the patient. As such, the boots became an important mode of unconscious intergenerational communication, having a unique role in the boy's developing psyche and masculine self.

Mendel did learn much later on in analysis that his father had another earlier significant experience related to boots. During his first years in the concentration camp he and a number of other prisoners were forced into testing a new boot for the German military. This "study" consisted of the men wearing heavy backpacks and being commanded at gunpoint to run in circles around the grounds for twenty-four hours while wearing the new boots. The manifest reason given for this torture was that the army wanted to study how the new material in the soles would wear and tear in combat. In fact, it was the men's souls that were more worn down. It was an impossible assignment which evidently provided much sadistic pleasure for the guards who kicked and beat the men when they fell from exhaustion. Mendel's father sported a hideous scar on his neck which resulted from being stabbed with a bayonet when he, too, dropped to the ground and did not get up fast enough to continue the drill. One day his father blurted out the story without emotion after this memory was triggered by a wartime documentary the two were watching on TV during one of his visits back home. Although Mendel had been well aware of the scar as far back as he could remember, his father had unconvincingly told him before that he had cut himself shaving. A similar attempt at covering over the horrors of his youth, like the story he gave about the numbers on his arm, it was another example of how his father would fictionalize his scars. In an effort to protect, he left his young son rather bewildered and not convinced but too apprehensive to be any more curious at the time. Indeed, how he survived the death march in the freezing winter weather was the ultimate test of "manhood," a rite of passage that was so unfathomable he could not even think about it until analysis.

As we considered how his father's life-and-death ordeals may have become symbolized by the old boots, the patient then associated to a recent incident with his fiancée. They had driven somewhere during the winter and as they got out of the car, it started to flurry. Mendel realized to his horror that she was wearing an open shoe and became enraged at her stupidity for being so unprepared for a possible storm and lectured her on the importance of having her feet protected from the elements. We recognized that some of the meaning of his overreaction was related to his relationship with his father, i.e., his anger at his father's "stupidity" over being unprepared and caught by the Nazis. This contempt warded off his own doubt whether he would have been any smarter or less loyal to his family. It also defended against his horror over his father's suffering, his wish to have prevented it, to have protected him and rescued him as well. This reaction also belied, on a deeper level, his aggressive wish to torture and destroy the father. Therefore, Mendel's reaction to his fiancée's meager footwear in harsh weather seemed to have been overdetermined by his identification with the weak and unprepared victim, his feelings of inferiority to this seemingly superhuman survivor father and to his identification with the aggressor. Psychosexually, the woman's inadequate shoe, a symbol of the inadequate or absent feminine phallus, may have activated his "castration anxiety," which was greatly intensified by the violence of the traumatic material. This incident served as an analyzable, extratransference illustration of intergenerational transmission that colored his daily life which was associated with multiple identifications (Blum, 1987) and shaped the formation of his masculine self.

Akhtar in his compendium of inanimate objects, describes the role of "things" throughout the life cycle for both developmental and pathological purposes. Feeling that we have generally underemphasized their importance, he notes "that psychoanalysts have paid inadequate attention to the constructive, sustaining, and symbolic significance of the inanimate surround in which the human mind evolves and functions" (Akhtar, 2003, p. 7). For example, he cites the challenges of negotiating the oedipus complex and recalls Anna Freud's descriptions (A. Freud, 1968), as he comments on the ways in which young children may try on the same-sex parent's clothing and possessions to compensate for their feelings of inferiority and helplessness in order to enhance their chance of winning the rivalry for the love of the opposite-sex parent: "The little boy wears his father's raincoat and his large shoes . . . " (Akhtar, 2003, p. 9). In this regard, Mendel's trying on his father's boots was developmentally quite appropriate and predictable. However, these particular articles were imbued with the legacy of his father's survival—an indigestible history of persecution, degradation, starvation, atrocities, unresolved grief, murder, guilt, and ultimately triumph—much of which was enshrouded in mystery and secrecy. Consequently, they became highly charged with the story of his father's life and, thus, provided a direct link to the unspeakable horrors of the Holocaust. As such, they took on the quality of a linking object (Volkan, 1981) which he described as "something actually present in the environment that is psychologically contaminated with various aspects of the dead and the self . . . it increasingly commands attention and with its aura of mystery, fascination and terror" (Volkan, 1981, p. 101). In such cases, the unresolved grief is transmitted from one generation to the next and is indeed very much a part of the burden of the second generation. And, because such an inanimate object usually belongs to the survivor parent's generation, it also has a quality of what Bollas has termed a generational object, a type of mnemic object which someone "identifies as generationally defining and that upon recollection brings him a sense of his own generation" (Bollas, 1992, p. 260). Indeed, it is an understatement to say that the Holocaust was a defining event in the lives of all those affected; it was so much so that it could not be metabolized in one lifetime (Brenner, 2004a).

NACHTRÄGLICHKEIT: "DEFERRED ACTION" OR DEVELOPMENTAL TRANSFORMATION?

Reis (1995), in his efforts to translate cognitive behavioral trauma theory into analytic language, has thought of the so-called trigger reaction in terms of a delayed quality of traumatic memory, reliving of trauma and the inherent disturbances in the subjective sense of time. He cites Bion (1962) and Ogden's (1994) emphasis on the analytic task of symbolic transformation of the patient's unarticulated experience which, according to Winnicott, cannot "get into the past tense unless the ego can first gather it into its own present time experience and into omnipotent control now" (Winnicott, 1974, p. 105).

Kitty Hart, upon her return to Auschwitz more than thirty years later, described her life-long challenge to put her ordeal in the past this way: "You see grass. But I don't see any grass. I see mud, just a sea of mud . . . open my eyes and see grass. Close my eyes and see mud . . . the watchtowers still look down. There must still be guns in there trained on you. I belong here. I ought never to have come back because it proved I have never been away. The past I see is more real than the tidy pretense they have put in its place" (Hart, 1981, p. 163). In this context, Freud's 1895 controversial notion of *nachträglichkeit*, loosely translated by Strachey as "deferred action," has been invoked to explain being frozen in time and becoming traumatized only after a triggering stimulus. Freud ambiguously contended that "a memory is repressed which has only become a trauma after the event" (Freud, 1895, p. 356). However, some writers, such as Blum, find this concept which focuses on traumatic events and memory antiquated, obscuring the importance of cumulative preoedipal trauma and disturbed object relations. He charitably sees it as "an unrecognized precursor to the contemporary concept of developmental transformation" (Blum, 1996, p. 1155). Yet, others prefer to embrace it and elaborate upon it. For example, Baranger et al. commend Freud for his departure from "the model of mechanical causality and a linear temporality on the past and present vector for a dialectic concept of causality and a 'spiral' model of temporality where future and past condition and signify each other reciprocally in structuring the present" (Baranger, Baranger, and Moms, 1988, pp. 115–116). Similarly, Modell sees nachträglichkeit as reflecting "that the ego is a structure engaged in the processing and reorganizing of time" (Modell, 1990, p. 4).

Regardless of this theoretical controversy, if, however, psychic trauma damages the ego's synthetic functioning and prevents an experience from ever becoming "in the past," one would be thrust in a state of timelessness (Bromberg, 1991) and a perpetual living of the trauma. Therefore, it could not become a memory to be repressed because it never stopped happening intrapsychically in the first place. So, instead of a benign event becoming traumatic after a future experience augmented by development, the opposite would be true. A traumatic event could only hope to become detoxified after it becomes part of one's past as a result of some experience in the future. For those survivors of genocidal persecution during the Holocaust, that developmental experience was having children. Becoming a parent held the most promise of any healing whatsoever.

Starting a new generation of Jewish children proclaimed ultimate victory over Hitler's decrees to destroy all of their kind. It would give them a sense of purpose or meaning to their senseless suffering and immeasurable grief to name their offspring for their murdered parents and siblings. But it also put a huge burden on many of the second generation to alleviate their parents' daily torment and to justify their own improbable existence (Kestenberg and Brenner, 1996). The developing child's psyche may have become appropriated by the parents, serving as a repository for their intolerable mental contents as well as becoming an auxiliary ego to assist in their negotiating a strange, new, postliberation world in a strange, new country.

And, for many who returned to their original homelands, the familiarity of the past was overshadowed by the hostility of the local townspeople over their return as well as a further collapse of time. One second-generation analysand from Eastern Europe described how, after his parents met in a displaced persons (DP) camp, they returned to his father's family's original apartment and, finding it abandoned, started to live there. Their child, the analysand, grew up in this apartment amidst the illusion of family continuity and an unspoken gap of time filled with a deadly silence. He recalled seeing remnants of old newspapers from the 1940s strewn in the corners of the cavernous hallways and stairways of the building which furthered his confusion over exactly what time period he was living in. As in Mendel's case, his potential space was constricted and consumed by the problems of which time zone he existed in.

In the analysis of children of Holocaust survivors, Kestenberg was emphatic about the need to thoroughly reconstruct the parents' lives, a feature of analysis not typically thought to be essential. In so doing, the "child," to paraphrase Hoffman (1995), then became the interpreter of the parent's experience in order to differentiate from them and free themselves up from the time tunnel which transported them back to the camps.

CONCLUSION

I would suggest that the inanimate objects incorporated by children that belong to their survivor parents be considered "transpositional objects." Such transpositional objects may resemble or function as linking objects and generational objects for the parent(s) but could then be used by the child for any possible developmental or pathological purpose. They might be used as transitional objects, fetishes or, in the case described here, for a more neurotic, oedipally based purpose which was incorporated into a young boy's masculine self. The extent to which such objects are present and how they might be utilized in other children of survivors requires much more research and attention to the possibilities in the clinical material. However, it appears that such items might promote unusual areas of weakness in the fabric of the developing child's mental space-time continuum. If stretched to a point of rupture, such tears could result in a psychic wormhole suddenly catapulting him back in time to the parent's Holocaust mentality. Recognizing and analyzing the role of such objects in the patient's psyche may facilitate a better understanding of his or her psychology. Although first recognized in children of survivors, intergenerational transmission of massive psychic trauma is not unique to the Holocaust (Apprey, 1993; Brenner, 2001), and its effects may be diluted in succeeding generations. This cultural transmission may be by way of the superego (Freud, 1940a) and through the incorporation of shared images of such tragedies which become woven into a large group's fantasy life (Volkan, Ast, and Greer, 2002). Such a legacy most likely contributes to the oral traditions and distinctiveness of a given family, an ethnic group, or a whole society.

NOTES

1. Loewald confronts his apparent contradiction about the futurity of the superego with Freud's view that the superego represents "the cultural past" as well as uniting the "present and the past" (Freud, 1940a, p. 206). In reconciling this disparity, he notes, "The superego then would represent the past as seen from the future, the id as it is to be organized" (Loewald, 1962, p. 267).

2. Although both were contemporaries whose genius helped shape twentieth-century thought, their meeting highlighted how different and incompatible their intellectual domains were, leaving whatever potential of integration of those worlds to future generations (Freud, 1933b).

3. To put this astronomical number in a human perspective, in the mere 120 milliseconds it takes for a visual image to evoke an affective reaction in the limbic system (Halgren and Marinkovic, 1995), that same light could travel over 22,000 miles. In other words, in the fraction of a second that it takes for the analysand to have an unconscious affective response to first seeing his analyst, a beam of light in his office could travel almost completely around the world.

6

Echoes of the Battlefield

> Two things in this war have aroused our sense of disillusionment: the low morality shown externally by states which in their internal relations pose as the guardian of moral standards, and the brutality shown by individuals whom, as participants in the highest human civilization, one would not thought capable of such behavior.
>
> —Sigmund Freud, 1914–1916

We should not be surprised that men at war suffer from the psychological effects of their experience, yet reasonably intelligent people may nevertheless be shocked to learn that killing and living in fear of being killed could have a deleterious effect upon the psyche. There is a societal need not to know that even for the most just of causes those in the military may return with many unwanted "souvenirs" of their valorous efforts to protect their country. These manifestations may be immediate or may take some time to make their presence known. According to the first independent study of those returning from Afghanistan and Iraq, about 18.5 percent have posttraumatic stress disorder (PTSD). Based on surveys of about two thousand returnees during August 2007 to January 2008, it was extrapolated that roughly three hundred thousand of the 1.64 million military personnel deployed are affected with PTSD or major depression. The estimated costs to society range from US$4.0 to US$6.2 billion. In this landmark report, *Invisible Wounds of War: Psychological and Cognitive Injuries, Their Consequences and Services to Assist Recovery*, the staggering and visible financial costs are revealed to us also (Moran, 2008).

The susceptibility to war trauma has understandably been a topic of importance as it has become increasingly evident that there are differences in resilience as well as in the nature of psychological response to the stresses of war. Factors such as a history of prior trauma associated with PTSD appear to increase one's vulnerability (Breslau, Peterson, and Schultz, 2008) and studies suggest that even a history of traumatization in one's parents may be a risk factor also. In such a study of children of Holocaust survivors, Yehuda (1999) concludes that "offspring of Holocaust survivors were significantly more likely to develop PTSD in response to their own traumatic events if their parents had chronic PTSD" (Yehuda, 1999, p. 113). Correlating the presence of low cortisol levels in the second generation with a greater risk of acquiring PTSD, she ascertained that such biological markers were strong indicators of psychophysiological transmission of trauma. We know, however, that there is more to trauma than PTSD and when it is enriched by intergenerational factors there may be myriad manifestations.

In this chapter, two men will be highlighted—one a career officer, a general, who figured prominently in the most sordid chapter of the Iraqi War, and another, an enlisted man who served in Vietnam and was wounded in combat in the Mekong Delta. Both of these soldiers were extremely principled and could not tolerate injustice or exploitation. Both of these men had a parent with severe war-related trauma and both of these men viewed their defining roles in the military not as war heroes or intrepid warriors. Their masculine selves were inextricably linked to different ideals.

GENERAL TAGUBA

The intergenerational transmission of trauma in military men may be inferred in the strange case of General Antonio Taguba who investigated the abuse and torture of prisoners at the now infamous facility at Abu Ghraib in Iraq. Taguba, whose military career essentially was destroyed by his extensive and uncompromising report in March 2004, unambiguously concluded that "Numerous incidents of sadistic, blatant and wanton criminal abuses were inflicted on several detainees . . . systematic and illegal abuse" (Hersh, 2007, p. 58).

His testimony on May 11, 2004, to the Senate Armed Services Committee reiterated his conclusions that the military police—young soldiers who acted as prison guards—were guided by higher-ups to soften up and prepare the prisoners for interrogation. This so-called Gitmo-izing of Abu Ghraib was the result of Guantanamo Commander Major General Geoffrey Miller's recommendations that the guards collaborate with the intelligence agents in "setting the conditions for successful exploitation of the internees" (Hersh, 2007, p. 63). Taguba insisted upon maintaining his integrity and ethics in the face of pressure and denials of knowledge of such a policy all the way up to Secretary of Defense Donald Rumsfeld. In reflecting upon his testimony, Taguba—not breaking his silence until his retirement in January 2007, after giving an interview with Hersh—stated "That's the reason I wasn't in their camp because I kept contradicting them. I wasn't about to lie to the Committee. I knew I was already in a losing proposition. If I lie, I lose, and if I tell the truth, I lose" (Hersh, 2007, p. 65).

Shortly after the hearing, Taguba's assignment was changed and he was ordered back to the Pentagon in order to "be watched." After a sarcastic encounter with Rumsfeld and a senior press agent in the locker room of the Pentagon athletic center, he realized he was being scapegoated; subsequent investigations were extremely limited in their scope and have failed to implicate those up the chain of command. Finally, in 2006, he was told by the Army's Vice Chief of Staff General Richard Cody that he needed to retire within the year. As he lamented to Hersh, "They always shoot the messenger. To be accused of being over-zealous and disloyal—that cuts deep into me. . . . There is no doubt in my mind that this stuff was gravitating upwards . . . the President had to be aware. . . . We violated the laws of land warfare in Abu Ghraib . . . the Geneva Convention . . . our own principles . . . the core of our military values . . . and . . . those civilian and military leaders responsible should be held accountable" (Hersh, 2007, p. 69).

General Taguba's courage to stand up to the abuse of power in leadership and oppose the degradation, sexual sadism, torture, and death of prisoners may be attributed to numerous psychological and characterological factors. Although he did not seek this historical role for himself—a two-star general was needed to do the investigation and he was simply available—what we learn from his background suggests that he was ideally suited to become the conscience of the military. Coming from a poor and very religious Catholic family, he was hard-working, industrious, and successful. In his early years, he was an altar boy and an obedient son. Significantly, his father—a native Filipino—was drafted in early 1942 in the midst of the massive Japanese offensive against General Douglas MacArthur's American Filipino coalition.

Tomas Taguba was captured several months later and became a Japanese prisoner of war. Imprisoned on the Bataan Peninsula, he survived the infamous Bataan death march, a brutal ordeal which killed thousands of Americans and Filipinos. Taguba's father somehow escaped and joined the underground continuously fighting against the Japanese until the end of the war. He then joined the U.S. Army in 1945 and retired in 1961. Interestingly, his son, the future general, grew up with little conscious knowledge of his father's military history, joining the Army himself as a career officer. Despite his qualifications and ambitions, he experienced such prejudice that he was criticized for "not speaking English well and having to pay myself for my three Master's degrees because the Army didn't think I was smart enough. So what? Just work your ass off. So what? The hard work paid off" (Hersh, 2007, p. 61).

Taguba's father broke his own silence in 1997 just ten years before the General broke his silence. When Tomas Taguba turned eighty years old, his exploits were finally recognized thanks to his son's investigative work documenting his eligibility for awards. During the ceremony when he received the Bronze Star as well as a prisoner of war medal, Taguba recalled "he had a big-ass smile on his face. I had never seen him look so proud. He was a bent man . . . but he stood up and saluted. I cried and everyone in my family burst into tears" (Hersh, 2007, p. 62).

Although Hersh does not attempt any psychological study of Taguba, he presents the reader with a fascinating profile of a man whose own father was a prisoner of war, subjected to murderous cruelty at the hands of his captors. We also learn that Taguba's mother had her own horrors from World War II. She lived across from a Japanese prisoner of war camp in Manila and often recounted in detail to her son how the prisoners would be tortured by having their fingernails pulled out and lived in daily terror of being capriciously bayoneted to death. So, while young Taguba could claim to know little about what happened to his father, he could easily recall what happened to other prisoners of the Japanese. Perhaps a defensive dissociative separation developed which enabled him to know and not know what might have or could have happened to his father while he could avoid being overwhelmed as a young boy.

We know that the studies of children of Holocaust survivors show that they may have had an unconscious wish to rescue their parents from the degradation and horrors of their incarceration. They may be living in a psychological "time tunnel" where they may exist in two time zones—the time of the Holocaust and the present-day reality (Kestenberg, 1982; Kestenberg and Brenner, 1996). Highly symbolic enactments, therefore, may occur on a regular basis where they live out elements of the parent's trauma woven into their developmental experience. It may be, therefore, that on an unconscious level the General in championing the rights of the rank-and-file prisoners of war in Iraq was trying to protect his father when he was at the mercy of the Japanese. For example, when he looked at photo images of "a naked detainee lying on the wet floor handcuffed with an interrogator shoving things up his rectum . . ." (Hersh, 2007, p. 58) or the sexual degradation of a father and son, he could not shirk his moral responsibility whatever the cost to his own career.

As one Lieutenant General who refused to look at the photos warned him "I don't want to get involved by looking because what do you do with the information once you know what they show?" (Hersh, 2007, p. 58).

The resolution of trauma may result in a mélange of identifications: with the victim, the aggressor, the rescuer, the innocent or indifferent bystander, and/or the witness. The unnamed Lieutenant General appeared to be more identified with the indifferent bystander who did not want to get involved. General Taguba, on the other hand, refused to identify with the aggressor and be "in their camp." Instead, he accepted his role as witness and (naïvely?) thought that others shared his moral outrage. He was in for a shock when during his first meeting with Donald Rumsfeld and staff on May 6, 2004, he was mockingly greeted by the Secretary of Defense with "Here . . . comes . . . that *famous* General Taguba—of the Taguba report!" Taguba later remarked with sadness: "I thought they wanted to know. I assumed they wanted to know . . ." (Hersh, 2007, p. 58). Taguba ultimately became identified with the victim himself for his refusal to look the other way or join in on the cover-up. In his words, "He [Rumsfeld] and his aides have abused their offices and have no idea of the values and high standards that are expected of them. And they dragged a lot of officers with them" (Hersh, 2007, p. 59). Not surprisingly, the torture of men involved attempts to destroy their sense of manliness and power, i.e., to dehumanize them and sadistically treat them, like female sexual slaves. Such documented acts included father and son sexual humiliation, forcing men to wear women's panties, having female guards ridicule men's genitals while they are being stripped naked and forced to pose for photos, senseless beatings, being dragged by chains around their necks and anally raping them with implements while they were shackled. Thus, the intentional dissolution of the masculine self appears to be a time-honored and universal strategy among torturers. At Abu Ghraib, Taguba concluded that the guards—to paraphrase an infamous alibi from the Nuremberg Trials—were simply "following orders."

It may be that from Taguba's perspective, being strongly identified with his father—the war hero and the degraded prisoner of war/victim—he had no choice but to stand his ground. This blend of identifications seen in another military man who was the child of a Holocaust survivor took a different but reminiscent form in this Vietnam veteran. This veteran has graciously agreed to have his interview with me published. Because of its length, I have made annotations along the way to highlight pertinent psychological themes.

AN INTERVIEW WITH A VIETNAM VETERAN

Part I

Ira Brenner (IB): First of all, I want to thank you for participating and being willing to talk to me about this.

Paul (P): You're welcome.

IB: As we've talked about, the focus of the book will be on trauma in men, and their resilience, and with what I learned about your Mom's experience in Eastern Europe, that adds a whole new dimension to things, so where would you like to begin?

P: Well, today is May 11th and forty years ago today was also a Friday and it was raining like hell and at 4:00 in the morning my Dad, brother, and I woke up and they drove me to Fort _____, which is in sort of downtown _____—that was the day I got inducted into the Army.

[*We begin our interview with an uncanny coincidence*]

IB: How old were you at the time?

P: Nineteen and a half. I was born in '47. I got drafted but I sort of got . . . I sort of . . . I volunteered myself to get drafted because I was out of college at the time, I was . . . I started in college at the right time right out high school. I didn't do very well. I felt. . . . We came from a small community and I felt pretty ill-prepared and probably even had some bad things happen when I started . . . when I did my freshman year of college, I mean, some people sort of got socially ostracized and, I mean, I don't know, my roommate pledged a fraternity so I went along with him—he was somebody I knew from Sunday School—and, so, I went through pledging and went through whatever it's called and then I became an active and once I became an active member, nobody spoke to me in the fraternity for the rest of the year and it was, you know, including, like, going downtown for social . . . and the people . . . I was totally ostracized and inexplicably, from my point of view, I had no idea what it was that I might or must be doing . . .

IB: You became inactive?

P: No, I thought I was part of the gang.

IB: So you pledged and became part of it . . .

P: Paid my money—whatever that was—got my little fraternity pin and then everybody kind of stopped talking to me.

IB: Everyone in the fraternity?

P: Yeah. My roommate talked to me but then maybe two people but other than that, nobody else did and it was . . . so it was very odd but back at the ranch I felt ill-prepared for college so then I started my second year and transferred elsewhere and basically I flunked myself out 'cause I knew I wasn't going to get the kind of grades and background to get into medical school 'cause that was always my intent, so that was in 1967. If you were out of college then, you lost your college deferment . . .

[P. is puzzled by events out of his control and to this day cannot explain the victimization and alienation he experienced. He became a social outcast and had to leave the safe world of the college campus after flunking out]

IB: Your 2S deferment?

P: Yeah. So I knew I was going to get drafted anyway so I thought, get the process over, so I went downtown to the Draft Board and said, I'm out of college. Can you put my, you know—I know I'm going to be on the list so put my name—I volunteered for the draft basically. I had worked in a pharmacy all during high school and even a little bit in college. I spoke pretty good German because my Mom and grandmother always spoke German and then I took German in high school and a little bit in my freshman year in college so I had this fantasy that the Army would send me to Germany to be a pharmacist assistant or something like that.

IB: You hoped to avoid combat.

[His fantasy of him being protected by a benign force looking out for his welfare]

P: Yeah, yeah. 'Cause I, I mean, I had no . . . I wasn't very athletic. I wasn't . . . I was afraid of guns—we weren't a family where we had guns so I didn't know anything about guns—so the Army decides in their infinite wisdom to make me an infantry guy—I mean, it was ironic at the time and forty years later it's still ironic. . . . It turns out—I found this out four or five years ago—that the Army in 1967 realized that in Vietnam a lot of the officers were getting killed—and I think that was actually before they were being killed by their own soldiers—they were actually . . .

IB: They were being targeted.

P: They were taking potshots at the officers so the Army actually apparently had this wise idea to . . . the other ironic thing was that in . . . you do basic training for two months and then the Army decides what you're going to become as a specialty and a bunch of us who were just like me had had one or two years of college, we all got sent to advanced infantry training in Fort _____.

IB: And there was some wisdom to that or is that what you later learned?

P: Which I learned four or five years ago but the Army . . . because so many people were getting, officers, were getting knocked off, they realized that they needed people that had, I guess, the intellectual potential to take over leadership if and when the officers got killed . . .

[*He theorized that he was being trained to be a replacement leader despite his abhorrence of violence*]

IB: I see.

P: And, so, my cohort that went through infantry training, I mean, almost to the last person, everybody had had some college or, you know, I had one friend who's a plumber but he's probably got some learning disabilities but he's one of the brightest guys you could meet even though he's very simple but he's got native smarts, so probably when they did the testing, so there we were, a bunch of, you know, scratching our heads going, what the heck are we doing in the infantry?

IB: But, at the time, I think, you know, it wasn't too amusing.

P: It was not amusing, no. When they lined us up and told us where you're going after basic training, a bunch of the guys actually cried. They were really scared out of their minds.

IB: And you weren't?

P: Somehow I . . . I knew it was bad news but I just thought, oh, somehow I'll muddle my way through.

IB: You had some confidence.

P: I had confidence in whatever.

[*Inexplicably, P. believed he would survive whatever challenges were presented to him*]

P: So we're probably up to about August of '67 now in advanced infantry training and started to think about this whole going-to-Vietnam thing and, first of all, when you're doing this infantry training, you sort of run around the camp doing physical training and getting in shape and in the military when you march and when you run, you usually sing some kind of song to keep the cadence so there was a lot of chanting and singing or whatever—I want to go to Vietnam and kill the Vietcong—and I didn't sing along when it came to those parts. I mean, I had no...there wasn't anything . . . I was able to, in a way, separate myself from what I knew I might be facing several months down the road. I was, like, I can't imagine myself being in a position to have to kill somebody. I mean, I did all the training that I had to do so that, you know . . .

[*P. remains alienated but this time it is from his fellow soldiers. He is a dove among hawks*]

IB: Marching, combat training, and all that? Chanting?

P: Well, I shot my rifle. It wasn't exactly—you have to do that, you know—it wasn't the best shot and I was afraid of guns. I mean, I literally was afraid of guns, afraid of bullets, you know, but you have to do it so I did what I was supposed to do.

IB: Do you remember any of those killing songs? Do you remember the lyrics of any of those killing songs?

P: Oh, yeah, yeah.

> I want to be an Airborne Ranger
> I want to go to Vietnam
> I want to be an Airborne Ranger
> I want to kill the Vietcong

That was it.

IB: That's what you guys ran around chanting.

P: Yeah, but I didn't.

IB: Right.

P: It just seemed morally wrong to even be thinking that or chanting.

IB: Sure. That was part of your protest at the time.

[*He refuses to sing group song, about killing the enemy*]

P: Yeah. But I did, you know, I mean, I also had a sense I had to keep my nose clean and not get in trouble. You know, I chose not to be a conscientious objector and go to Canada like other people because I thought that anything that I did that might be considered breaking the law would interfere down the road with going to medical school. I always had my eye on getting back, getting my education and I was going to be a doctor. I mean, that was never a question to me. So I toed the line enough . . . I mean, I never got caught breaking any rules. I kept my nose clean and a lot of people didn't but, so, but, you know, they're trying to instill in you a warrior, I guess, kind of feeling and there's other talking about going and killing and a little bit of talk about, if you do all this, you won't get . . . you'll be okay or you won't get killed so here are the things you need to do and I thought most of those a bunch of garbage. I just had a sense that . . . almost like when you go to any kind of . . . when you go to medical school and they teach you for four years and you get done and you go, they didn't teach me anything that you use in reality. I had a feeling that this is . . . somehow at nineteen, I still had a sense that it would be . . . this experience might be similar. So, I did have probably, I mean, one of the most significant experiences of my entire life, so I was somehow . . . during August of '67 I wrote a letter to my family doctor who I had talked with a little bit after I had my horrible freshman-year-of-college experience, so the summer between my . . . and he and I, you know, I guess he did counseling—I don't know what you'd call it—but, so, we had a relationship so I wrote him a letter and I said, you know, I said, this idea about going to Vietnam, I said, you know, I said, I realize I might get killed and it doesn't bother me but I worry about how Mom and Grandma would react if that happened and that was my Mom and my grandmother. Grandma was, like—my Mom's mother—a very significant person in my life. I mean, my . . . you know, they talk about everybody in life, if they're lucky, somebody tosses them a life preserver? That was her role in my life.

[*P. was dubious about his indoctrination, maintaining his own set of values and using his family doctor as a good male transference object given his absent father. He worries about the effect of his possible death on his beloved grandmother and mother*]

IB: Your grandmother.

P: My grandmother, yeah.

IB: You weren't worried about your father's reaction?

P: No. No. No, that . . . no. It didn't occur to me.

IB: Or sibs?

P: No. Just Mom and Grandma. So he wrote me a letter back—he always called me the formal version of my name—he was the only person that ever called me that—he says, I guarantee you if you want to die in Vietnam, you'll die in Vietnam and it was like this wake-up call that . . . I mean, I didn't realize that there might be, that I might have more control over how I did once I was there than the next guy had. I mean, so, really, it was like another . . . it was a life-saving event in a way because I think a lot of people went there and they just had sort of a fatalistic, pessimistic idea that I'm probably going to get killed. I went over and I said to myself—because I changed my internal dialogue—and I said, I have to do whatever I can to not get killed. I had a feeling just because I sort of knew the statistics that I'd probably get injured but I figured that . . . I thought, well, you know, if I'm lucky or whatever, it'll be a relatively minor . . . you know, it'll be something not too bad. I'm trying to capture for you how anxious I felt sort of leading up to going over there. Somehow I think because of that letter that my doctor sent back to me, I think I had a more optimistic attitude than most of the people. I think I wasn't less scared but I think I was handling the anxiety in a different way. I mean, I can't tell you if I was in denial but I was thinking how about how am I going to . . . I was thinking strategically. How am I going to get there, keep my wits about me . . .

[*The doctor instilled a change in P.'s psychological attitude from passivity to actively fighting for his survival. P. had an upsurge of narcissism and began to value his life more as the doctor cared enough about him to write back*]

IB: And survive?

P: And survive. Keep my eyes open and somehow not be in . . . just hopefully not have anything terrible happen.

IB: So, obviously, you were . . . your mission for going over there was not to kill as many Vietcong as you could or get a medal or do some major patriotic thing. It was basically to do your time, not break any laws and *come out alive.*

P: Right, and I had . . . I wasn't that politically astute then but I had a sense that the whole thing was a sham before I got there anyway and that was . . . you know, this is late '67 when I went over and, you know, the protests had started in Washington but, you know, I just . . . I had a sense that there was something, you know, a scam, a sham, but I didn't know enough politics to know the whole story but I had a gut feeling, so my sense was to take care of myself, try to survive . . . you know, when you go there, you know you have a year, a 365-day assignment, so everybody . . .

IB: Unlike how it is today.

P: Right.

IB: It seems to be an open-ended contract.

P: Yeah, with Iraq, it's a horrible thing—and, by the way, we ought to talk about . . . we ought to make sure . . .

IB: Yes.

P: . . . whether it's today or another time, to talk about how Iraq comes into my thinking.

IB: Absolutely. Absolutely.

P: So when I got there . . .

IB: When did you get there?

P: I got there, let's see, I dilly-dallied . . . they send you to a place where they process you, then put you on a plane, so it happened to be right around a holiday so I got a day or two delayed for going to services—and then I got another couple-day dilly-dally delay because I went to the Red Cross center and donated a pint of blood so everybody who did that got a day so I was trying to delay the inevitable.

IB: It didn't come off of your 365.

P: No, no. You still had, yeah, so I got there around mid-October of 1967 and you do a little bit of training and then you get sent to the unit that you're gonna be with, so by some quirk—there was, like, four or five of us that had been in training together and we cohorted—we just showed up at the same place and they sent us to the same place, the same unit, so we were in this . . . they sent us down to this—I was in the _____ Infantry Division which . . . we were in the Mekong Delta—and before we went over there everybody . . . you know, in the Army there's rumors—I don't know if you were in the service—but in the service, the service basically operates on rumors if you're one of the low-rank guys and I was an enlisted guy—and the rumor was the Delta is the worst place to be and, so, I thought, oh, shit, here I am in the Delta. They sent us down to the Delta. The Delta is basically . . . there's no terrain. It's just flat. There's some trees here and there. It's mostly rice paddies and rivers and streams.

IB: No place to . . . no shelter.

[*He is sent to the infamous Mekong Delta—a dangerous place with no place to hide*]

P: No place to hide kind of, you know, and, so, I took a look around at that and I said, oh, that's not very good, and then this camp that they sent us to was in this little . . . there was a small—I don't even know what you'd call it—it's not a main camp, it's like a . . .

IB: Satellite camp?

P: And it was in the middle of a rice . . . basically in the middle of a rice paddy. The defensive perimeter was 55-gallon drums that were filled with dirt so those were about as tall as your chest or something. I mean, we were basically out in the middle of, you know, we were exposed. I mean, I looked and it's muddy and mucky 'cause October was sort of the end of rainy season. It's just a pit. I mean, it was really . . . it was a pit! The whole thing was, like, this is really . . . it was absurd, you know. If you look at it in retrospect, you laugh about how primitive everything was. I mean, the building—we lived in these tent structures that had wooden floors but they were tents. In the Delta, the Vietcong were the enemy. At the time I was there, our enemies were the North Vietnamese and the Vietcong, they did guerrilla warfare. Guerilla warfare is they'd sneak up on you; they don't follow any rules; they don't wear any uniforms; you don't know who they are so you imagine, okay, here I am in this tent and if they send mortars in, then we're just sitting here and a mortar can go through a tent like, you know, so, you go, boy, this is like completely exposed.

[*P. is understated, in a dry-witted way, as if to humorously ward off the utter sense of vulnerability he must have felt*]

IB: How many were you in this camp about?

P: The whole camp . . . the camp probably had 6 or 700 people. My company had about 100-plus people . . . so I got there and this place is a pit and it looks pretty frightening. You're exposed. The good news was there was a rumor that the company commander—the CO—had been the kind of . . . we heard this and this made some sense to me that if the guys before I got there, if they'd been out on patrol, if anything happened to any of the men, they would find the nearest village to wherever that bad thing happened and burn it down and his idea was to let the locals know that Charlie Company wasn't to be messed with. The other thing you learned is that they always knew who was going out in the field, like the Vietnamese, the Vietcong, you know, so, when we went on an operation, my first operation, we basically . . . it was like going for a hike, so you walk out of the base—we didn't ride on vehicles, we didn't ride on boats at that time—so we went for a hike, so there's a hundred guys lined up with all this equipment hanging on them making more noise than you can imagine, so the first thought I had was, this is bullshit. I said, if you're making this much noise, you're attracting attention . . .

[*Now, in a detached, reporter-type way, P. recounts how vulnerable he and his comrades were to guerilla attacks and how absurd the military maneuvers seemed*]

IB: Sure.

P: So my first thought was, there's something bad going on here. If we're not smart enough . . . you know, I'm not a GI Joe but I knew enough to say, this is wrong. You know, we shouldn't be jingling and jangling . . .

IB: Not a good strategy, right.

P: It's like who's paying attention to detail? Who's really . . . but I was pretty pissed off right from the moment . . . and then knowing that—it's almost like people, the guys, you know, they know how many bullets we have, they know how many grenades we're carrying, you know, and some of the locals were Vietcong, so you walk through the village and everybody's looking at you, you know, and you know that some of them are people that at some point later might be shooting at you, so this is October . . .

IB: You were pissed?

P: I was pissed! I was pissed because I said, this is dangerous. This is really . . . this scared the hell out of me because I thought the way you operate . . . you know, I somehow knew enough about guerrilla operations that I said, you know, they're sneaking around out there—and I guess I had the mental image of the Revolutionary soldiers versus the Redcoats. Like the Redcoats would stand up, you know, fight like a man and our guys hid behind the trees, but I thought, they're hiding behind the trees, the Americans should be hiding behind the trees. Parenthetically, I had a couple—this is fast-forwarding a little bit—but I actually had a couple company commanders that tried to operate as guerrillas would and their higher-ups—the officers that oversaw them—actually punished them by taking them out of the field because they weren't following protocol. I mean, I was smart enough to realize that there was a lot of bullshit going on—and, unfortunately, I can keep score in my head—so I was sort of building up this count of all the bullshit things that I saw. This is from the moment I got there basically, so the first day we went out on a hike or on an operation. . . . So, the company commander that used to burn the villages down—they were called hooches—he actually forbade the guys to walk on the rice paddy dikes because that's where the booby traps were so he made people walk in the water but for some reason the day I got there we were walking on the rice paddy dikes so I'm not sure . . . the guys really hated him for making them walk in the muck and the water but he was trying to keep them alive and keep them from getting injured. It was actually October 26th and the way I know that is that from my very first day out, we go for a walk—I have no idea how far we were from the base camp—and there was a river that we had to cross so we were, I guess, water-trained—our company was; I didn't know anything about it; I was just following everybody else—and, so, they threw a rope across the river and somebody went across the river and I think the third person across actually the rope slacked up. He was loaded with ammunition—he broke the rules—and . . .

IB: What rule did he break?

P: Well, he should have unloaded all his stuff that was wrapped around him. He basically had an anchor around himself and the rope slacked and he drowned. That was my first day. His name was _____. I can show you his name on the Wall. I didn't know him 'cause I had just gotten to this unit.

IB: So you witnessed him drown?

P: No, but I was pretty close.

IB: But—you heard about it.

P: I knew about it. Yeah, I mean, I knew exactly what happened and . . .

IB: I mean, how did the news get to you if you didn't actually witness it?

P: Well, you're all kind of milling around . . .

IB: You can see what's happening over there, yeah.

P: Well, he was like . . . I mean, you know, you're sort of walking in a line, you know, like ants marching to the picnic table, and the word passes back and we had to stop—we couldn't keep going—and I was actually dreading this idea of crossing this river, I mean, there's something about that that I thought . . . 'cause I wasn't very physically strong and I just didn't have confidence in my physical abilities, so he drowns, then we're kind of standing around, then probably, I don't know, an hour later or something when people are trying to get organized, they looked around, they searched—he ended up being washed down the river; they found him, I think, a couple weeks later—but, in the meantime, we're walking along and I'm sort of on this bank of the river—there's really no defined bank; it's just all muck—and, all of a sudden, I'm up to my knees in mud and I can't move 'cause there's a technique of walking in the mud in the Delta so that you don't get your feet stuck but I hadn't learned that since it was my very first . . . so I'm actually stuck in the mud. There were a few sniper shots that you could hear, you know, here and there, and I'm, like, this is it, you know, like, I'm done and I'm, like, holy shit! and, luckily, one of the guys who had been there—the old-timers—a good old boy from the South sort of solved my dilemma. I was standing there for . . . it seemed like an hour but I was probably stuck there for, like, ten minutes . . .

[*A soldier drowns during his first operation and P. gets stuck in the mud and totally exposed to sniper fire. He fears he will be instantly killed but is saved by an experienced soldier*]

IB: Were you guys still in single file?

P: No, we're starting to move . . . scatter around a little bit. I didn't want to yell because I thought if I yelled and if there happened to be any Charlies around then I'd be a target, right? So I'm just, you know . . . I wasn't incontinent but when I think about it in retrospect with a smile on my face because it was kind of . . . there's an absurdity to it, right?

IB: In retrospect.

P: Yeah.

IB: At the time . . .

P: So this good old boy . . . and a lot of the guys were from the South so one of the good old boys who was an old-timer came and pulled me out.

[*His rescuer is a "good old boy" old timer from the South and knows how to free him up and yanks him free*]

IB: How did he do it?

P: He just yanked and, I don't know, he just knew how to do it. There's a technique so you don't sink in the mud yourself. I didn't lose my boots. A couple guys actually lost boots 'cause they got . . . not that day but other times people got stuck in the muck, so to speak, so that was the last time . . . I learned how to walk, you know, you don't let yourself sink in and keep moving, so that was the first day and I remember getting back to the base camp, you know, I was completely covered with mud and . . .

IB: Shaken up pretty good, I would think.

P: I was more concerned about _____ the guy that got washed down the river—denial, displacement—but I realized that that was senseless, his death. I didn't know at the time that he was carrying his ammunition and he shouldn't have been but I knew something had gone wrong and that somebody hadn't paid attention to the details like they should have, so I really got a sense that something really bad is going on here, so I knew that if I was going to keep myself alive and intact, I had to learn quickly and what I did strategically, I'd go on down to some of the guys that had been there for 325 days and I ended up . . . for a couple days I was carrying the ammunition for this tall, skinny guy from Georgia who was a machine-gunner and I carried his ammunition and he had been there for a long time—he was this quiet . . . I don't think he said 10 words—but what I did for the rest of the time that I was doing that kind of stuff was every time he'd move, I'd move exactly the same way . . . I did whatever he did 'cause I thought, he survived, he didn't have a scratch in the whole year . . . ten months he'd been there and I did everything that he did so I started realizing, the way you survive is you see what the old guys had done.

[*Knowingly, he intellectualizes and expresses concern for the man who drowned with all of his ammunition weighing him down*]

IB: You imitate. Now, you carried his ammunition. Was that a deal that you had with him?

[*He looked to those who knew how to survive and imitated them and stayed close to them*]

P: No, that's a job.

IB: Oh, okay. So, in other words, that's just how your assignment works and that's how you met him and then you . . . .

P: Right. Right. I'm not sure if I, like, picked him out. I can't remember . . . yeah, the new guys did get the scut work . . .

IB: Sure.

P: . . . so somehow . . . I don't know exactly, I mean, I knew he had been around and he just seemed to me to have a pretty finely-tuned instinct. He seemed like a natural soldier, I think. He knew what he was doing , very confident, he was cool, you know, sort of Clint Eastwood-y . . .

IB: Sure, sure.

P: There was something about this guy _____ that . . . I was new. I was going to do what he did.

IB: He was the right guy to . . .

P: And then probably . . . so we did a few of those walks-in-the-woods-kind of thing and nothing else really happened, so my company—Charlie Company—it's a bit confusing—we were Charlie Company and the enemy was Charlie—so Charlie Company led a charmed life for several months after I got there because we were known in the vicinity and the locals and the Vietcong didn't mess with us.

IB: So that strategy clearly helped.

P: So what Captain _____ had done really had a lingering effect—and Captain ___ left soon after I got there—but the locals knew who we were and they did pay attention to that, so we lived a relatively charmed life and that was a unique experience.

IB: Did you hear rumors about what was happening in other camps around the Delta at that time?

P: Not much, not much. I mean, occasionally you'd hear that somebody got in trouble and, you know, we might have to go and try to bail them out but usually—and we did that a few times but by the time you get there, everything is done because the way guerillas operate is, they shoot at you and then the minute you figure out where they are . . .

IB: They're gone.

P: They're gone. They don't hang around to let you shoot at them.

IB: Sure.

P: They're not stupid. We were the stupid ones because we thought they were stupid and, you know, it's the old . . .

IB: Right.

P: . . . chauvinism. So then I did something that probably would seem inexplicable to people but four of us got called in to the new company commander. He asked if we'd be interested in being his radio operator. So there were a couple things that an intelligent person knew when they went to Vietnam: one—try not to get sent to the Mekong Delta—well, I was there already; two: don't be a radio guy because you have an antenna sticking up four or five feet above your head; it's almost like when you see a bicycle rider with one of those flags whipping around and you know there's a bicycle rider; even if you can't see him, you see the flag so the word around was don't be the radio guy because the Vietcong will shoot at you. I had a different idea and I said I would do it because what I learned would tell me how I can survive this mess. My logic was, the more I know what's going on, the better I'll be able to keep my bearings and keep an eye on everything and I thought I needed to know what was going on, because if you have an infantry company, you know, there's 100 guys, there's four or five officers, there's four platoons and each platoon is broken into four squads and each squad has a squad leader and then . . . so there's, like, eight to ten guys in each squad, so you're really hearing smaller organizational units . . .

[*He defies the logic of the crowd and opts to be a radio operator carrying a tall visible antenna*]

IB: Right.

P: . . . and, so, I realized that if you're in the squad, you're so far removed from knowing what's going on, I said to myself, that's dangerous. It's less dangerous to know what's going on even, you know. I played an odds game. I said the odds are better—as I saw it—for me—to know what's going on, to have the antenna sticking up from by backpack, than to be just one of the guys following along.

IB: Sure, because if you're the radio guy, you'll hear the communication.

P: I'll know what's going on and I'll be the company commander's radio guy, not one of the platoon—each platoon actually had a radio guy—so

I was, like, the radio guy for the company commander so I knew what was going in our group but then you also communicate back to the battalion and then usually the battalion has the helicopters, you know, surveying what everybody's doing.

IB: And you were one of the invited people to be a . . .

P: Yeah, he picked, you know, four or five of us. My friend who was the plumber was one of them and he didn't have any college but he was a smart guy. He volunteered and then one of the guys that had been a friend of mine—he and I actually had consecutive service numbers so we got inducted standing next to each other in _____—we went through basic training together—we went through advanced training together—he got married in the one month between when we finished infantry training . . .

IB: Before you went to _____.

P: . . . so he invited me to come and be an usher at his wedding which I did so we were like friends, I think . . .

IB: Sure, sure.

P: He volunteered not to be the company commander's radio operator 'cause he thought that would put him in jeopardy so he and I had to split up a little bit so three of us—the other guy, there was another guy, sort of a creepy guy, so he had had some college, so he was one of the guys that had some smarts...

IB: As you were saying, the more educated . . . the enlisted guys, yeah.

P: He picked the guys that understood what was going on . . . I didn't leave the Delta. I mean I left it but, you know . . . we stayed there the whole time. We left this crappy base camp, though, after a month-and-a-half or something. So then I became the CO's radio guy and from that point on I didn't really have to shoot my rifle because if we were getting . . . so then eventually we were on some operations and we got ambushed and, you know, we were getting shot at and then, you know, from the enemy, they were in front of us, and then kind of behind us a half-mile away was the base camp and they were shooting artillery over us, lobbing it, you know, onto the . . . supposedly where the Vietcong were and, so, there was one incident . . . my infantry reunion guys always talked about this night where a few of the artillery rounds landed on us, I mean, literally . . .

[Being the CO's radio operator enabled him to know about the attacks, get help and not have to fire any weapons]

IB: The trajectory wasn't . . .

P: They hadn't adjusted it, so we lost a few guys because of our own . . .

IB: "Friendly fire."

P: Yeah.

IB: Did you know it was your artillery?

P: Oh, yeah. Oh, yeah, and one of my jobs . . . so I was operating my radio and one of my jobs was to get people back—there were several people that had communication but I was one of the people that said, your range is wrong, and I tried to do whatever . . . so then my job transformed and I actually became . . . what I realized is, I'm the caretaker for the guys . . .

IB: Yeah.

P: So I kept an eye on what was going on, I had to take care of the company commander, I knew where we were 'cause I had a map too—if you're in the squad you don't have a map usually—so I had a map. I always had to know where we were. I learned how to read a map—the military taught me—I hadn't been a Boy Scout—so I always knew where we were, I knew how many . . . you know, we had to order re-supplies, you know, we need, you know, 5,000 this and 100 C rations, I mean, I knew everything, you know, so I was like the CO, CEO, COO . . .

IB: COO . . .

P: . . . and everybody else's, yeah.

IB: And there was almost a maternal caretaking quality as you're implying.

P: Right, and I'm the oldest of four kids in my family so I was always, you know, that was my role in the family, you know, big brother taking care of everybody, you know, Mom is sort of—I mean, we'll probably have to go here too—my Mom is sort of not exactly a dedicated mother, okay, 'cause she's from a society where—a complete diversion, but . . .

IB: Maybe not.

P: Yeah, I know. Where she came from they had nannies who took care of the kids, so had she grown up the way she would have grown up, she would never have had to do any child care so she's got four kids, right? so she ain't prepared, so somebody had to care of the family, you know, so I always did that, I mean . . . so I was kind of used to taking care of other people but I rose to the occasion, I mean, I really, I was in my element taking care of people and keeping an eye on what was going on and knowing what was happening and I formed a good friendship with the company commander. He was a guy . . . I think at that time he was a couple years older and he had had, like, three years of college or something like that but he looked like . . . he had, like, Buddy Holly glasses, you know, it's the 1960s, so he looked very geeky.

[*He was the big brother, mother's helper and caretaker at home and assumed that role in Vietnam*]

IB: Like a Geek Squad kind of guy, huh?

P: Yeah, yeah. He looked intellectual but he was a good guy and, so, you know, I mean, your days are kind of spent . . . you know, somebody sends you out on a mission. When you work . . . so my job, since I worked for the company commander, I had to . . . like, three or four of us all were with him, the radio . . . 'cause you have a radio to talk to the guys in the company, then you have another radio to talk to the battalion, you have a third radio, so we were kind of a group. We kind of clung together, you know. Usually we walked in the middle . . . if we were out on a large "hike"—I don't even know what they call those stupid things—but if you're wandering around the countryside, we would be in the middle of . . . so there would be, like, forty guys in front of us and forty guys in back of us.

IB: You were protected.

P: Probably not if you think about it. I mean, if you're Vietcong, you're going to say, let's see who's in the middle. Look at all those . . . look at those three radios and there's one guy that doesn't have one and everybody seems to be talking . . . you know, if you're watching from the trees or from the little . . . the Vietcong dug holes in the ground and they had little periscopes, they'd peek, you know, I mean, so they're watching us. You knew they were watching you. So, we were kind of . . . we didn't have to even really think that we might to have to be, you know, the radio guys, I mean, we might have carried one or two clips of ammunition so we really . . . we had to carry our radios, we had to carry smoke grenades . . .

IB: So you didn't carry a rifle anymore.

P: Oh, yeah, no, no, you had to carry a rifle. I only fired my rifle—I think I probably didn't even fire ten shots out of my rifle the whole time I was there.

IB: You look happy when you say that.

P: I'm so happy. I mean, I had no . . . you know, I thought about the scenario. What if I was face to face with a bad guy and what would I have done? And I'm not sure what made me think of this but probably a couple weeks ago I was thinking about that scenario again. I don't know what brought it up but I was actually thinking, had I been . . . I think I was talking with somebody about the movie *Letters from Iwo Jima* or something, you know, I was imagining that scenario and I was thinking about what would I have done, you know, would I have . . . I would have fought for my life but I'm not sure how easy it would have been to take another person's life, you know, and, honestly, I mean, I also knew enough at that time—you know, I was about twenty by then—so I had . . . I watched . . . a lot of the guys seemed to have no compunction about killing if it came to be that they had to kill somebody, and I had a lot of compunction against it . . .

[He wonders if he would have killed the enemy if he were about to be killed himself]

IB: Of course.

P: . . . and I don't know if those were the guys that had tasted, you know, that had killed somebody and nothing happened back at them, I mean, I realized that killing . . .

IB: What do you mean?

P: Well, if you kill somebody, I had this feeling and I can remember this clearly, thinking, so, if you're in Vietnam, you're walking around, there's some bad guys, you shoot 'em and you kill them, they don't then get up and kill you back like they do in cowboy movies 'cause we're all the cowboy TV generation, so I had this hypothesis, I guess, so if you have to kill somebody and nothing bad happens to you, then you realize killing isn't hard. Killing's relatively like falling off a log, which is what you do when you're there.

IB: It gets easier.

P: It's easy and, so, I felt, I mean, I still to this day feel incredibly relieved that I didn't have to do that 'cause I don't know what that would have done to my head, you know? it wouldn't have made me somebody who thinks killing . . . but I think it would have changed me. I would feel worse now about the experience than I do 'cause I'd have to say, look what I did, you know? so, in retrospect, the experience, I thought, is . . . you know, there's sort of a dividing line in the algorithm—kill somebody else/don't kill somebody else—and I thought people could kill other people, I think it still haunts them, you know? in a different way than others are haunted by our experience.

[*He wonders how he would have changed if he became comfortable with killing*]

IB: Something that you know from being friendly with these guys . . .

P: Oh, yeah!

IB: . . . from the reunions, from the nightmares, from what you guys talk about.

P: Did you say nightmares?

IB: Yeah.

P: I don't know what goes on in their heads, you know. I mean, a lot of the guys have nightmares but I don't know . . . I haven't asked them specifically. It would be interesting. Is your nightmare about you killing somebody or just sort of being there with people . . .

IB: About to kill you?

P: Yeah, or people get blown up or have seen bad things, horrible things happening.

IB: Witnessing terrible things.

P: Yeah. That I don't have a sense of . . .

IB: But you clearly get the sense that those guys who killed are especially burdened by that.

P: It's my hypothesis—I think, I think that they are.

IB: And you certainly feel that you would have been?

P: Yeah, I mean, you know, just intellectualizing, I mean, I read—I don't know that I ever told you about it—there's a guy named Jonathan Shay, a psychiatrist in Boston at the VA. He wrote two books. One is *Achilles in Vietnam* and *Odysseus in America*. *Achilles in Vietnam* is about the experience, you know, when you're in Vietnam and then *Odysseus in America* is about Vietnam veterans coming back and he . . . I think, I'm trying to remember how he formulates this . . . I think that if you're—I'll have to go back to it—I'm losing my train of thought, so . . .

[*He becomes quietly overwhelmed, having difficulty concentrating, as he ponders the psychological fate of those burdened by actually having killed others. He, at this time, thinks of himself as having been spared*]

IB: About the division of the algorithm—killing or not killing—and whether or not there's a burden, especially that is what you imagine is how you would have felt.

P: Yeah.

IB: What's happening right now is we're talking about powerful . . .

P: I'm trying to think about what . . .

IB: I'm wondering if there's something being evoked in you right now about what we're talking about because this is really powerful stuff.

P: Yeah.

IB: What are you feeling?

P: Well, I'm . . .

[*Unable to feel at the time, he intellectually "reports" on being ambushed on January ___ and wounded on February ___ in a detached and dry-witted way. Ironically, the tape broke while being transcribed, necessitating my asking him to repeat these most traumatic experiences of his tour of duty*]

Part II, Twelve Days Later

P: So, the question how did things go after I left here last time was really interesting because I went home and I felt . . . even though I'm comfortable talking about all this and I talk about it a lot—I don't tell war stories but I talk about it openly—I felt . . . I did feel a little strange when I got home, sort of *as if my envelope, my protective envelope, had been made porous, not ripped apart, but it just felt*—I don't know if it's exposed. Exposed isn't the right word. You haven't heard my story.

IB: I haven't, even though you and I have known each other . . .

P: Right.

IB: In a different context so you're wondering if that, you know, is a factor also.

P: Yeah. I don't know. I don't know. But it wasn't bad. I mean, you know, I handled the feeling, I mean, I was able to sleep that night and didn't have bad dreams . . .

IB: It was the anniversary of your . . .

P: The day I was inducted into the Army.

IB: . . . your induction day. Yeah, that's . . .

P: Yeah, yeah.

IB: That adds another load to it.

P: Right, right. Yeah . . .

IB: I have a lot of respect for anniversary reactions.

P: We left off the story January ___ and that's the day where our company got really badly ambushed and definitely splayed out, I mean, there's no way I'm ever going to forget January ___, you know? The feeling that I had that day, though, I mean, I have a feeling that I do something to suppress that, you know, that feeling that I was . . . you know, because my rifle got stuck in the muck and even though I didn't . . . my job wasn't to use my rifle, I think that that could have been a day that we got overrun and not having a functioning rifle, I mean, if it came down to protecting myself or not being able to protect myself, you know, I mean, that was a bad moment.

[*He is unprepared for the ambush and his rifle gets stuck in the mud, the way he himself got stuck during his first day there*]

IB: You were pretty vulnerable.

P: That was, like, yeah . . . that was, like, a very vulnerable moment that day and, you know, I think it was embarrassing to have . . . I mean, all the other guys are getting the shit kicked out of them and, you know, I'm sort of not unhappy that I wasn't in the middle of the rice paddy but I couldn't do very much except take care of my radio and call in help and all that which is what I did, I mean, that was my job and I did it well, but, you know, I couldn't shoulder my rifle if I had had to to protect the guys and, so, there's always that nagging feeling that I have of letting people down, you know . . . I mean, even though . . . I mean, I think about it very rationally and I mean, in a way I didn't let anybody down because I did what I was supposed to do and, thank God, nothing happened where I had to use my nonfunctional rifle but, yeah, there I was, you know?

IB: I'm wondering if this is a subtle manifestation of survivor guilt.

P: Yeah, yeah.

IB: You know, it comes out in all kinds of ways and, as you say, not everyone walked away that day.

[*He acknowledges survivor guilt over not having been able to protect his comrades*]

P: Right, right. That was actually the day . . . that day I think, that was the biggest loss or the biggest number of people that we lost in our company, I think, ever, from the day our company arrived in Vietnam—which is in late—before I got there—which is in late 1966, early '67—to, I think, they rotated them out, I think, somewhere in 1969 and January 10th was the biggest one-day loss of people—injured and dead. If you go to the Wall, you know, when you go to Wall in Washington, it's organized by dates . . . it's organized by the date of death . . .

IB: Ten guys, you said?

P: I think ten guys died, yeah, and, you know, just fast-forwarding to the last five or six years when we started to have reunions? the guy who was one of our medics, he's got this incredible memory, and he says, not everybody who died is listed, so he knows . . . so even the records are just incomplete, so that's the survival feeling, you know, I mean, it pisses all of us off, you know.

IB: That these guys aren't remembered properly.

P: Yeah. You know, they're not sort of logged in.

IB: Do you remember their names?

P: I remember a few of them, yeah. I remember them as people too, I mean, a lot of them were people I knew. One was a crazy Hispanic guy—he was one of the funny guys, so he was somebody everybody kind of liked a lot. Yeah, I remember some of them. I remember . . . you know, when you see the list of names, I mean, I knew a lot of them, and, you know, the people that got injured that day . . . I think we kind of left off the story where I was holding my one friend's head in my lap that night after things had quieted down and before the "dust-offs" came to pick people up and . . . I mean, it was like the freakish war movie you see, you know, when the choppers landed, I mean, we were putting the wounded guys on the choppers and then we were putting dead guys on the choppers, you know, and it was dark, the lights were kind of eerie and it was kind of foggy, I mean, it was, like, out of a movie. Without any question, it was not . . . I mean, it was really . . .

[*He recalls the bizarre, eerie scene as his wounded buddies waited to be evacuated*]

IB: Surreal.

P: It was very surreal and it was also very painful to . . . you know, 'cause we . . . like I told you last time, we really had led a charmed life—our company—and it was really the first time we'd taken that many . . . we'd been at the receiving end and I think probably in the back of your mind you always know . . . at least I always thought that at some point whatever charm Charlie Company had . . . carried with it, people would be dissipated and they would know we had new leadership and they would know we had new guys, you know, grunts, and they'd know that we were vulnerable and that we weren't going to retaliate in the way that was effective in terms of keeping the locals on guard against us, so our lucky charm ran out of electricity or whatever, so a couple days later, we're back in base camp and I actually—again, like I mentioned, I had pledged to my friend's new bride that I would take care of him—so I basically told the first sergeant, I'm going to Saigon to see what's going on with him and I didn't ask permission, I just kind of said, I'm going, and so I found what I think was some kind of fly plane that went . . . I was fifty, sixty miles down in the Delta so I hopped a plane—just walked over to the landing strip . . .

IB: You said, I'm going and he . . .

P: I told the first sergeant—they probably thought that he and I were gay, you know, I'm convinced of that to this day that, you know . . .

IB: That you guys were lovers.

P: They probably thought something was going on, okay? He is kind of an effeminate guy, so, I mean, you know, they probably thought something was going on. Nothing was going on but, you know, I was just being responsible and I wanted to see him before I somehow tried to get through to his wife to let her know firsthand how he looked, so I made my way to the hospital—I forget the hospital there . . .

IB: So this wasn't insubordination, this wasn't abandoning the post?

P: No, no, 'cause we were kind of standing down to recover . . .

IB: Recovery time.

P: And, I mean, if I had to, I would have been insubordinate but I was a good enough trooper that I think the guy knew that I was doing . . . I was just doing something on . . . based on my moral whatever and . . .

IB: As they say—moral compass.

[*He hops a plane to Saigon to find his wounded buddy in order to keep a promise to his buddy's wife to protect the man*]

P: Yeah, so I went to this hospital and found him and he was all . . . he had shrapnel in his back, he had shrapnel in his face, he actually lost vision in one of his eyes but I made sure he was alive and made sure that he was okay.

IB: He was communicative?

P. Yeah.

IB: He actually knew . . .

P: Yeah, yeah. He actually . . . I brought him some of his stuff—I don't even know what I brought him—probably some of his stuff from his locker or something and just kind of checked in on him and I checked in on a couple of the other guys and I can sort of vividly remember just walking around this place as if I had, you know, I mean, it was like . . . again, it was like almost—not magic—but it was, you know, it wasn't surrealistic, it was just, you know, I was just walking around checking the guys, you know? Almost as if I were an officer, you know, doing the right thing, checking on my boys, you know? and one of the guys—this medic with the good memory—he got injured twice—this was his first injury—he actually got . . . I don't know what got him but he had a scapular fracture so something exploded next to his back and fractured his shoulder blade. Like, in all of your years in medicine, have you ever heard of a fractured scapula?

IB: A fractured scapula!

P: That is something I never have, but the concussion from that paralyzed him temporarily. Whatever smashed into his back, he was temporarily paralyzed, and I said to him—and he remembered this thirty-some years later—that I said to him, "Don't go back out in the field. You're good. You know, you've done enough. You're not going to have to go out"—and it took him about five or six weeks to recover so he actually went back out on patrol, but it was after I got injured, so I didn't see him again until thirty-some years later when we started having reunions. So I saw people that I needed to see.

[*They meet 39 years later at a reunion and reminisce*]

P: When I was in Saigon—and then I had to make my way back down to the Delta—so I left the air base, and I actually ran into a high school friend—there's one of my . . . and he and I went drinking with a bunch of Australian infantry guys—they were hanging around there—so we went drinking, I mean, it was almost like a party and it was, you know—thinking about it forty years later or thirty-nine years later—it's, like, how strange is that, you know? I mean, it's four or five days after January 10th, you know, we lost all those guys, you know. I think when I got back to the base camp, there was actually a memorial ceremony which I have pictures of and, you know, we had ten rifles, you know, they were stuck in the ground and their helmets on top and their boots in front of them, I mean, just like you see pictures of—those were our guys, you know. I remember being tearful that day. That was a tough day but, you know, I mean, you're all twenty-year-old guys and who's gonna cry in front of the other guy, right? And I can remember, though, sort of feeling tearful . . .

IB: But had to suppress it.

P: Sucking it in, yeah. I'm sure the other guys were doing the same thing.

[*His suppressed grief over the losses continues*]

To my memory, not much happened for a while. There's, like, a blur. I'm sure that I could think of some things that happened but off the top of my head I can't remember 'em and then I eventually probably went on a few operations or something but then I ended up getting injured on February 11th—I think it was Lincoln's birthday, his real birthday—so the day I got injured was a really weird day. We were going on an operation so we had to—oh, I know—back up . . .

IB: Before February 11th.

P: So backing up a little bit—so the other thing in terms of scared shitless, my company, we sort of did several different things but one of the things . . . we were part of what was called a mobile rivering force and we were connected to the Navy. We worked with the Navy. We were on the Mekong River—that's where our base was—and, so, part of the time we were actually living instead of in our base camp in these barracks kind of things, we went from that crappy place that, you know, tents and real primitive down to this base camp that had sort of like 2 × 4—I think they were two-story buildings even—that was sort of like more like a regular Army thing—it was a big base—and then when we were operating out of the boats, so then we kind of moved out to these barges that were anchored in the middle of the—I don't think it was the Mekong River but it was a big branch of the Mekong River—and these things were like . . . they had been Navy barges and then they built like a four-story structure, like a dormitory almost, above it, okay? So we lived on a boat on those things for a while . . .

IB: And they're anchored.

P: They're anchored in the middle of the river, yeah, so in a way it's safer because we're out of mortar range . . .

IB: How many hundreds of yards offshore were you?

P: Well, probably half a mile—it's a wide river there—so a little bit safer. In the base camp, you know, you can get . . .

IB: Was the dormitory, the floating dormitory, patrolled by boat?

P: You don't really need . . . you need to keep an eye out probably for sampans that come too close but they kind of knew better—you know, they would have been shot at—so you're relatively safe, you know, and the Vietcong didn't have scuba equipment—if they had scuba equipment that could have been, you know, but probably even if you did, you couldn't have swum through it, there was a huge current . . . the current was pretty impressive—so as part of the mobile rivering force one of the things we did was we floated around in these little boats that almost looked like the duck boats that show around the tourists in the cities and some of those boats like you saw in pictures of World War II that had a ramp in front of the boat that flipped down and then the soldiers ran off. So, what we did when we were on what we called "on the boats" and on the river is we would drive up and down the rivers, which are probably a little wider than your office, I mean, they're not big, and the goal is to get attacked because in the Delta you never knew where Charlie was and the only way you found him was when he attacked you so our job was float up and down the river, "hope" to get attacked, then the next thing was the boats, the Navy driver of it, turned the boat to the embankment, you know, jam it into the bank, flip down the ramp in front and we were supposed to run into the barrage of oncoming gunfire, machine guns and whatever, and that would be how we found them 'cause we had no way of finding them, so, fortunately, when we were doing that kind of nonsense we didn't get ambushed but the feeling of terror from that is something that I never forgot and I don't think any of the guys—you know, first of all, just kind of the sort of John Wayneism of it all, you know, John Wayne would attack the machine gun onslaught and, of course, all the guys would survive, so we knew better . . .

IB: You all sensed it was a suicide mission?

P: Well, you knew some people were going to get hurt and killed. You know, I mean, you knew that you'd probably had more people than Charlie had so that at some point if that did occur you'd win. . . .

IB: By sheer numbers.

P: Numbers, you know.

IB: How many guys were on each boat?

P: I think it was a platoon on each boat so it was about forty guys and we just kind of . . . you're huddled in this wet, you know, weirdo thing, you know, we're not Navy people; we're Army guys, but we just . . . that was our assignment and that's what we did and actually about a month after I left, one of the guys that did get . . . that was involved in one of those, you know, flip-the-ramp-down-and-run-into-the, charging into the onslaught, one of the guys that all of us kind of liked a lot because he was just kind of a likable, cute guy, you know—his name was _____. He was like a teddy bear, you know—so one of the letters I got from my friend said that _____ got killed . . . you know, I mean, you just sort of knew the scenario, so in the interim between January 10th and when I got injured February 11th, you know, was sort of like this what if, you know, what's going to happen, that kind of thing. Somehow we just didn't end up getting ambushed, so then on . . .

IB: The Charlie Company charm coming back?

P: I think it was more that . . . it felt more like since we had taken so many losses, injured and killed on the 10th, that we weren't fully operational or something—I'm not quite sure what the whole story was—so eventually we got a bunch of new guys which we called cherries—you've probably heard that expression if you've talked to Vietnam guys—so we got a bunch of cherries—probably, like, twenty-five or thirty cherries—and that was really bad news because those guys had no clue what to do and that, combined with the terrible company commanders that we had, that was, I mean, all of us knew something bad was probably going to happen or at least we were worried it would. February 11th, the day I got injured, we were assigned to go out on a mission, the whole company, so we showed up at the little landing area where the helicopters were sort of parked and we said, here we are, and they said, who are you? And we said, we're Charlie Company, and they said, well, we're not taking you. We're here to pick up somebody else, so there were, like, you know, fifteen helicopters and there was ninety or one-hundred of us, whatever, and we're all staring at each other and at about probably near noon—maybe even a little bit after noon—somebody decided that, yep, in fact, they were there to take us out, so it was like this, you know, you knew something bad was going on. Those kind of things actually didn't happen that often. They were usually pretty well, somehow well-coordinated, so bad vibration . . .

IB: You had some foreshadowing.

P: Bad vibration, right? Definitely a bad vibration so we got on the choppers and we went about five miles northwest of our base camp and as we were landing we started taking sniper fire so when I rode in the chopper there's like—I don't know if you've seen pictures of those six- or eight-passenger choppers that we rode on but there's, like, a bench to sit on and then a couple of us—I always sat on the floor, at the door I'd be hanging out, I was kind of, like, sitting there . . .

IB: That was your spot.

P: Well, somehow, again, I mean, it seemed like I could get out quicker if I was sitting there, you know, even though if the chopper banked, you know, you'd kind of go, uh oh, I hope they're not banked, you know—they don't slide out; it was a stupid thing—but, anyway, so as we were coming in, we started taking sniper fire and I even remember, like, you know, flattening myself back on the floor 'cause you knew the bullets were coming—you can sort of tell by the sound of a bullet if it's coming in your direction; it's sort of a different crack to the sound of the bullet..

IB: So you pulled your legs back inside and . . .

P: No, I just lay [down] flat so that I was less of a target, so somehow we landed and jumped out of the chopper, hid behind, you know, a rice paddy dike. The rest of the company, you know, they're kind of . . . choppers have to land, you know, they can't all land at the same place so they kind of land at some kind of a formation on the ground and, so, the majority of the guys were kind of in front of us and they were, like, hiding; they had their heads down, they weren't doing anything, so these were really all new guys, including . . . must have been a couple of the platoon leaders, the sergeants and the lieutenants, 'cause what you're supposed to do . . . this sniper wasn't even, like, we weren't getting shot at by a lot of people but they were all hiding and what we were supposed to do is to shoot back and the guys weren't doing that. The company commander, who doesn't know his rear end from third base, he doesn't know to tell them to start shooting and that day the radio guys that went with him weren't the . . . it was me . . . there was another guy that wanted to become a radio guy so he was subbing for one of my buddies, so I was kind of, like, taking care of him . . .

IB: Like one of these senior guys out there.

P: Yeah, yeah, I was, so the company commander has no clue so I finally just said, screw him, I got on the radio, I said to the other . . . I think I was on battalion radio which means that my frequency is tuned to the battalion; the other guy was tuned in to our guys on the ground, so I think I grabbed his radio and said, you guys need to start shooting at these . . . I mean, 'cause the CO was just, you know, like apoplectic almost, you know, he just didn't know what to do . . .

[*In the chaos of being shot at by snipers, he goes on the radio to give orders to shoot since the CO was apparently paralyzed by indecision and inexperience. P. had "bad vibrations" that day*]

IB: You were not in radio contact with the CO though?

P: We were together, 'cause we all . . . remember, we all walked around and we all huddled together, we all . . .

IB: So did he know you were calling to give the order to shoot? I'm trying to understand. . . .

P: I tried to kind of be diplomatic . . . I mean, you know, I mean, my memory is a little bit vague but, I mean, I think I kind of said, you guys need to start shooting, you know, something that wouldn't threaten him but that would get something happening 'cause we were pinned down; we couldn't get to where the rest of the guys were and at that point we didn't have . . . so you have helicopters that drop you off and then there are other helicopters which are called gun ships and those things come out and they'll just shoot the crap out of wherever the bad guy is supposed to be so we didn't have a gun ship out yet but we were calling for one to come out and help us out, so I'm not sure . . . I think they took a few shots . . . our guys took a few shots in the direction of where this guy was shooting from so he quieted down a little bit so then the CO and the other radio guy and I were going to run—there was a clump of mud or something—we were going to run from one clump of mud across the paddy to a paddy dike so we could be near . . . getting toward the guys 'cause we were sort of separated but there might have been a few guys behind us too but most of the group was in front of us, so, you now, again, we're running with our radios on our back and it's just me . . . the other RTO and me. The CO, I'm not sure where the CO was and I think he said, you guys run across there and I'll see what happens. I'm not sure actually but I think I said to the other guy, we have to get up with the other guys or something—and I'm not sure if I was the one who initiated it—in any case, so we're in the middle of this rice paddy and there's water—some paddies are muddy and some are wet—so there's water probably six inches . . .

IB: The time that you get stuck in? . . .

P: No, not really. The river banks you get stuck in. The paddies are sort of clay-like . . . so we're running across this rice paddy and the other guy got shot somewhere around his beltline—I couldn't exactly tell where but he was holding . . . so he's laying face up in the water, in the muck, screaming and so I kind of—I'm not sure, I crawled over to him, or you know, I kind of went over and I was trying to help him and I tried. . . . I was taking his belt buckle off because I just wanted to do whatever I could first-aid-wise and I had both hands out helping him and I got shot and it turned out—I didn't know this at the time but the same bullet went through both arms so it just skimmed under my skin on my right forearm so it went through and through and what happens with bullets when they get a slight impediment like soft tissue is that they splay out—and I do remember that from way back in basic—so the bullet then hit my left arm and kind of smashed in a big area of my left forearm so when I looked down there was this . . . it looked like a glob of blood, didn't see any skin there, like it was just a two- or three-inch diameter hole in my arm is what it looked like so the first thought I had was—so my hand went numb—so I thought that meant that that artery, so I thought, bad news, artery has to bleed out so I started trying to do something to get a tourniquet on myself.

[*He got shot in the arms while coming to the aid of a wounded comrade*]

IB: You're still exposed in the rice paddy.

P: We're both lying on our backs by this point but I'm not making myself a target anymore but we're both . . . and we're alone. I mean, like, there's nobody out there. Nobody's shooting at this guy that's shooting at us yet. Gun ships maybe were just starting to come onto the scene to shoot and quiet him down but nobody would come out. Usually you're carrying, like, a first aid, like a compress, it's a bandage that everybody usually carries with them. For some reason, I didn't have mine. I might have used it on him or I might have used . . . so I didn't have one to put on myself so I had a belt, which is just like a regular belt 'cause I had a hunting knife that I carried with me so I ripped that off to make a tourniquet for around my arm and eventually the sniper stopped shooting at us and eventually one of the other guys did come over and put his bandage on my arm and eventually got a medic so it was just like everything was screwed up, you know, it was like everything was just totally screwed up. The CO didn't know what to do. I didn't have my stuff, you know, I wasn't prepared in a way. The other guy, the other radio guy, he was such a rookie and such a new guy, to this day I don't know his name and I keep trying to find some way to get a list of people that were in our company on that day to see if I could just recognize his name by going down the list. I can't even get that so I have no idea what ever happened to this guy.

IB: The guy who was shot in the waist?

P: Yeah.

IB: So you don't know if he made it or not?

P: I think he made it. I mean, I think . . . so eventually . . . the shooting quieted down, they got us to a piece of relatively dry land, whatever, and a medic came and gave me a shot of morphine. I smoked the only two cigarettes in my life that afternoon—literally—I haven't smoked before but I said, this seems like a time to have a cigarette.

IB: If ever there was.

P: I knew I was alive, I mean, I knew I wasn't going to die. I knew that . . . I had a feeling something not good had happened but I remember having a thought that whatever comes of this I'm going to make the best of it, that, you know, somehow make it to medical school and become a doctor and I'm standing out there in the middle of this nonsense thinking about, you know, I'm going to put it together, whatever it is and whatever I have to do.

IB: 'Cause at that point you still weren't sure if you were going to lose the arm or not?

P: I guess I didn't think I was going to lose my arm. I don't know, somehow I just didn't think I would and also I had some faith in whatever the doctors were going to be able to do to take care of me, you know, which you have to have. If you're in a car accident in the upper part of the mountains and you go to the hospital and the orthopedic surgeon comes in after having six beers, you still think that he's the best orthopedic surgeon in the state, right? So I had confidence that whatever, you know, that the doctors would somehow be able to put me back together. So, then—I'm focusing on screw-ups because . . .

IB: What kind of marks do you have left on your arms?

P: Oh, I have scars—I'll show you—so then I actually called in my own . . . since I had the battalion radio, I called in my own dust-off including . . . you have to give the coordinates on the map so they know where to come and, you know, we're five or ten minutes away from base camp and we're sitting there, like, forty-five minutes and we're like, well, where are you guys? and they said, well, we don't see you guys—obviously, they switch you over if you talk to them, so it's, like, well, you're not here and we're here so they read me the coordinates where they were and they had gone five or ten miles southeast instead of northwest, so it was a real screw-up.

IB: It was a comedy of errors.

P: It was really a screw-up, yeah, it was probably like some movie. But I was okay because I had my morphine and I was pretty . . . you know, morphine is good stuff, right?

IB: Oh, yeah.

[*He performed his own first aid, radioed for help and rescued himself*]

P: I liked that and eventually they got us back to our base camp on dry land and they have, like, a field hospital that's basically an air-inflated plastic Quonset hut, so I remember they couldn't get an IV started and the guy tried five or six times and I said, you do it one more time and I'm going to beat the shit out of you. I remember just kind of being a little . . . by that point I was getting pissed off.

IB: It takes a lot to get you pissed off like that.

P: Me? No, no, not at all. But, again, you know, I mean, when you're being taken care of you shouldn't get pissed off at the people taking care of you but by that point I said this is, you know . . . so eventually I remember some guy, somebody, I think it might have been the anesthesiologist, put a subclavian—I don't know if it's a subclavian line or he knew there was a vein, a clavicular vein or something, and he found a vein there, but he just knew anatomically. I think that was my first IV in my life, so I wake up, you know, late that night and had no idea what . . . the doctor came and told me a little bit about what's going on. This was during the Tet Offensive in '68 so we're getting . . . so the base camp gets mortared so here we all are on these rickety, metal frame beds and we all have to sleep on the floor . . .

IB: In a plastic bubble.

P: Yeah, in a plastic bubble. I was, like, everybody else gets to go into the sand-bagged bunkers. We're laying on the floor and that happened three nights so three nights in a row we're basically sleeping on the floor, so. . . . The doctor—I actually remember the guy's name—I have no idea where he was from but I remember his name and he came up and said, it got your radial nerve and so you're probably gonna not be able to do certain things but we'll be able to put your hand into a functional position and then there'll be maybe tendon transfers—I had no idea what that meant— but he explained it to me and it turned out he was exactly right in terms of my prognosis, so . . .

IB: You needed all that.

P: Yeah, yeah, but, you know, I also had my ticket home and I knew I was going back. A lot of people that got injured had to go back but I lost my supination of my left hand so that meant I couldn't hold a rifle 'cause everything else, you know, short of the supination I might have theoretically had to go back but I knew that I wasn't. . . . I knew I had my ticket home and then it was, like a week of, you know, three days in the Delta and four days in Saigon waiting to sort of. . . . I had to get stabilized and I think they to debride the wound one more time before and then they took us to Japan, but, so for seven nights, you know, and the Tet Offensive was going on and it was, you know, it was . . . in Saigon we were in a real hospital but, I mean, when you've been out in the field and you sort of can have some mobility and then all of a sudden you're in a building, that was actually a bad . . . that was a bad feeling, being in a building and not being able to have my stuff, being able to maneuver, had no boots, you know, I didn't even have shoes, you know, it was, like, total . . .

[*He was told he would have a permanent limitation of his arm but he had his "ticket" out*]

IB: Pretty trapped there.

P: I was trapped. I had no equipment, you know, and I had my instincts so I knew what to do, right? But that was a pretty weird time.

IB: Pretty darn scary time, I would think.

P: You know, it was scary sort of counting the minutes to get out of 'Nam, you know, counting the minutes until the plane took off and even . . . I think the last night we slept in a sort of Quonset hut-type thing at the air base and so three nights in a Quonset hut in the Delta, three or four nights in this hospital and then the last night in this Quonset hut thing and thinking, you know, there's mortars coming in again, you know, there's still one more chance for them to get me—get all of us—and finally the plane takes off and that was like (he claps) that was it, you know. (Claps three times) I was out, you know.

IB: And you knew it.

P: And I knew it, you know.

IB: What was that like? Leaving your buddies behind.

P: Did I think about that? I don't know. You know, you're really of two minds when you're there. One mind is, take care of my own rear end, you know? And, so, that part of me was, like, I'm out of here. You know, I've got my ticket home. The other guys, you know, I guess I wished everybody could come home and, you know, I mean, again, I knew that the whole thing was a sham so I'm also—at least three minds—so the third mind is, like, this whole war is just a sham and people are getting killed and maimed and injured and psychologically maimed for nothing and it's a joke. We're not helping . . . the Vietnamese people don't want us, we're not stopping Communism, we're probably not going to win it but we were fighting it but we don't know how to do guerilla warfare, on and on and on, so it was like . . . so there's this level of absurdity, you know? So just wishing all the guys could be out of there. I guess I sort of cherry-picked the people that I, you know, I hope this guy makes it and that guy, I mean, the people that I knew . . .

IB: Your friends.

P: My buddies, you know . . . I think, though, I was more self-focused and I was taking care of myself.

IB: Survival mode.

P: I had to get out of there.

IB: Yeah, sure.

[*Not thinking about leaving his buddies behind, he focused on survival and leaving Vietnam as quickly as possible*]

P: And then . . . so from Vietnam you have to go to Japan. They have these three big hospitals there so that's where you had to get more debridement if you need it and you get stabilized and then they sort of give you your—those going back home, those going back to the field, so, I mean, I was going back to the world, as we called it, but that was a very weird time because I didn't know anybody. There wasn't a lot of chitchat—at least I wasn't chitchatting with anybody—I wasn't feeling very good probably from some of the medication—I think they had me on Darvon, Darvon compound. Do you remember Darvon compound? Did you ever take it? Darvon compounds, the first time I took it, I remember lying in my bed and feeling like I was about a foot above the, I was levitating. I had bandages . . . you know, I mean, my left arm had like a half . . . it was a plaster—I think they call it a half-cast, a cast but not employed around the arm so they had just a shell and then the rest of it had gauze and stuff and . . .

[*The painkillers and trauma made him feel depersonalized*]

IB: So it was between a cast and a splint?

P: Yeah, an Ace bandage. My right arm had just a little skin wound but there was a bandage on it so I couldn't wash, I couldn't . . . I didn't have any, you know, and they had to give you kind of a toothbrush and a comb and whatever but I could barely take care of myself, you know.

IB: Your hands were affected . . .

P: Go to the bathroom, yeah. My right hand didn't affect my function but I remember . . . so I was the walking wounded so I had to go to the cafeteria for my meals—they didn't bring my meals, you know, in my hospital bed—so I remember the first time I did that, that you walk through, you put your food on your tray and then you have to carry your tray to a table and I didn't have the strength to do it. I mean, I did. I mean, I somehow was able to do it but, I mean, I barely had enough one-handed strength at that time to carry a tray and I remember that was a pretty grim time 'cause they didn't have . . . there really wasn't anybody that came . . . I mean, none of the nurses really came and said, how are you doing, buddy? Nobody really, you know. It was really hard.

IB: No USO there to . . .

P: They were there. Well, a Red Cross person gave me some money 'cause I didn't have any money and, you know, you could buy Coke and chips and that kind of junk—there was something—I didn't have a nickel to buy anything 'cause I had my . . . I did have money when we went out in the field but I had it in my helmet 'cause in the Delta you carry all kinds . . . so I had it in my helmet and when I got . . . when they took us back to the field hospital at our base camp down there, you know, they took all my stuff so I had nothing. I had no wallet, no money, no nothing . . . I mean, you know, the important thing was to buy some goodies, that was what I was thinking about. The Red Cross gave me ten or fifteen bucks, something like that, and I had a little pocket cash, but nobody really talked to me. I was just, you know, I was all alone and I'm okay being alone, in my own thinking, I guess, I'm a lone person but that was a pretty . . . that was, like, a very weird feeling, you know. I wasn't thinking of my parents at all, you know, I wasn't thinking, boy, I wish they could be here. . . .

[*He felt very alone and unable to care for himself*]

IB: Yeah, I'm wondering if they knew, if any of your next of kin were notified . . .

P: When you go there, you sign in, I believe, you give them authorization to notify them, you know, they . . . so what I said is if I get severely injured, notify them. Otherwise no, so I got hit February __. February __ I wrote a letter and I said something, I got injured, dah, dah, dah, I'm okay and I dropped it in the mail. February __, the next day, I wrote another letter, doing fine, still here in the hospital, you know, blah, blah, blah. Today's

Dad's birthday. Hope he's having a good birthday, blah, blah, blah, so they
got the second letter first so they didn't . . . and it came from me. It didn't
come from the Army so when I got to Japan they had actually . . . they got
the letter before I got to Japan. They called the Congressman and his office
tracked down where . . . so when I got to this hospital in Japan, the clerk or
the person checking me in said, your parents called. I'm sure I was the only
person who'd ever been there whose parents called before he got there. I
called home and my job, as far as I was concerned, was just to say, you know,
this is what happened and this is what they told me and I'm fine, you know.
But it was a very weird feeling . . . at some point, they, you know, like I'm
still walking around with these little slippers and, you know, pajamas and
whatever . . . hey, you're kind of like, can I get some clothes here, you know?
so there was a place where you could get a few items of clothing and all they
had were Army, they didn't have . . . so they had Army, like, regular shoes,
right?—I'll never forget this—so they didn't have . . . at the time my shoe size
was nine and a half, the only shoes they had were size seven and I took 'em
so I'm walking around in size seven shoes with my nine and a half feet just
to have shoes and just to feel a little bit better, you know.

IB: Have a little integrity, a little dignity . . .

P: Yeah, yeah. . . . I was . . .

IB: Pretty helpless.

P: Yeah, yeah, and, in fact, I was off the pain medication and . . .

IB: Feeling down at all?

P: I don't think so, you know, I was just kind . . . I think I was just kind
of nonplussed, I mean, just kind of, like, oh, well, you know, like fatalistic,
like it happened and on to the next, you know? but I don't remember feeling down or angry, you know? You know, when I had surgery later, I remember . . . it was almost—I've certainly had a hernia, whatever, a tonsillectomy
or something—and I remember . . . and, so, after surgery, I remember three
or four days after surgery, I started to . . . I'd feel this, oh, somebody actually
cut into my body and, you know, like, this is really like . . . this is a pretty
unusual event, you know, having somebody have that ability to do that to
you . . .

IB: The bullet was lodged in your left arm?

P: No, no, it went through.

IB: It went through both arms.

P: Yeah. But what was interesting is I don't remember having that . . . so, it's almost like, you know, years later, I'm talking about, surgery years later I'd have that sort of a shudder, like, oh, my God, I had surgery but I didn't have that feeling . . . 'cause, you know, you had to have . . . I had surgery on the 11th, the day it happened, I had some kind of procedure in Saigon, I think, but maybe not, definitely had general anesthesia again in Japan, 'cause then they sewed it up with these metal sutures, these wire sutures, to close the skin, then I had two or three surgeries and I was back in the States before I got discharged.

[*He does not remember feeling very much about his surgeries . . . "nonplussed"*]

IB: So the reconstructive stuff . . .

P: Yeah, yeah, yeah. But I never had that sort of post-op shudder that I had years later so it's almost like when I had, you know, as I think about it, that reaction years later was what I should have been, you know, the shudder for . . . holy shit, I just got shot! you know and it got my radial artery, you know, so I knew . . .

[*He had a delayed emotional reaction but did not realize what was happening*]

IB: It did get your artery.

P: I didn't know that until, I don't know, a couple years later I got a letter from somebody doing research on arterial repairs and I had been coded, you know, they had, you know, a code for whatever, artery repair, and so they wanted to know how I was functioning or whatever, and it was the first I knew. . . . I mean, I knew I had the radial nerve. I had lost median nerve function but that actually came back but I didn't . . . and I suspect I had it but when . . . so what I saw on the day of the injury I didn't see squirting blood. What I thought years later is probably that bullet had cut the radial artery but it probably cauterized it too. I don't know if that happens but . . .

IB: Sometimes the artery goes into spasm . . .

P: Yeah, yeah, yeah.

IB: If the artery's cut and it sort of creates its own tourniquet.

P: Yeah, yeah, yeah, tourniquet, so I thought either of those two possibilities. So the life-threatening part of it, 'cause, I mean, you know, I . . . the vulnerability I felt with subsequent surgery, I mean, as I think of it, as I reflect on it, was excessive, you know, I mean, not to react to getting shot and that, you know, not to react very much has always been interesting for me to just observe about myself.

IB: So you underreacted to all of this?

P: Yeah, I really think I did.

IB: Did it ever catch up to you?

P: Yeah, yeah. That would have been about . . . the timing is . . . the year it caught up to me . . . it either had always been caught up or it really caught up to me about seven years ago when I developed my PTSD but, according to my wife . . . one of the ways I figured that I had PTSD is I started going to the reunions which this is, I think, are going to be our sixth or seventh one that I've gone to yearly, and at the first or the second one, one of the guys comes up to me and says, you got it. You need to go get checked. And I went, what? He said, you know, PTSD, you need to go to the VA and I went, what do you mean? I mean, I didn't . . . I'm sort of on the verge of diagnosing myself with PTSD, but one of the guys kind of saying to me, you know, you're in trouble and you don't know you are. Now, this is a guy who had been, like, he'd been a sixteen-year-old when we were over there. He looked . . . he was tall and skinny and somehow looked a little . . . so he lied to get into the Army. He was a doofus then and he got a head injury and developed this . . . he had this memory problem that he couldn't forget anything and now he's an engineer or whatever, but he was the guy that came up to me and said, you have PTSD and so I . . . that's kind of how I put it together that I had it.

IB: What signaled it to him? You guys were hanging out at the reunion or something?

P: So a year later, at the next reunion, a few of us were talking and this guy's always been a yacker and, so, he said, yeah, he said, you know, when we were in 'Nam, he said, you were always, like—some word he used about me—like you're always, like, zeroing in and you're going for things and you're . . . not intense 'cause I'm not . . .

IB: Focused or something like that?

P: Sorry?

IB: Focused.

P: Focused, focused, and just goal-oriented and he said, you showed up here for this reunion, you were, like, lost. He said, I thought you were having a nervous breakdown. That's what he said about me and, I mean, he was just a country boy really—a smart country boy, you know?

[*He appeared "lost" at his reunions and one of his buddies told him he must have PTSD and needed help*]

IB: This is after thirty-some years?

P: Thirty-some years. So I said to my wife . . .

IB: Medical school, marriage . . .

P: Right, to a mental health professional, don't forget. So I said to my wife a couple years ago . . . I said, so when did—this might have been three years ago—when did you know that I had PTSD? and she said, oh, about thirty years ago but they didn't even have the diagnosis when we got married, I mean, we got married in the 1970s, they didn't have PTSD until somewhere in the 1980s. . . . So, how long did I have it? My wife said, oh, thirty years at least but I didn't know that I had it. You know, once I realized that I had it, I mean, it really flooded me and then I thought about—you know, I did a little reading about it, you know, I tried not to read too much because I didn't want it to interfere with my therapy—but I realized that I was explosive. I realized that I was hypervigilant and I was always ready to do something if need be. The one thing that . . . so when we all getting back from Vietnam and, you know, this is in the late 1960s and you'd read stories or you'd watch the news and they talk about a Vietnam vet who'd be walking along the side of the road and a car would backfire or somebody might shoot off a firecracker or something and the guy would dive behind something, so while I'm in the hospital . . . so eventually I ended up in the hospital, so my travels went from the Mekong Delta to Saigon to Japan to the Army hospital there, so while I'm at the Army hospital and you start to hear and watch the news and they talk about Vietnam veterans, you know, kind of combat veterans, infantry guys, doing all these things, you know, that everybody thought was a little bit odd and, so, I said to myself, I can't do that. I mean, even though . . . I said I just have . . . I said, I have to overcome . . . if I have the urge to do that, I'm going to have to override it somehow, so the one thing that I didn't do that other Vietnam vets did a lot of was dive for cover, so what I did if I heard something that sounded like it might be incoming is I assessed it and I kind of said, okay, gunshot, if it's a gunshot, is it coming in my direction or not? If it's fireworks, I can handle fireworks. If it's a car backfiring, I can handle a car backfiring, so rather than . . . so, you know, so I did something for one of my potential symptoms but . . .

[His wife had known it for thirty years but he could not recognize it in himself]

IB: Did you feel an urge to dive for cover in these kinds of . . .

P: Oh, yeah, oh, yeah, oh, yeah.

IB: But you had a rapid assessment system in your mind, I guess, to appraise it.

P: Yeah, yeah. On the other hand, I was—and probably less than I used to be—but I'm still pretty intolerant of people putting other people in dangerous situations so, for example—this is something that I . . . I tell this story all the time and I'm completely not proud of it—but, on the other hand, I did the right thing. I mean, during residency, when I was an intern in the ICU and I had to go transport a patient and he was supposed to keep watch but he slept through and lots of patients were in trouble when I got back and I got into a fight with him, a physical fight with him, and, you know, to this day I'm the one that's accused of doing something wrong.

[He cannot tolerate people endangering others and became violent one time during his residency]

IB: You slugged him?

P: Yeah, and . . .

IB: And he knew why?

P: He knew why. Everybody knew why but somehow I was . . . in a way it didn't seem to matter and to me, because of what I saw happening to guys in war, okay, where you do something like that and you put other people in danger, so when I see something that's the equivalent of that I react and I'll react physically if I have to, okay? And I justify it and I learned that other people don't do that, so, once . . . I mean, again, this is within the last few years, once I learned that I have PTSD and how it affects me and how it affects my interactions, so I've had to kind of look at . . . I mean, even though I can justify by my own logic, it's still not how other people do things. Other people don't beat up the junior resident when he doesn't take care of the patients in the ICU, okay? Nobody does that. I'm the only person that's ever done that to my knowledge or one of a few, okay? and there are other things that I will do in the face of authority where I think there's a betrayal coming that's gonna endanger people, so that's . . .

IB: I wonder if there were any official repercussions in your training around that?

P: If there were?

IB: Yeah.

P: Oh, you mean, like if I ran into my old chairman tomorrow, he would say, remember that time you . . . what they did is they hung it over my head forever. They kept reminding me, do you remember that time you got into . . . the chairman stayed . . . he was around for a long time and whenever we'd . . . not every time we'd get together but every other time we somehow would get together, he would bring it up, not in a yuck-yuck-yuck kind of a way, I mean, in a . . .

IB: In a very . . .

P: As if something, I mean, I didn't get it until, again, until way in retrospect. I didn't get it that what he was saying is that was really inappropriate, you know?

IB: That that was a serious thing that you did and they were pretty upset about it?

P: It's called assault, battery, I think. I think it's got a name. I mean, I think this guy, had he been smart enough, could have taken me to court, my fellow resident.

IB: Did you hurt him?

P: Sorry?

IB: Did you hurt him?

P: No. I was never very strong so he was stronger than I.

IB: He didn't fight back though.

P: He did, yeah. He pushed me back, but, you know, I've done that with a lot of bullies in my life, you know, confronted them and, you know, they push back but then, you know, but he was still a lazy, you know. . . . Two years later, he became a Fellow and I was the senior resident when his wife was admitted. You'd think he wasn't having a little problem with that? He was having a big problem with that.

IB: Wow.

P: We'd look at each other, making interesting kind of eye contact.

IB: Wow. What were your eyes saying to each other?

P: Fuck you, I think, and you'd better not mess with my wife is what he was saying to me. You know, I was going to do the right thing . . .

IB: Of course.

P: . . . but I was saying, it was irony, isn't it?

IB: Oh, boy.

P: Payback, but, so, you know, I mean, I really have been kind of plagued by the PTSD stuff without . . . so when you asked did it ever catch up to me, I mean, you know, I didn't kind of have like a, oh, I don't know have . . . I didn't have like a sort of this hubris about it like, well, lots of guys have it but I don't but I just thought, I'm glad I don't have it, you know? I mean, I didn't know I had it because I didn't read much about it. I mean, I knew I didn't dive for cover and, you know, I thought I was functioning, but, you know, every opportunity to have some kind of a confrontation or to be, according to everybody else, over-reading a situation, you know, and sort of looking at it . . . you know, I mean, like something flying over—a helicopter, you know?—anytime anything like that happens, I mean, I just, you know, I—hopefully not present tense but past tense—you know, I re-acted to something analogous as if it were that consequential even though nothing is that consequential. Once you're out of the combat zone, there's very few things that are of consequence and I would react as if . . . but I always thought, well, it makes sense to me, you know? This guy's doing something that's going to hurt other people and, you know, and my reac-tions would be inexplicable to other people and, you know, just painfully so. I mean, you know, I'm a good person by my own estimation. . . . And to be doing things that would be so shocking to other people, you know, like where is this coming from? you know, and not sort of saying to myself, I wonder what they think about it but just, this is really weird, I mean, I just do what seems right but it's wrong, you know, and it's like this . . .

[It took him a long time to realize that some of his behavior was inappropriate and related to PTSD]

IB: But it has felt so right to you!

P: Right. And, you know, again, I mean, in therapy I sort of started realizing, you know, and part of PTSD is that you see black and white and I'm a person that preaches gray, like when I teach or I teach our patients, I mean, I'm in gray. I'm not in . . . but when it comes to other things, I mean, I'm very, you know—I think less than I used to be—but . . . and I didn't realize that even, and for somebody who embraces gray, I really . . . I mean, you know, and preaches it and I thought I embodied it but then I, you know, once I started looking at myself more carefully, I realized that I didn't and I went down several notches in my own estimation, you know, that's been really painful to just kind of . . . I mean, I don't think I'm narcissistic and I don't think I'm self-congratulatory but that's not how I get my strokes but to realize that I was impaired and didn't know it, you know, that's taken a . . . it took some wind out of my sails, you know, and I was impaired, I mean, I really was impaired and it's so funny to think about...well, I hadn't made this connection, but one of the things that really, really, really pissed me off in the several years after I got back from Vietnam was not the physical injury to the guys but the psychological injury to the guys and I just had this thought, which I hadn't had before, isn't it interesting that my impairment, as it turns out, is psychological more than physical and I hadn't thought that about myself until this . . . I mean, I thought, well, I mean, I probably do—I have my own neurotic stuff—but I didn't think that I had any Vietnam stuff.

IB: And you just had this awareness.

S: Two seconds ago, yes. Yeah, isn't that interesting that my impairment over those long number of years was psychological too and, I mean, different . . .

[He suddenly realized during the interview that his problems were more psychological than physical]

IB: In a more occult way.

P: Yeah, yeah. Somebody who's keeping it hidden from me, that censor. I mean, you know, for me, that's really painful, you know, that's about as much pain as I feel, you know, to let myself down, to not conduct myself, you know, the way I expect myself to conduct myself and. . . . You know, my values are still right. I mean, it wasn't the value part, it's sort of the interactional part. I thought I was lucky, I mean, I thought I was lucky that it didn't seem to have . . .

Part III, Nine Days Later

P: So one of the things that I have to say . . . I mean, so when we started the session last week, you asked me how I had been and I told you that the previous week when I left here I felt like my envelope had been perforated so this week, you know, after last week's talk I was fine and I didn't have, you know, I slept, I was fine, I felt intact, I mean, you know, not distracted, I played tennis that night, you know, and everything—you know, so I was functioning okay—but I think that, as you mentioned, what you said just now about the psychological part, I mean, you know, I'm aware inside of myself of . . . I think I do expend some energy to put this aside and it's something that I don't feel is a good thing for me to be doing. I don't think it's healthy but, on the one hand . . . on the other hand, it's necessary and it's just part of my mental economy, you know, my . . .

[*He is now more aware of how he wards off feelings and memories of Vietnam*]

IB: What would happen if you didn't expend that energy to keep it off to the side?

P: I think I'd be distracted. I think I'd be . . . you know, I think that . . . so, going back to December 1967, January 1968, okay? It had become clear that we were . . . that our charmed life was almost coming . . . you know, we weren't charmed anymore. We lost the company commander who sort of knew what he was doing . . .

IB: The guy who burned the villages down.

P: Well, he left right when I got there but then the person that took over from him—my friend _____—_____ knew what he was doing so we were okay with _____ but then after _____ left, which was sometime in December, then we got these bozo commanding officers and there was a little more heat and you could tell that we were getting shot at more, there were more encounters, and you could tell that something was changing for Charlie Company and I think that all of us . . . I mean, you know, the communication about how . . . you kind of go, oh, shit, you know, something was gonna happen here, you had a premonition, so I think all of us—well, I can't speak for anybody actually—but I think that there was a sense that something is gonna happen.

IB: There's an ominous feeling.

P: Too many good days had gone by. We're in the Delta. We know that the Vietcong are, you know, it's their . . . they own it, right?—at least I knew that—and you knew something was gonna happen and then there was this prospect of being on the boats where, you know, I mean, this is sort of filling in a gap—I didn't mention this in the first session; I mentioned it last week so it will be redundant—but I think sort of anticipated getting on those little boats and going up and down the rivers and . . .

[*He reviews how his company's "charmed life" changed and he became more afraid*]

IB: Becoming targets.

P: . . . hoping to get shot at and then having to leap into the machine gun fire, I mean, I think the prospect of that was pretty . . . if I let myself think about that, that's really frightening, I mean, that's just more frightening than just about anything because not only are you on the river in a boat but what you're supposed to do is counterintuitive, I mean, the intuitive thing, in my opinion, if somebody's shooting at you is to get the hell out of the way, you know? and so I was frightened that what's gonna happen when and if this ambush finds us—again, and the goal is that's how we found them 'cause otherwise we couldn't find them—so what if they find us but also I think I was also aware of here, again, the Army has these, you know, "genius ideas." Instead of getting away from being shot at, they want us guys to walk into it, okay? And so the feeling of being humanly disposable, okay? We're a bunch of twenty-year-old guys, right? And we're disposable basically and, you know, I thought about that a little bit on Memorial Day on Monday. I always go to the Vietnam Memorial, which is in _____ and I don't pay much attention. . . . I just go there to think about what the . . . and, you know, it struck me, you know, again, that war, the Vietnam War, is about, you know, some, I mean, had I been in World War II I think I would have fought like a banshee, I would have done my job, but the Vietnam thing was obviously nonsense so I'm thinking, okay, so here we are riding around in these little, tin boats, tin-can boats—actually they were more like shoeboxes; it was like if you waterproofed a shoebox and played in your bathtub, that would be more like what this was—so these steel shoeboxes floating on these narrow rivers and running into the machine gun fire if it came at us and somebody had done some bean-counting, obviously, and said, yeah, some of them are going to die and I knew that we weren't fighting Communism, there was no cause, it was nothing, it was all about nothing, and, so, it's frightening and it's also the futility and the betrayal and, over the past four or five years, I've learned . . . I've done some reading and—I think I mentioned the first week we talked—the book by Jonathan Shay—*Achilles in Vietnam*—and what he really finds out about it is betrayal, that betrayal is a huge part of trauma, especially military-type trauma, and, so, the betrayal of trust, the betrayal of just, I mean, it's . . . they toss you out there and you become, I mean, you become less than a potential statistic, I mean, you don't exist, you know, you're not . . . you don't count and that feeling came back since you and I talked last week, maybe because it was Memorial Day and I was thinking about the guys, you know, just sort of the process of losing people, especially, you know, in these wars that we've had in the past thirty or forty years which have been for nothing, you know, just some political or economic gain for somebody and, so, to be rendered nothing and to be . . . you know, I don't like . . . the word "cannon fodder" sounds trite but to be put in somebody else's gun sight—the enemy, so to speak—and just by our own people so that we can find them so that some fuckin' colonel or some Westmoreland-type guy could report back to Lyndon Johnson or Richard Nixon or whatever that here's the body count, okay? So if you remember watching the news back in the 1960s, you know, the body count was the big deal and the body counts for the most part were fabricated and they were made . . . they were to make somebody look good.

IB: Are you describing not being cannon fodder but being bait?

P: Bait, exactly, exactly, exactly. There was live bait.

IB: Yeah.

[*Our talks and the Memorial Day holiday revive feelings of betrayal by the leadership and being used as cannon fodder or live bait to flush out the Vietcong*]

P: Yeah. In that sense, you know—I'm going to try to sort of regroup for the purpose of the interview—so I was already thinking about that, so then _____ loses his leg, okay? On New Year's Eve. You know, I get into this fight with the colonel. It's clear to me, you know, it's becoming more painfully clear how we are bait and how, you know, we're just . . . we're pawns, you know, again, we're not human but we're also, you know, our lives are getting more and more at risk and then sort of culminating in a way, in the weirdest way, on January 10th when . . . so, leading up to it were these completely rotten company commanders—it's interesting that over the three weeks my negativity about them has escalated, isn't it? I'm noticing that.

[*He becomes more aware of his anger at the incompetent leadership*]

IB: Well, your expressed negativity.

P: Yeah, yeah, yeah, you know, I mean, I'm, you know . . .

IB: Is that new to you or just . . .

P: No, no, but I'm editorializing, maybe I'm—I think I'm hyper-bolizing—but I guess I'm just sort of . . . you know, I'm letting sort of . . . I'm letting myself go back there and feel what it was like, you know, and sort of purposes of our talk so that was just one more, you know, one more blow to my sense of integrity, you know? Like this is really bad stuff, you know, in our language of Vietnam, this is bad shit. Something is gonna happen. Something bad is gonna happen. Bad leaders, you know, bad Colonel _____ bad Westmoreland, you know, so January 10th we were sent out to rescue one of the other . . . you know, the battalion has four or five infantry . . . an infantry battalion has four or five infantry companies so we were C Company—Charlie Company—so they're either Alpha or Bravo—A or B—Company was getting attacked so we were sent out to rescue them, to back them up—I forget; there was a word for it that I can't remember it now—bail, you know, reinforce them but that isn't it . . . so when we got caught, when our guys got caught out in this huge, open, rice paddy, you know, it was like . . . the other thought that I probably had some level was this is it, you know, this is what I was . . . I knew this was coming, this whole . . . something has been building up, so I anticipated it and it happened and then my rifle got stuck in the muck, you know, and several of my friends got wounded badly or killed. None of my sort of one-to-one friends got killed but people that I had bummed around with and, you know, just joked around with and stuff but people that I knew were generally the guys lots of people liked. I mean, one of the guys that died . . .

[*Ominous forebodings prior to their ambush on January __*]

P: Somebody at one of our recent reunions—this has happened . . . this story has come up about three times at our reunions—that _____ actually knew he was going to get killed and probably that day.

IB: Huh!

P: He had a premonition about it and I sort of knew that before we went out but, you know, I can vaguely remember knowing that he thought

his number was up. . . . He said it! He talked about it. He just knew, yeah.
I mean, you read that in war stories . . .

IB: You do, you read that. Did you hear . . . did you see that, rather, in
other guys?

P: Not that I can remember. Not that I can remember. Not off the top of
my head exactly. So that fact that the guys were out there, they're getting . . .
they were just getting, you know, bombarded by the mortar mercilessly and
they have no cover—and I knew that—and I couldn't do anything, you know,
I mean, whatever I was able to do was inadequate, I mean, whatever anybody
was able to do was inadequate 'cause the whole thing ended when Charlie
decided to end it—not our Charlie Company but the Vietcong guys—I mean,
it didn't end 'cause we did anything effective, I mean, you know, if we called
in artillery or gun ships came in to . . . we didn't even know . . . you know,
you're getting shot at, you know where bullets are coming from—you can tell
by the sound—if you're getting mortar, you don't usually know the direction
and mortars have a funnier noise when the shell drops in the tube, you know,
you just sort of melt but you can't, you can't, the hearing, you can't direction-
alize, so calling in the gun ships or calling in artillery, which is about all we
had to protect us, you know, it was inadequate so it was just, you know, it
could have been worse than losing ten guys that day. I don't even know how
many people got injured but, like I said at the end . . . last week, I mean, it
was enough guys that we had to go out for quite a while. I mean, it was major,
there weren't many people left in our company and I think when I . . . so, you
know, when I put my friend on the chopper to get him out that night and
then that hellish kind of a scene with the weird light, I think what probably
kept me pushing ahead was that I was taking care of him, you know, I was
taking care of him for his wife as I had promised her and I was pretty single-
minded about that, you know, as I said last week, but the fact that you sort of
have a premonition and then something bad happens . . .

[*They were totally at the mercy of the enemy and he felt utterly helpless to help
himself let alone anyone else*]

IB: When you got shot.

P: Well, the day I got . . . you know, I think I always had a premonition
. . . I had a sense that very few people didn't get injured so I figured I'd get
injured. I mean, I, you know, I didn't know how or in what way and I certainly wasn't trying to enhance the process, I mean, you know, but I just . . .
I mean, I thought statistically speaking, there ain't that many people that go
back home that didn't get some kind of a mild injury, I know, you mean, a

piece of shrapnel, a pierced something or, you know, but it was what I had seen. It was usually pretty minor so the day I got shot was more . . . I didn't have a premonition about myself. First of all, this is a screwed-up day, you know, and any time things are screwed up—more than usual—I mean, the Army is, you know, I mean, the Army . . . everything is screwed up anyway. If you haven't been in, it's hard to explain that but, you know, it's probably, like, if you have a family of Mom and Dad and six or eight or nine kids and you're trying to get everybody ready to go to some event on time and it takes twelve times longer than it does with Mom and Dad, you know, so probably something like that, a bunch of people, you know, organized and getting from here to there, so everything was always screwed up, you know, that's just the way it is. I wasn't . . . I don't think . . . I wasn't that big of a . . . not obsessive, in a certain way, I'm not a control freak but seeing that that's how things functioned, I mean, that made me very uncomfortable knowing that bad things happen when things are disorganized. Does that sort of regroup us from . . .

[He had his own premonition of getting wounded]

IB: Yes, it does. Thank you. I guess I wanted to talk to you a little bit about Iraq and this idea that you brought up about the expendability of life. I wonder if that's also a segue into the Holocaust.

[His mother was a child survivor of the Holocaust and he had told me he was very interested in discussing the impact of her experience on his, also]

P: Well, the Iraq . . . it certainly is . . . it certainly was . . . actually the moment of that Tuesday morning, that September 11, when the Towers were in flames and then when they collapsed, I instantly fast-forwarded—or fast-reversed—I don't which—and I said, American . . . young people are going to get killed again because of this and, you know, I didn't know where or how but, I mean, as I was sitting there watching the TV . . .

[He instantly knew there would be another war when he saw the World Trade Center in flames on 9/11]

IB: You knew.

P: I knew instantly what was going to happen and I have such little faith in the people who lead this country that I knew they were going to screw it up royally. I have less than no faith in the Pentagon, in the military, 'cause those guys, you know . . . as lots of people have said, they're still . . . whatever war they're fighting today, in their mind they're still fighting the previous war so they're not even present . . . in the present tense; they're in the past tense, so once . . . so I knew some bad things were going to happen to American kids, you know? I predicted pretty much that they were . . . once they said, you know, it was Osama Bin Laden, I actually predicted to myself that they would somehow make sure that he wasn't caught because what I knew the Pentagon needed and what I figured Bush needed was a good diversion big-time . . . well, Bush and those guys, the politicians, needed a diversion. The Army, the military guys, need a place to play with their toys, their military toys, so when they sent them to Afghanistan, the first thing I said was, let me see how they're doing it. If they're driving around in cars and, you know, sort of pushing their weight around, then I knew they were going to get people killed for nothing. When I saw them on burros and a lot of the guys were walking around in Afghani caftans, for ten minutes I said, they're do-ing it right. They're gonna catch him. And if you can think that there's a chronology—at least that I have in my mind—that all of a sudden they stopped doing that and so I knew that the fix was in and they didn't want to catch him and then, soon after that, they started contriving to go in and assassinate Saddam Hussein in Iraq, so once they started doing that, from a military point of view I saw them doing the same thing they did to us in Vietnam and I knew that the leadership was incompetent and that they weren't going to find whatever they needed to find and people were gonna, you know, die uselessly, needlessly, you know, and be bait for who knows what, so I actually had—once Iraq started—I actually had a mild kind of flare-up of my PTSD, I mean, I got . . . I was coming out of it but I really had to kind of dig and, you know, sort of what I had to do so that I didn't sort of fall back into my PTSD funk. What I had to do was stop watching the news, stop reading the newspaper, and you know, I sort of have always loved . . . my grandfather, who I sort of worshiped a little bit, I mean, I always pictured him sitting in front of the TV watching news so somehow if Grandpa sat in front of the news I sat in front of the news watching TV news and I had to stop . . . basically I had to stop watching the news so I stopped watching the evening news. I stopped completely. I stopped reading certain sections of the newspaper because I was so angry and so hurt and so . . .

IB: You were overstimulated.

P: Yeah, and, so, it took me back and I was . . . and even . . . the one place that, you know, that my reunions with my guys, which were sort of safe, turned out to not be safe because these guys thought it was a great thing to go into Iraq and get the terrorists who did this and I didn't even try to push the argument and say, guys, this isn't the boys who did this to us, you know? this isn't the right place, you know? Thy got . . . they're simple people, a lot of them, and they got snowed by the way the rest of the American public got snowed.

[*He had a flare-up of his PTSD after the invasion of Iraq*]

IB: They didn't know about displacement.

P: Yeah. So, the Iraq thing did and does . . . you know, I'm not sure I have language that I can use in public to tell anybody how bad I feel about it.

IB: How about in private?

P: No. I just, you know . . . it just . . . it infuriates me and, you know, Sunday's *New York Times*, you know, the front page picture of the Sunday *New York Times* is a picture of fifteen or twenty amputees in a gym playing some sports game, okay? at the . . . actually at the U.S. Olympic Center preparing or starting practicing for the Para-Olympics as if it was a wonderful thing and I'm looking at those guys and I had to invoke whatever defense I had . . . you know, I had to not look, you know? The horrible thing is it provokes me to think about things that are immoral. I mean, you know, I think like somebody needs to be, you know . . . but other than . . . the same thing that we did to Saddam Hussein, we need to do to some of our so-called leaders, okay? 'Cause they're basically doing the same thing but somehow making it a moral cause and justifying it and it's not justifiable from my point of view, but I feel like I have a different perspective because I was there and I've been in that situation and . . .

[*He is morally outraged at the exploitation of young men sent to fight such wars*]

IB: You've become a military authority.

P: I think I am, yeah. A weird talent to have, but, you know, it's not that difficult, I mean, people that were in the Army can also look at it and have the exact same authority that I do. It isn't very difficult.

IB: But I think someone who's been traipsing around in rice paddies and getting shot at by snipers and not just reading about it but being there and seeing bravery, cowardice, incompetence, the futility, the confusion, the inefficiency—it's just the whole enterprise.

P: Yeah, yeah.

IB: And I think that puts you—and everyone else there—in a very different category.

P: The painful part is that even among the people, among my compatriots who were there, there's only one or two who actually . . . who I can even speak openly about it because most of them are sort of gung-ho and that was, you know, I had to put on the brakes in a couple conversations when I realized where they were and where I was and I wasn't in a . . . one thing I'm not going to do is get in an argument with my boys . . .

IB: And apologize.

P: . . . about those kind of things, right? Being able to feel what those . . . so, in Iraq, when those guys are anywhere . . . so there was a picture that I saw—it might have been in the newspaper, you know, I don't read it but I page through it—there was a picture of, I guess, some guys that are searching for these two and three people that were supposedly taken prisoner by the Iraqis so it showed a line of them sort of walking toward the cameraman . . . it looked to me as if they were walking down the road. One of the soldiers walked by, I think, a father and a little boy. In Vietnam, sometimes little kids were booby-trapped to do something to you as well as, you know, adults so I thought, this soldier is, you know, he's oblivious to that or maybe, thank God, maybe the Iraqis don't do that but the Vietnamese did that, but I thought about, okay, so that soldier in a way is not acting appropriately and then, as I looked at this line of soldiers, it said, you know, the caption was "Searching for the Missing Americans" but basically they're walking down the road looking in front of them. It didn't look like they were looking for anything. It looked like they were going through the motions, okay? And it's going through the motions, when I see that—anything that makes me think of that—drives me bananas, okay? And the place where it affects me, you know, translates to day-to-day life. If I see people doing things, going through the motions, and it was one of the things that sort of got me out of pediatrics and I see a victim, I see a system, I see, like, a bureaucracy where I can imagine a chain of events and people being victims at the end of that chain, I lose it and then I can't be there anymore. You know, I'm a lot better now than I was two years ago but . . . so when I see those kind of things happening, you know, so I look at that picture and that picture means more than just . . . first of all, it's complete bullshit. These guys, if they're searching for their missing comrades, they're not doing any kind of searching that you and I would want them to be doing, okay? They're going through the motions. As I said, that . . . that's not acceptable. That's not how . . . maybe I'm being, you know, childish and grandiose and fantasizing that they have to use some kind of magic to find these missing guys—I don't know, but whatever they were doing in that photograph wasn't it and, you know, it takes me back to watching the news after I got back from Vietnam and they're showing, here's the Americans, we are doing battle with the Vietcong, I'd watch the news, that's not what was going on. That's not what's going on at all in that news clip, you know? so it's all fabricated, okay, so . . .

[*He is cynical about people's motives and cannot tolerate the indifference of bureaucracies which victimize the common man*]

IB: Out of ignorance or out of willful intent to mislead the viewer?

P: Maybe a third possibility which is that you can't always . . . I mean, if you send a news crew out, there's not always going to be a battle but they have to show them doing something so if they're shooting across the rice paddy and you could hit the water buffalo or something, you know, or, you know, somebody thinks they heard something so they're shooting but there's really no back and forth, it's really one-sided and yet the news people have to call it...they call it a battle, so I see those kind of things and I guess it makes connections for me, you know? About what people do to other people. It was interesting, I sort of did chuckle to myself after a talk last week where I said to you how, you know, after I got back from Vietnam I was really upset about the people and I thought that I had, you know, I had come to a pretty . . . I mean, I had a physical injury but I thought I was pretty okay . . .

IB: Psychologically.

P: Psychologically, and remember I said I was really upset about the people who were damaged psychologically, you know, so I chuckled once or twice since last week about that discovery that here I am among the same group that I had been so concerned about, you know, but I've never . . . you know, I mean, I hadn't thought about it.

IB: Yeah, that's what you said.

[*He is still digesting his new insight about the extent of his own psychological wounds*]

P: Yeah. I don't know why but I still . . . I guess I still think that even though I've had my, you know, many decades of sort of subclinical PTSD and whatever, I guess I still, you know, if I said, am I functional or not? I guess I'd still say I'm functional as compared to some of the guys who really aren't. I went to medical school, I did residency, I ran a pretty damn good practice in _____ you know, so, you know, so I . . .

IB: Married, family.

P: Yeah, I mean, you know, I have friends, you know, I mean I . . . you know, I do good things in the community so it just . . . and then a lot of the guys, the other guys, do too. It's not that they're completely dysfunctional but . . . I just always saw it as . . .

IB: Someone else's issue.

P: Well, I saw a lot of people being really hurt and maybe losing whatever possibilities they might have had for . . .

[He counts his blessings and sees how much worse off others are]

IB: So let me ask you this: what effect, if any, do you think your mother's experience has had on your ability to cope with this or any of the residue? Do you see any connection? And if so, what? Again, my ears perked up when you talked about expendable human life.

P: Yeah, yeah, and I thought about some Holocaust connection there. My mom and her brother were part of the kindertransport which I mentioned to you—not on the tape, I think—but . . . so they were sent to England. According to my Mom . . . my Mom's main memory is that . . . you know, I actually—I think I sent you an e-mail—I found them on a list and they were with a family that had a very German name actually and my Mom said . . . I said . . . I called her up and I said, oh, you were with somebody—I forget the name—and she said, he's a Nazi. His brother was a Nazi and his brother actually bought my Mom's, my mother's maternal uncle's business in their city. There was a German guy who somehow had an English connection but he was a Nazi, according to my Mom—which I hadn't heard until three weeks ago after you gave a talk about the kindertransport—long-winded, I'm sorry.

[His mother is a child survivor of the Holocaust, saved by the kindertransport to England]

IB: No, not at all. This is . . .

P: There's something . . . so the concrete story was that they were sent to England but then my grandmother and grandfather and a couple of my . . . my grandmother's brother and his wife got out using a fake passport, pretending like they were going on vacation but using a fake passport that my grandfather had been able to get—passports (plural)—and so then they were in France so then my Mom and my uncle left England and went down to France to join their parents and aunt and uncle and then my aunt and uncle—my Mother's aunt and uncle—had left—they had two young boys, younger kids than my Mom and uncle.

IB: Is this the one that just passed away?

P: The one that just died a week-and-a-half ago, so my grandmother's brother and his wife had left their two young children back in the village and the story goes—and I only heard this partway carried by the wind—that my grandmother walked back and forth across the border day after day after day to negotiate to get the boys out and she eventually did, and I knew those guys—they lived in _____ but occasionally they would travel . . . they were well-to-do so they'd show up in the United States occasionally, so I had . . . one of them now still lives in Europe so I visited him a couple times, so those two guys owed my grandmother their life really, which was never acknowledged very much and they never, you know, there was, like, this big wall of denial . . .

IB: Denial of what? The dangers or? . . .

P: Well, probably just about anything, everything you could imagine—the fact that their parents left them behind, that my grandmother instead of their own parents had to trek across . . . walked across the border. You know, my image is that Grandma just had guts and courage and, you know, was a different kind of human being than her brother and did what she had to do. She was heroic, you know, in a lot of ways, so that's some of the, you know, sort of the concrete realities that I know of. You know, like a lot of families . . .

[*His idealized grandmother was courageous, heroic, and tireless in trying to save her family but a climate of massive denial pervades his family*]

IB: How did she let you go to Vietnam?

P: My grandmother?

IB: Yeah.

P: I don't think there was any way out of it. I think she was badly hurt 'cause I was the oldest grandson and she was pretty good at making sure—there were five grandkids—she was pretty good at not letting anybody feel like they were the favorite so we all felt like we were her favorite but, you know, so I was one of her five favorites but I'm not sure there was anything anybody could do and the day, I mean, the day in October when they took me to the airport, October 1967, so my Mom, my grandmother, my sister, my brother and my Dad, you know, at the airport and my sister started to cry and my Mom said, women in our family don't cry . . .

[*When he left for the Army, his sister started to cry and was forbidden to do so by his mother*]

P: So there we are, standing in the airport, I'm starting to walk toward the plane, my sister who at that time would have been fifteen, she started to cry, and my Mom elbows her and says, women in our family don't cry, invoking my grandmother's . . .

IB: Do you know what she was alluding to at the time?

P: No, no. I mean, it's interesting that I didn't know . . . I didn't think about what that really meant on an emotional level until within the past few weeks when I looked up the kindertransport and all of that . . .

[*His leaving for Vietnam revived repressed memories of his mother's leaving on the kindertransport where his mother was stoic and did not cry*]

IB: Since the program.

P: Yeah, since your talk.

[*He attended a talk I had recently given about a man who helped children in Nazi Europe*]

IB: Yeah, yeah.

P: So . . .

IB: But you grew up knowing something about the stories.

P: Not very much.

IB: What did you know? What was the "headline" family story growing up? You knew your Mom wasn't born in the States . . .

P: The nuts and bolts was that they had escaped after Hitler invaded. Kindertransport didn't come up until years later. They didn't know about that, did they?

IB: It wasn't a term that was used.

P: Yeah, yeah, it wasn't known or it wasn't . . . so we didn't 'til I . . . there was sort of a vague knowledge that my Mom and uncle had been sent to England. Then I knew they were in a displaced persons camp where ___ _____ was, as it turns out, but not at the same time. Then they were sent to a displaced persons camp in _____. Then they bought passage on a ship that was supposedly coming to the United States, probably full of Jews from Europe . . . they had money, I mean, I don't know how . . . they had money. They weren't . . . so they had some money but not . . . so . . .

IB: What was the family money from? Family business or whatever. Do you know?

P: My grandfather's company, yeah, my grandfather's family owned a factory where they made _____ and they were probably a factory where they made _____ and they were probably one of the first to do that and they were all over Europe . . .

IB: Big company.

P: There's a guy now who's a _____ maker—my Mom buys _____ there now and again—who's from their town or from near their town— and says they were the Rockefellers of that country. That's what this guy said to my Mom, so my Mom goes around patting herself on the back for what she lost and what she has now. . . . So they got on this boat—again, this may not even be correct—they were in this displaced persons camp, they got on a boat and I think it was supposed to go to the United States but maybe it was going somewhere on the west side of the Atlantic, not the east side of the Atlantic, and this boat was one of several boats that actually drove around the Atlantic for one year and nobody would allow the people in.

IB: Like *The St. Louis?*

P: She doesn't know and I have no way to find out now that my uncle's dead. My Mom knows . . . my Mom's an airhead so she says, I don't remember nothing. She has always just . . . she's got a decent IQ but she doesn't know anything.

[*His mother is an "airhead" who copes by remembering nothing, probably employing dissociative defenses*]

IB: That was part of her . . .

P: That's how she has always been, okay? That's her reaction to her stuff—so she would have been about twelve or thirteen, I think she was probably twelve when the boat left that side of the Atlantic.

IB: So, let me understand. First they went to England and were safe and then they came back . . .

P: They came to France because my grandparents got out of _____ . . .

IB: So the war was still going on when they came back to France.

P: Well, but I don't know if it had started in France yet.

IB: But it was before 1945.

P: Yeah, this is 1939.

IB: Right, right. So, in other words, they could have stayed in England relatively danger-free . . .

P: Yeah.

IB: . . . but came back into Europe—war-torn, mainland Europe—well, the kindertransport was in '38 right until the invasion of Poland, okay? So it might have been 1939 or 1940 that they went back into Europe.

P: Right. I think I can remember seeing my Mom's report card from the school where she went to in France. I think it was 1939, so she has this report card from a local school.

IB: So they didn't stay in England.

P: My Mom and my uncle were brought back to . . . they were reunited with their parents.

IB: Because their parents thought that they . . .

P: I don't know . . .

IB: . . . had gotten free?

P: It's not clear . . . who knows? I'm never going to find out, you know? Actually, after your program, I called my uncle—it was around the time of his birthday—'cause he and I haven't talked for several years—we had some problems—we were pretty close for a long time so I called him to wish him happy birthday and to tell him about your program and, you know, your talk and everything—and he gave me some detail—I told you in the e-mail that he almost bumped into Mr. Winton, Sir Nicholas, so he was in touch with some of the kindertransport people but my Mom wasn't so then my uncle got sick and few days later and. . . . In 1990, he had a tumor the size of a football so he had a huge operation, and then a year or two later had more tumors removed but because he was a mean SOB he stayed alive way longer than almost anybody else with that kind of cancer . . .

[*His mother and uncle returned too soon to Europe to reunite with their parents, who mistakenly thought everyone would be safe. His uncle also survived and then lived longer "than almost anybody else" with his malignancy*]

IB: What a survivor . . .

P: Yeah, yeah. We decided that it was because he was a mean SOB. That was his way of coping with having lost what he lost. So they're on this boat. My uncle, the guy who died, they say that he got polio and both of his arms were paralyzed for a while and the doctors did something and one of his arms was fixed and one wasn't so he actually had a . . . I bet he had Guillaine-Barre or transverse myelitis . . . I mean, I don't . . . he never had any postpolio syndrome 'cause most . . . I don't think anybody that I have ever heard that had polio didn't have some postpolio . . .

[*His uncle developed paralysis of his arms*]

IB: Some atrophy in light of that?

P: Well, his arm was completely atrophied but there's a postpolio syndrome where people get symptoms of some neurological stuff years later which he never got but whatever the diagnosis . . . so he had one arm basically. That was his . . . it was his left arm. I got shot in my left arm too so figure that one out, boss! I mean, you know, interesting, isn't it?

[*He realizes that both he and his uncle have damaged left arms and marvels at the coincidence*]

IB: Yes, and I am just listening . . .

P: Yeah, I know. I'm listening too . . .

P: So then . . . so the boat . . . so somehow my uncle bought his . .
. when the boat stopped in _____ he bought his way into _____ so he and
his wife and those two boys got off in _____ and that's where they stayed.
I think other members of the—I don't know—there were other members
of my grandfather's family on the boat and somehow they ended up in
_____ too. My grandfather's sister had earlier come—like in the
early 1930s, I think before Hitler or right when Hitler was starting—had
come to _____ so somehow eventually they got into the States
. . .

IB: Sponsored?

P: . . . somehow they got in. So, growing up, so Mom felt . . . Grandma
was stoic, Grandma was dignified, Grandma, as one of my high school
girlfriends said or college girlfriends said, when your Grandmother walks
in the room, we all feel like we should all stand up. She just was dignified—she had gone to finishing school in _____ and, you know,
I mean, she was a real, solid citizen, a lady, polite . . .

IB: Very cosmopolitan.

P: Very European. Very . . . she looked like all those little ladies with
their hair perfectly done and always dressed perfectly and, you know,
just . . . she always, you know, seemed perfect until, I mean, at some point
I realized . . . she could do wrong but she didn't do much wrong. I mean,
that was . . . I idealized . . . all of us idealized her, okay? so she was . . . so
then . . . and my Mom . . .

IB: Your Mom was born in . . .

P: 1927.

IB: 1927. So she got here in 1940?

P: Yeah, plus or minus, plus or minus. So right around the time she
would've gotten her "princess crown" had she been a young lady staying in
Europe—that's when they got chased out—and so my mother was, I think,
forever pining away for whatever life she might have had, you know, back
in the good, old country—or the old, good country, I don't know—she had
me before she was twenty and she turned twenty a couple months after I
was born so my Dad is seven or eight years older than she . . .

IB: He's American born?

P: Yeah, he was born in this country, so my Mom—I'm trying to think how to describe her—I mean, it's all about her. My Dad was sick recently. I'd call up—how's Dad? I'm doing lousy, she would say, 'cause Dad doesn't talk on the phone very much. She's never really let us have a relationship with Dad because she's worried, I think, we're going to say something about her. She's hypervigilant, I mean, she's got all of the symptoms of chronic PTSD. I mean, she's hypervigilant, she's sort of . . . she doesn't explode, you know, like in the way . . . you know the way that alcoholics explode? so she's not explosive like that but, I mean, you can be having what you think is a regular conversation . . . you'll say something that she'll take personally and she'll go from 0 to 60, you know? kinda like I noticed that I did a lot of when I, you know, I recognize some of my own PTSD symptoms. She . . . I don't know what age this started but my Mom doesn't get up until, like, ten in the morning, okay? so I would be the one that made breakfast for all of us kids and got everybody kind of . . . I don't know if I made sandwiches for lunch but, I mean, you know, you know, she was never there to . . .

IB: You were the responsible kid, the oldest.

P: Yeah, I took care of people.

IB: All of your life.

P: Yeah. For which I, I mean, you know, I'd rather be that way than, you know . . . my youngest brother is—in my opinion, he's pretty . . . you know, so he's the youngest, I guess that's the youngest brother's . . . but so her deal, my Mom's deal, was, I could have been—what was that character in the movie? "I could have been a contenda," you know?

[*He describes his mother's lability, fixated child-like behavior, inability to reconcile her own losses and her doting on the youngest child, not letting him grow up either*]

IB: *On the Waterfront.*

P: Yeah, Marlon Brando. So my Mom probably, you know, I think, had this thing, I mean, even though they got out and, you know, it was almost like she never has grown up and she's 79 and it's too late to change now. She's still in . . . if you interact with her long enough and you have some psychological understanding, you know, you kind of go, this is not an adult. This woman is not an adult and, so, you know, in

some ways, I think . . . you know, so when I was in 'Nam and even when
I was doing all the other things I've done in my life, you know, I mean,
I have taken care of, you know, I've taken care of other people and I've
done it right and I always said, she does it wrong. You know, I always
had that conscious awareness, you know, and after some therapy I've
also had different . . . but I mean, you know, it's like she really doesn't
. . . you know, if there are two ways to make a decision, she'll do the
wrong one and so in the weirdest way, I've been lucky because that's how
I would have wanted . . . I mean, if I had to choose paths in life, that's
what I would have wanted to choose, so I have a feeling . . . so when
you say, how does any of this connect? You know, I mean, it probably
connects in the weirdest way that being functional was like a reaction
against her being not functional so my being functional in a bigger sense
was how I managed even though, you know, I had to go through all of
that stuff in 'Nam and, you know, I guess I just always had a sense of
. . . you know, and in Jonathan Shay's book he talks about the mission,
we're always on a mission, okay? So, I mean, so you're going out and
you're going to find, you know, engage the . . . do whatever your job is
for the day, engage the enemy or whatever, and be successful at it and
have a mission that succeeds, okay? And do you want to hear something
really interesting? I've had this . . . I think, the first one or two reunions
when I went to and we started with the Vietnam, with my infantry guys,
I sort of was sitting around thinking, I wish we could go out on a mission and do something and succeed at it. I mean, I had . . . I just said,
I wish there was something we could all do together, you know, like go
tromping in the woods, go to a fishing hole . . .

[*His mother was traumatically frozen in her childhood, and growing up, he took
care of her as well as his siblings. His caretaking role in Vietnam appears to have
been a repetition of his role in the family*]

IB: That would work out.

P: Do something in the woods, not sitting around in this hotel where
we could, you know, make up for all the shit, you know? And the unsuccess
of getting our asses kicked, you know, again, even though we didn't but we
were in that place where you get your ass kicked.
IB: And you see your Mom as a child who's still back in her trauma
somewhere.

P: Totally, yeah. Sadly and totally.

IB: You feel she has no idea.

P: I don't think she wants to have an idea, you know? I mean, anytime there's . . . anytime over the years where we would have a somewhat psychological discussion, she would say, I don't want to . . . I don't understand myself and I don't want to. I mean, she would say that, you know, and I remember that from the time I was pretty young.

IB: It's such an interesting contrast in the way you describe not knowing, not wanting to know—what did you call it? Airhead or bubblehead?

P: Airhead.

IB: Airhead, okay. Airhead. On the other hand, hypervigilance, tuned into something—danger, disruption, some sensory input.

P: But that's PTSD, that's PTSD, yeah. Those are . . .

IB: And an airhead is PTSD.

[*Mother fluctuated between hypervigilance and not knowing. Grandmother was extremely competent and he identified with both*]

P: It is, yeah. Yeah, I mean, you know, the shadow that my Grandmother cast was . . . you know, Grandma was infinitely competent so there ain't no way my mother would've been minimally competent but Grandma didn't put it in . . . she didn't throw it in your face, I mean, she was like . . . she was like somebody that if you'd watched her in action, you would have said, she looks to me like she's been analyzed by somebody really good over there but I don't know that she ever was. Again, she didn't talk about it but if she had been, it would have been one of those three-month analyses because she was of that age, right? It wouldn't have been on a five- or six-year interminable psychoanalysis . . . but she acted as if . . . you know, because when we would talk and we'd talk about bad things, she'd say the kind of things that I've heard . . . you know, ah, you just have to put it past you or you have to, you know, not exactly, you have to not get so upset about things, you know, these almost like homilies, you know, like, you know . . . they're not trite either . . .

IB: So she had a lot of wisdom.

P: . . . very wise, very, you know, potentially coping, good coping skills and then my uncle, on the other hand, he got by . . .

IB: Your mother's brother . . .

P: My mother's brother that just died, he got by . . . he's close . . . you know, it's as if he had been in one of the camps, so he was kind of a dead guy, you know, how a lot of the guys that came out of the camps were dead? But he was never in the camp.

IB: He had a parallel experience to your mother.

P: Same boat, same camp, same trip, same everything, he got paralyzed, you know, I guess at one point on the ship when I think he had both arms paralyzed he—I heard this in the past, five or ten years—he contemplated throwing himself overboard 'cause, you know, he, you know, he was a teenaged guy—he would have been fourteen or fifteen—and he had no arms, right? I mean, he's helpless, so fast forward, I mean, you know, so he has one arm, you know, he becomes . . . he's got a . . . he spoke, like, eight or nine or ten or eleven languages, you know, fluently, and, you know, who knows what language he thought in, you know, he was a brilliant businessman, he could go to the racetrack and win $20,000 a day, which was one of the ways he made money, maybe more, you know? he always had a wad of cash in his pocket that's probably more money than you and I make in a month, you know, just knowing how to, that horse, you know, and, you know, and if you were on his team, he was engaging, he was intelligent, he was cosmopolitan, he knew everything but if you were, like, some of us in his family who he decided weren't up to his standards, you were dirt or less, you know, trailer trash, so he ran hot and cold, but, you know, but everybody tried to get something out of him but he wasn't going to give anything, you know, he was a dead guy, I mean, he used sex just for . . . you know, he told me about his sexual exploits, you know. I mean, in my family, we don't talk about sex. It's not that we're prudes; we just . . . you know, it doesn't seem appropriate.

[*His uncle was brilliant but dead inside, like a concentration camp survivor. His arm was useless, but he was a narcissist and got invested in his intelligence and devalued others he deemed inferior to himself*]

IB: A private matter.

P: Yeah, so, I mean, he didn't tell me the details but, you know, he made . . . it was just, you know, he would talk about that but it was, like, he was really a dead guy and it was . . . it was always interesting to me to think about how he had not been in a concentration camp but yet it seemed like he was—you know what I'm talking about, right?

IB: Yeah. Sure . . .

P: I don't think I'm making up this language.

IB: You're not . . .

P: Yeah.

IB: So where's your father in all this?

P: You know, I . . . my Dad's kind of losing it cognitively over the past two years so I've been trying to have little conversations with him about what he did during World War II 'cause it struck me that we never talked about what I did in Vietnam so I had an entrée—the Clint Eastwood movie, the Iwo Jima movie . . .

IB: *Letters From Iwo Jima.*

P: . . . and the book about, you know, the American book, *Flags of Our Fathers*, which I read, and I found out that Iwo Jima was . . . let's see, I think they moved up the chain so I think Saipan was right before Iwo Jima—maybe after; I forget—but my Dad was on Saipan during World War II so I finally found an entrée that, you know, 'cause my Dad was always pretty angry—his father had always ducked out—my Dad's father had come over from . . . supposedly from _____ but he probably escaped the pogroms around the late 1800s and he was considerably older, so Grandpa was—from my Dad's point of view—he was, like, kind of an autocrat, I think, you know, or dictator, so my Dad . . . the family lore was about Dad and Grandpa battling, you now, endlessly, but by the time we came around, my Dad was an angry guy but he was starting to turn it inward. He was angry at Grandpa and then probably angry at my Mom but never in sixty-plus years has never . . . my Dad's an intellectual. He reads the *Times* and he, you know, up until he started losing it cognitively, I mean, he . . . he's a very . . . he knows what's going on in the world and then there's the airhead that he lives with, right? Who doesn't know nuttin' and she reads . . . I think she doesn't know anything, doesn't want to know anything . . .

[*His father was a World War II combat veteran, fighting the Japanese on Saipan. He was angry, reticent, and very intellectual*]

IB: He's eight years older?

P: My Dad's seven and a half, eight years older.

IB: So he was twenty-eight when you were born—roughly?

P: Yeah. So we've all scratched our heads and said, how in the hell can he put up with her? and occasionally she'll say, I don't know how he puts up with me—and she hasn't said that lately, my mother—but my Dad . . . at some point, you know, you could . . . you know, when we were young, he was angry. You know, it was the early . . . it was the 1950s, you know, and I figured in retrospect, you know, the post–World War, my grandfather was trying to control him, you know, my Mom probably couldn't live within the budget of whatever money my Dad made because she was a princess, of course, and, you know, had to have whatever she . . . she didn't buy jewelry and—we didn't have that much money—but I don't think she was a very good budgeter. So my Dad . . . so despite all those strikes that could have been against her, my Dad has put up with her for sixty-some years and we're all, you know, we're all just, you know. . . . He never told his wife to go f____ herself, you know? Because that's what she needed. She needed a slap upside the head, you know? and my Dad . . . well, my Dad has all this bottled-up anger that he's really had to bottle, I mean, really, really, really bottle up, almost like, you know, you'd have this nuclear stuff and they'd case it in this molten glass stuff so that it . . .

IB: Yeah.

P: Okay? and that's his anger. That's my analogy for his anger but he's never had it . . . he's never . . . and he won't, I mean, you know, she's never . . . he's never really lashed out at her the way all of us wish that he would have, you know, like a normal. . . .

[*His father has enormous bottled-up anger and never confronted his wife's child-like entitlement, much to P's disappointment*]

IB: So he's not taking it out on his kids.

P: He did when we were young. He did some. My brother bore the brunt, you know. I was a goody two-shoes.

IB: If you had it to do over again, would you have handled the Vietnam enlistment any differently? You said leaving the country was never an option.

P: You know, I mean, I didn't want to be a felon and not go to medical school 'cause I was always . . . in my mind, I was always a doctor. I guess I trusted that I would be okay. I think I just . . . and I don't think it was teen-ager bravado like the teenagers that are driving 100 miles . . .

[*His teenage omnipotence and unconscious identificatory factors transmitted from his mother's survival appeared to have fueled his bravado*]

IB: Your mother and her brother left relative safety and went right back into the war. They made it okay.

P: I didn't know that at the time.

IB: Not consciously, anyway. I am just speculating . . .

P: You know, you know, I . . . you know how there are people that when you talk about doing a residency and how you regale stories of being up all night and all the hours . . .

IB: Sure.

P: . . . and there's some people that'd say that was terribly bad . . .

IB: Right.

P: I was never one of the people that said you shouldn't do that and, even though I have all the negative feelings about the military, I also wouldn't say, you shouldn't go . . . I mean, there's something that I gained by being in the military, you know? Would I do it again? I might—as stupid as that might be—but I think the gains are more than the deficits. There's risk. I mean, the risk is, you know, obviously enormous. The risk part is bad but the gain part is, you know, there's something . . . I know more about the world, you know? I have more control, okay? And, for me, I mean, that's an important issue. Does that make any sense?

[*In a displaced fashion, he confirms this hypothesis and is convinced he needed this life experience in Vietnam to gain a sense of mastery over the senseless dangers in the world*]

IB: Sure. It makes as much sense as anything else.
P: I'm more informed.

IB: Yeah, absolutely. You saw what happened on September 11 and you knew in a split second what was going to happen.

P: I was on the phone with my cousins and telling them.

IB: I believe that not everyone could have known that, you know?

CONCLUSION

In his profound reexamination of Achilles in Homer's *Iliad* written twenty-seven centuries ago, Shay highlights the great bard's observations of two major themes that pervade the history of military engagement: "the betrayal of 'what's right'" by a commander and the onset of the berserk state" (Shay, 1994, p. XIII). In his interview, Paul poignantly describes his disillusionment with the leadership and the absurdity of the military strategy as he experienced it whereas General Taguba could not simply go along with the degradation and abuse of prisoners at the cost of his own illustrious career. Paul also emphasizes the pivotal experience of soldiers learning to kill and what he imagined would have happened to him if he had crossed that fateful divide. Grossman's study of the conditioning process and learning to kill and the devastating psychological aftermath (Grossman, 1995) suggests that Paul's struggling to preserve his humanity and compassion is at the core of his identity. In both cases, these men had a parent who survived the degradation and helplessness of war albeit in vastly different ways. Taguba's father was a prisoner of war and survivor of the Bataan Death March in the Philippines at the hands of the Japanese whereas Paul's mother was a child survivor of the Holocaust whose separation from her parents and total disruption of her life was due to Nazi persecution of the Jews. While we do not have psychoanalytic data from either of these men, we may infer that their identities as military men were profoundly influenced by their parents' victimization in World War II. Their own identities with the victim and their tireless championing of the rights of those caught up in the cycles of madness associated with war figured prominently in how they saw themselves and how their masculine selves were constructed.

7

Forged in the Holocaust

Never give in. Never give in. Never, never, never, never—in nothing, great
or small, large or petty—never give in.

—Winston Churchill, 1941

Resilient: (1) Returning to an original position, springing back, recoiling,
etc.; also looking back. (2) Elastic; resuming an original shape or position
after compression, stretching, etc. (3) Of a person: Readily recovering from
illness, shock, etc.; resistant to setbacks or adversity. From the Latin "re-
silire": to leap back or recoil.

Psychological resilience following overwhelming life experience has become the subject of great interest in recent years. In addition to its obvious
importance in the military and the significance of revictimization in childhood survivors of sexual abuse, the events of September 11 have brought
the issue home to all of us. Social catastrophes on our soil have shocked
us into realizing that no one is immune from terrorism and its traumatic
effects. At a subsequent ISTSS (International Society for Traumatic Stress
Studies) Convention, plenary sessions and symposia included such titles
as "Stories of Healing and Resilience: The Power of Culture and Community," "Turning Trauma and Recovery into Art: Creative Languages of Injury
and Resiliency," and "Fostering Intergenerational Resilience from War and
Genocide." The latter symposium dealt with American Indians, parents
with PTSD, and the aftermath of war. Some of the research in progress presented preliminary data supporting the fact that some people with a prior
history of trauma do not have an increased likelihood of developing PTSD
in response to a major event. Since then, the interest has grown exponen-

tially in the study of the precursors and conditions which lend themselves to acquiring resilience. For example, in those sexual abuse survivors who do not experience revictimization, resilience is associated with the perception of being in control and feeling competent. Given the power of compulsion to repeat (Freud, 1914a, 1920), the in-depth psychoanalytic studies of this phenomenon would greatly enhance our understanding. From a statistical standpoint, studies of disaster relief workers at Ground Zero suggest that only a significant minority develop PTSD. In comparing their adaptive styles with those who did not develop PTSD, it is hoped that large-scale studies will also shed further light on resilience. According to self-reporting questionnaires, certain patterns were observed such as having self-directed anger but not self-blame, seeking support from others, being accepting and having the capacity to see the positive side of things. Such findings have then been operationalized in order to teach resilience to at-risk populations, using a psychological style that minimizes or does not address unconscious factors. This new field of "Trauma Preparation" offers a cognitive/behavioral model consisting of five stages: anticipation, pretrauma, trauma, posttrauma, and recovery. While such models and strategies might seem foreign, superficial and perhaps even a bit naïve to the psychoanalyst who has the opportunity to explore the psyche in microscopic detail, the need for large-scale interventions is a reality in today's world. Most relevant to this chapter, however, is the fact that this brave new world of trauma studies owes much to those psychoanalysts who had the courage and fortitude to listen to Holocaust survivors when no one else wanted to or was able to. As Judith Kestenberg often commented in the Holocaust Discussion Group at the American Psychoanalytic Association that when the survivors first came to the shores of the United States, they may have wanted to talk but people could not tolerate to hear about the atrocities and their incalculable losses. Survivors quickly learned to shut up and did so for about forty years. Psychoanalysts with rare exceptions also had great difficulty in listening, as many were survivors or refugees themselves who retreated into a clinical world of orthodox Freudian theory, overemphasizing psychic reality over painful external reality.

MASSIVE PSYCHIC TRAUMA

One of these rare pioneers is Henry Krystal, M.D., whose 1968 book, *Massive Psychic Trauma*, has been a most powerful but quiet presence in my bookcase for many years. I did not realize that this most valuable contribution was also having a profound effect on one of my patients until I moved offices and rearranged my bookcases. Frantic until she relocated it on a different shelf, this woman then revealed how fascinated she was by the title, imagining that it was her biography. Each day as she lay on the couch, she would commune with the book and get an odd sense of reassurance as the title would mirror her state of mind and remind her that her problems were deep and longstanding. She imagined that the answers to the riddle of her childhood were written on the pages of this mysterious book, fantasizing that there were very thin slices of her skin lying in between its pages or perhaps were the pages themselves. Like the grotesque lampshades of Buchenwald crafted from the tattooed skin flayed off the bodies of prisoners who were selected and murdered specifically for this uniquely depraved Nazi art, the patient's own fantasies were saturated with Holocaust imagery. If only she could open the book, she would then know for sure what had happened to her and connect to her body and claim it to be her own. It was fused with her father's war-ravaged body and she experienced the sexualized, traumatic reenactments on a regular basis with him in a dissociated, dreamlike state. Over time, she was able to harness her defiance and unwillingness to completely submit, a trait originally used in the service of resistance in treatment, to confront adversity and create the kind of life she could only imagine in her happier dreams. This refusal to surrender, a key to her resilience, was catalyzed by our hard work in analysis and is a quality of mind that we may see under the most unspeakable conditions of genocidal persecution and contribute to the formation of a certain kind of masculine self.

Genocide is the ultimate narcissistic injury. It is intended to obliterate the individual and his kind of all traces of his past, present, and future. The term for this "crime without a name" was coined in 1943 by the jurist Raphael Lemkin when he learned what was happening to the Jews of Europe (Marrus, 1987). It occurs when a human being is progressively deprived of his rights, his possessions, his home, his loved ones, his dignity, and ultimately his right to live simply because he is a member of an identifiable group. The resulting assault on the ego is utterly overwhelming and when flight to safety is not possible, regression in the service of survival may be necessary in order to avoid the depletion and total despair that may lead to suicide. On an individual level, Ferenczi (1929) in his essay, "The Unwelcome Child and His Death Instinct," described how maternal aggression intensifies the internalized aggression of the unwanted child, who is more prone to get sick and die. When this paradigm gets enacted on a large scale, the helplessness and impotent rage may contribute to the demise, or near demise, of a whole people. Although other groups, such as gypsies, homosexuals, and Jehovah Witnesses, were mercilessly treated as well, the German government's "Final Solution to the Jewish Problem" did not allow any exceptions for the Jews. By the end of World War II and the liberation of the concentration camps, it has been estimated that two-thirds of the Jewish population of Europe and about one-third of the worldwide Jewish population was murdered. Of the 18 million civilian deaths in Europe, one out of every three, or 6 million, were Jewish. Over 1.5 million children were included in this incomprehensible number.

Krystal's follow-up studies with over 1,000 Holocaust survivors for forty years offered him a unique perspective. He played a key role in establishing the legitimacy of psychological damages due to persecution and in our current understanding of the nature of posttraumatic stress disorder. He essentially focuses on three elements: (1) the stages of the traumatic process, (2) those factors in the psyche which prevent psychic trauma, and (3) the sequelae of trauma. I will briefly review them, link them to developmental theory, especially Mahler's and Winnicott's, and offer some of my own ideas based on my work with Judith Kestenberg. I will then present highlights of our current understanding of the neurobiology of resilience. In describing the stages of the traumatic process, Dr. Krystal describes the catatanoid reaction which is beyond fear, one of physical submission and essentially becoming a robot. If it does not progress to a malignant state leading to death, it actually may have some survival value as dissociative defenses would appear to underlie this zombie-like state. He also describes a different kind of death in the concentration camps, preceding the so-called Musselman state, one of total depletion and punctuated by intermittent, ineffectual rages. In my own interviews with death camp survivors, they would often report how necessary it was to avoid fellow prisoners once they reached the point of no return in this deteriorated, dying, old man state as it could be quite infectious to others. Krystal concluded that in this chronic robot state there is a symbolic death and a permanent death imprint characterized by desensitization and identification with death and the dead. Despite all that is now known, it still remains unfathomable to most to appreciate the enormous challenges for survivors of such trauma to have bounced back in any way, let alone resume any semblance of a "normal life."

The second element that he describes is one of prevention. He notes that the efforts of the ego to bolster the stimulus barrier are essential, resulting in a defensive constriction of perception. An example might be the functional blindness seen in the Cambodian refugees which he feels is different from a conversion reaction or repression and is more akin to repudiation or disavowal. In my view, here too we may consider an underlying dissociative process which links these phenomena. Indeed, I have seen a number of patients with dissociative identity disorder (formerly known as multiple personality disorder) who, in their various dissociated selves were blind or deaf or had other functional sensory impairments which serve the same purpose of not seeing, hearing, or knowing. In the traumatic state, the information processing is impaired and the disturbances of perceptive, cognitive, sensory, motor, affective, conscious, and regulatory functions serve as a way of warding off overwhelming input, so they go beyond typical ego defenses.

The scope of attention is severely narrowed as in a hypnotic trance.[1] This constriction due to external overwhelming factors is in contrast to the constriction of perception due to upsurge of instinctual strivings where one's external world narrows as Hartmann has described. He says that "The animal's picture of the external world narrows and broadens as the demands of his instincts become stronger or weaker; its center shifts according to whether he is hungry, in heat, etc., to those elements which are directly related to the gratification of the instinct" (Hartmann, 1939, p. 58). Here, the constriction of perception is for a different purpose. Krystal also makes sure that we are aware of the role of luck and constitutionally good health in those who survive and these factors cannot be overestimated at all.

The third element is the sequelae of massive psychic trauma. Krystal observed a persistence of cognitive disturbances in the forty-year follow-ups, in which many survivor testimonies have a constricted "facts only" quality to them. Here, there are isolated memory fragments, disturbances in registration and recall, and not the continuous chronology that we might expect. There is defensive reprocessing of memories, amalgams of dreams and fears, and the generation of traumatic screen memories to ward off the totally unthinkable. Also, in the catatanoid reaction, he invokes the model of primary repression resulting in a black hole in the information processing system (Kinston and Cohen, 1986). Here, too, I think this inability to integrate such massive assaults on mind and body are in the realm of dissociation and present a major challenge in trying to do analytic work with this population. Krystal also posits that there can be four different kinds of splitting of one's self-representation. One can be on a fixation on the past. Another is believing and not believing what has happened and how. A third involves a splitting of identity which, again, is more in the realm of dissociative disorders. Despite his opinion that it is rare in the Holocaust population, there has been a largely ignored population of hospitalized, aging, Holocaust survivors in Israel, consisting of patients who have been chronically hospitalized for decades, diagnosed as schizophrenic who, after some review of their condition, actually may include a number of severely dissociated child survivors (Laub, 2002).

The fourth element is that there can be splitting within the self between the victim and an identification with the perpetrator. Here too we may expect disavowal and dissociation, massive repression, and splitting. In addition, there is an ability to adequately mourn, given the magnitude of the losses and the nature of the circumstances during the genocide. Simply stated as a task that is impossible to complete in one generation, it then became the task, responsibility, and inevitable burden of the second generation and beyond. It has been an essential part of the legacy of trauma for the children of survivors to consciously and unconsciously continue the mourning a generation later, for their parents' unresolvable losses. Indeed, it is traditional for Jews of Eastern European backgrounds to name their children for deceased relatives, so many children of survivors were named for Nazi murder victims who had been very close to their parents such as their own parents, siblings, and even children from earlier marriages. In connection with these losses, there may be survivor guilt, the unanswerable question of where was God when all this was happening, resulting in enormous conflicts over faith and Jewish identity, as well as alexithymia. It is important to consider that even these symptoms themselves, from an adaptive standpoint, are a creative effort on the part of the human psyche to try to solve the problem of overwhelming trauma. That fine line between adaptive and maladaptive, mastery and repetition, as well as transcendence and denial, is what resilience is all about.

INFANTILE OMNIPOTENCE

Krystal's particular interest in the death camps, the signature of the Third Reich, led him to conclude that "Healthy infantile omnipotence is the most important asset and the emotional mainspring of extraordinary reserves for dealing with life's stresses and potential trauma" (Krystal, 2003, p. 4). He believes that "Almost every survivor has preserved a secret spark of omnipotence which whispers to him that he is very special and so he managed to survive the incredibly overwhelming and humiliating near-death experiences . . . but these secrets of unspeakable horror translated into the language of infantile omnipotence and narcissism may be concealing this message: 'Do you want to know how it is that I survived? The secret is, my mother loved me!'" (Krystal, 1997, p. 159). Citing Kumin's (1997) work on synchronous pre-object relatedness as well as Schore's (1994) ideas about right hemispheric communication between mother and infant as the psychophysiological foundation of the requisite secure, healthy attachment, he emphasizes the developmental aspects of omnipotence in contrast to its use defensively.

Winnicott's contributions corroborate such a formulation. Influenced by Klein who elaborated upon Freud's assumption of infantile omnipotence and narcissism, Winnicott emphasized the developmental aspects of it being the result of good-enough mothering and the infant's own creativity. The mutual influence of the child's activity in discovering the wonders of the mother's breast in concert with her attunement and availability allows for the creation of the breast as a part object in the transitional space between the two. However, since omnipotence is the product of collaboration between the dyad, things can go awry. Most notably, a "false self" personality organization may develop to compensate for the failure of the dyad to reinforce the infant's omnipotence. A pseudo-compliant, social self, capable of reacting and eliciting some type of response from the other, perpetuates the illusion of omnipotence but it is disconnected from the child's "true self." According to Winnicott, the life-long, intrapsychic fantasy of omnipotence manifests itself readily in the analytic situation where "there is no trauma that is outside the individual's omnipotence . . . in infancy, however, good and bad things [do] happen to the infant. . . . [T]he capacity for gathering external factors into the arena of the infant's omnipotence is in the process of formation" (Winnicott, 1960b, p. 590). Accordingly, those who have been totally shattered by massive psychic trauma cannot resurrect an illusion of omnipotence without feeling that everything that has happened was their fault—such negative omnipotence lends itself to "if only . . ." fantasies (Akhtar, 1999) and profound survivor guilt.

Margaret Mahler's views about omnipotence are relevant here as well. She proposes two stages of omnipotence within Freud's phase of primary narcissism, a time which occurs in the immediate period of life after birth. The first stage, "normal autism," is characterized by no awareness of the maternal caretaker as he/she exists in what Ferenczi described as "unconditional hallucinatory omnipotence." Mahler's second stage, symbiosis, is then characterized by a vague awareness of an external, need-satisfying presence which, paraphrasing Ferenczi, she described as a "conditional hallucinatory omnipotence." Many months later, during the fifteenth to eighteenth month of life during the practicing subphase, she observed that the toddler's elated mood, the feelings of omnipotence and conquest associated with locomotion and muscular activity, gave way to a deflation owing to a more realistic appraisal of his or her place in the world, i.e., being puny, helpless, and dependent upon a mother who is a separate being. Gender differences have been noted at this time, such as the girl's tendency to become more depressed than the boy, whose masculine self is beginning to coalesce, and the young child may cling to the illusion of the parent's omnipotence a bit longer (Jacobson, 1964). Developmentally, his increased cognitive capacity associated with the newly acquired ability to stand upright is not only a milestone of the greatest evolutionary significance but it also ushers in a period of enormous narcissistic vulnerability.

This "species-specific human dilemma . . . arises out of the fact that on one hand the toddler is obliged by rapid maturation of his ego to recognize his separateness, while, on the other hand, he is as yet unable to stand alone and will continue to need his parents for many years to come" (Mahler et al., 1975, p. 229). In what sounds like a formula for resilience, Mahler and associates then conclude that "The reestablishment and regeneration of self-esteem and confidence in the world [of the practicing subphase] will generally depend upon the pace and the timing of the replacement of omnipotence by sound secondary narcissism" (Mahler et al., 1975, p. 216). It is then, during the rapprochement subphase, when healthy self-esteem may develop and that the foundation is laid down for the regulation of such mental processes.

NARCISSISM

In my own collaboration with Judith Kestenberg (Kestenberg and Brenner, 1995) with child survivors, we studied resilience in child survivors from a standpoint of "narcissism in the service of survival." We wanted to elaborate upon Freud's notion that narcissistic libido is derived from the soma (1920), noting that a narcissistic investment in every vital part of the body would guarantee survival and well-being. In addition, we considered that primary narcissism has its own developmental line as various organs and zones gain prominence and are more cathected than others. Also, the movement patterns which are present in every living tissue could act as conveyors of libido and aggression. One of the main patterns would be that of a rhythmic alternation between growing and shrinking of the body shape. Growing to take in vital life- and comfort-giving substances, the organism expands as it grows. To expel noxious substances, it shrinks. These patterns of growing and shrinking are linked with the affects of comfort and discomfort, as well as intake and discharge. They are part of the motor apparatus and they underlie primary narcissism and diminish as we get older but never disappear as long as we still are living. We considered primary narcissism as a psychic reflection of growth and maintenance of life whose early manifestations are seen in the smile of contentment, Spitz's first psychic organizer.

A second source of narcissism would be from self-love and self-admiration when the child feels loved, approved, and admired by important objects. As Freud autobiographically stated about his own emerging masculine self, "If a man has been his mother's undisputed darling, he retains throughout his life a triumphant feeling and confidence of success which not seldom brings actual success along with it" (Freud, 1917a, p. 156). Another relevant movement pattern is that parts of the body extend to reach pleasant stimuli and withdraw from unpleasant stimuli. This pattern underlies attraction and repulsion, forming a basis for anaclitic relationships, the substrate of what Freud described as "secondary narcissism." From this theoretical foundation, we distinguished between primary narcissism with its sources in the body and two kinds of secondary narcissism—one that arises from withdrawal from the object due to lack of love, and the other when libido is drawn from the loving object. Furthermore, not only can the body or the whole self be invested with libido but also the mental apparatus or even its component structures, i.e., the id, ego, or superego. We then reasoned that if the ego could be selectively invested with narcissism, then in further differentiation, selected ego functions like memory or motor skills could also be highly cathected, sometimes at the expense of others. So, we theorized that, from an economic viewpoint, a redistribution of narcissistic libido might be necessary in order to maintain physical survival.

A MAN WHO SURVIVED

Joseph Drexel (1980), a political prisoner who was tortured in Mathausen for his anti-Nazi beliefs, wrote that he was forced to sing during his tortures. He used the songs as "an enlivening drug" which revitalized him. Oftentimes he felt a split within himself: his body was tied to the table and beaten and one part of him felt the intolerable pain, the threat to his life as well as his desire to give up and die, while the other floated "without sensation and devoid of gravity but in a strange, spatial congruence with a martyred body" (p. 118). We speculated that his depersonalized overcoming of gravity and space was a revival of the primary narcissistic triumphs of early childhood associated with movement. Drexel was kept in solitary confinement in the dark. He was afraid of the darkness which, to him, equaled a constriction and loss of space. However, he invested it with a narcissistic fantasy that the night simulated the wideness and infiniteness of space. In so doing, he could imagine that his thoughts could flow and when they were carried by his waking dreams, he felt "held by the invisible spirits and suspended on the wings of memories" (p. 11). Here, being carried to safety seemed to be linked to nonverbal memories of a man, threatened by extinction, who conjured up feeling born again into a safe, holding environment. By retaining his dignity and self-esteem, and by regaining faith in his own ability to resist the pull toward death, he found the will and the wherewithal to survive. Of course, it is well known that in other circumstances, dignity may have been retained but death could still not be averted, as young girls and boys went to the gas chambers singing their national anthems.

In those who did survive, short respites from deprivation or torture could allow them to regain their narcissistic equilibrium by enjoying bodily care. When Drexel was able to rinse himself with water, he felt a well-being that reminded him of having been freshly bathed: "A strong will to live flowed through my blood vessels" (p. 105). It is also remarkable that a tortured person can become very aware of his or her inner organs. In this prephallic, narcissistic regression under life-threatening conditions, Drexel declared his love for his heart which he addressed as if it were a beloved child in its mother's womb: "I held my breath and listened to its uneasy beats and a strange, almost affectionate love pulled me towards a small, courageous, bundle-like organ and its secret and wonderful, soft and unerring force. You small, wonderful being in my chest . . . I could trust you now . . . you would not disappoint me" (p. 102). In this vein, another source of narcissistic nourishment for child survivors came from the parting words of a loving parent, which fortified his wish to live. Identifying with the mother, the child could then minister to his own body just as the mother or father did when they were alive. The parent would seem to love the child from beyond the grave which inspired the will to survive.

TERTIARY NARCISSISM

The confrontation with death, therefore, has a profound effect upon the psyche (deWind, 1968). A redistribution of narcissistic libido may occur naturally in the normal course of aging and with a gradual awareness of the inevitability of one's death, the maintenance of self-esteem, self-worth, and the right to live all have to be reconciled with the recognition of the inevitability of death. When one is forced to confront this normal developmental task prematurely, it is out of phase and requires a tremendous reorganization of psychic forces. In a sense, it is the antithesis of a fixation. We tentatively agreed to call such narcissism "tertiary," that is, a return to the overcathexis of the body to life-saving, ego functions and associated aspirations to live a long life. In such extraordinary, life-threatening circumstances, the ego and bodily functions which maintain self-preservation would become invested or fueled by this tertiary narcissism. Invoking the reservoir analogy of narcissistic libido (Freud, 1923), we postulated that primary narcissism could coalesce with secondary narcissism under such circumstances, which was forged into this tertiary narcissism. It could then provide for additional resilience which, in the case of child survivors, enabled them to endure until liberation.

The persistence of this putative redistribution of narcissism might explain some of the sequelae of massive psychic trauma. So, with child survivors, the extent to which the Holocaust experience affected and colored their psychological growth would be influenced not only by the nature of the trauma, the stage of their development and their premorbid mental health but also by a continuation of such a narcissistic configuration. I saw this dynamic in action on a group level one evening during a local meeting of child survivors where the affirmation of life was dramatically enacted when the hostess lit a fire in her fireplace but curiously forgot to open the damper. Within seconds, the room which was packed with unsuspecting child survivors filled with dense smoke. Without panic, several people sprang into action opening the doors and windows, thereby "rescuing" everyone from what was rapidly becoming a gas chamber. Functioning as a collective psyche, their unspoken communication about protecting each other and their seeming readiness for danger was quite striking. Altruism and a sense of belonging (Kestenberg and Kestenberg, 1988) associated with the survival value of group formation was demonstrated quite well here as it seemed that the group's will to survive increased as each person recognized his value to the other. Thus, the group's narcissism increased in the face of danger which was successfully averted. Many child survivors reported that they often sensed that it was a triumph just to wake up alive each day. From a large-group perspective, similar observations can be made about their collective strength. Shortly after September 11, when air travel slowed to a trickle, a national meeting of child survivors had very few cancellations.

Despite the meaningless of time and the dangers that lie ahead, finding and having something to eat became a source of great pride and accomplishment. Appropriating a piece of clothing, such as a coat or a pair of shoes, was similarly a sign of great resourcefulness, along with finding shelter, escaping, running fast, eluding guards, etc. In addition, a number of child survivors attributed their survival to certain highly valued traits or skills in themselves, which would reflect their primary narcissism. For example, having an Aryan appearance of blond hair and blue eyes was mentioned quite frequently. One woman recalled a harrowing train ride with her very Semitic-looking parents as false papers were being scrutinized. She felt that her looks confused the German officers and they naturally assumed that she was not Jewish. She would not have been betrayed by the circumcised penis which for boys became a death sentence as it revealed their hidden Jewishness. Indeed, she felt a sense of omnipotence because she had saved herself and her parents. The pride that she had had in her pretty face prior to the war took on lifesaving significance during persecution in contrast to the phallic narcissism of the boy which would need to be manifested in more surreptitious ways. For example, fluency in the German language was highly prized and had survival value. A male survivor credited his survival with a command of German so that he was able to translate and communicate with the Nazis. They, according to him, thought he was special, which made him feel protected. Feeling protected is related to feeling loved and infant observation suggests that narcissism is heightened when the child is loved, approved of, and admired, as it requires the baby's capacity to incorporate the good that comes from the outside. He feels better when he is fed, cared for, and caressed. He then becomes more precious, owing to the good care which has been given. Thus, a loving object's behavior is another source of secondary narcissism which is antithetical to the first source of secondary narcissism, which arises from the lack of care or pain associated with the object.

THE PROFILE OF A RESILIENT MASCULINE SELF

The survival value of the deployment of manic defenses in the face of danger and unresolvable mourning cannot be emphasized enough (Klein,

1935, 1940; Winnicott, 1935; Akhtar, 1992; Brenner, 2004a). Akhtar, synthesizing Klein's ideas which were elaborated upon by Winnicott, observed that the manic defense is characterized by denying internal reality, a flight to external reality, the keeping of parental introjects in a state of suspension and the use of opposites. To this formulation I would add that the flight to external reality under these circumstances also includes the energy to adapt to or literally flee from external reality. While the awareness of this response to traumatic loss is not new and certainly not unique to the Holocaust, I have been struck by the presence of this potentially adaptive defense especially in adolescent survivors more than in infant survivors, latency-age survivors, or adult survivors. Parens's own account of his escape from a camp very much illustrates this point (Parens, 2004). As many experts have previously noted (Katan, 1961; Zetzel, 1965; Jacobson, 1957; Wolfenstein, 1966; Krystal, 1988), adolescence is the time of life for the maturation of affects which facilitates the capacity for grieving at a higher level under normative circumstances. While there is controversy over the extent to which younger children can truly mourn their lost objects under the best of conditions, the adolescent is better prepared for a number of reasons. Specifically, there is the opportunity for a second individuation which reinforces object constancy (Blos, 1967), the acquisition of abstract thinking promotes a deeper comprehension of death, greater physical strength facilitates alloplastic adaptation in order to alter one's environment (Hartmann, 1939), and sexual maturity enhances the capacity for new and enduring object relationships to supplant the loosened ties with one's parents. As a result of these changes, there would be more potential manic energy.

In a rather unusual article in *Fortune Magazine* (Loomis, 1998), five male Holocaust survivors who became multimillionaire entrepreneurs and philanthropists were profiled. There were a number of common denominators in these men which support the hypothesis that a manic defense associated with an omnipotent fantasy fueled a resilient masculine self in them:

1) All five went through at least part of their adolescence either in hiding, in slave labor, or in concentration camps. They experienced this crucial developmental phase under murderous, life-threatening conditions of genocidal persecution.
2) All five suffered object losses, including the sudden separation or traumatic loss of their fathers, either before or during the war. The loss of the father who was unable to protect them deeply affected their Oedipal dynamics, male identification, and increased the need to become more resourceful and self-reliant in order to survive.
3) All five were described as either very bright, precocious, mischievous, defiant or energetic at an early age. Constitutional factors and a drive for mastery may have been important factors also.

4) During their confinement, all five broke the "rules" and risked their lives trying to stay alive and to save other people's lives. They had progressed beyond the rigid, rule-bound superego of the latency age child and have enough flexibility or even a split in their superegos (Kestenberg and Brenner, 1986) in order to make quick, risky, and heroic decisions.

5) All five had unshakable confidence, optimism, and a conviction that they would and should somehow survive. Omnipotence prevailed.

6) All five were either described by loved ones or described themselves as having traits consistent with such omnipotence, defiance of authority, ruthlessness at times, and a manic defense. For example, "this drive, this incredible drive . . . "; "working six days a week . . . [and having] the attention span of a gnat"; "He was crazy. I didn't have a husband"; "I've been through the war and I'm not going to take any crap from anybody"; "I figured I could handle just about anything"; "Business is war. I don't believe in compromise. I believe in winning."

One of these men, Sigi Ziering, survived from the ages of eleven to seventeen with his mother and younger brother. He had to assume the paternal role of provider and protector while living through hell. He did not show any emotion for over twenty years until May 1997, when he, along with 105 other founding members of the U.S. Holocaust Museum in Washington who donated at least US$1 million each, were treated to a parade of flags representing the U.S. Army divisions that liberated the camps in 1945. In his speech, Ziering proclaimed, "Today, I cried because the worst memory of the ghetto and the camps was a feeling of total isolation and abandonment by the rest of the world. This feeling of utter despair and hopelessness weighed more heavily on us than the constant hunger, the beatings and the imminent death facing us every minute." Ziering, whose indefatigability earned him a Ph.D. in Physics, a career working on nuclear reactors, space projects, and ultimately becoming the CEO of a very successful company which developed radioimmunoassay materials, never forgot about the element of luck either. In describing the selection process at a camp he landed in prior to liberation, he mused, "With German precision the guards went at their jobs alphabetically (each week) and never got to Z" (Loomis, 1998, p. 82). Yet he did not rely on chance or divine intervention. He was tireless and very productive. Living out the stark motto on the iron gates of the death camps, "Arbeit Macht Frei," he bluntly stated his philosophy of life and secret of survival. "Unless you work, you're destined for the gas chambers." He outwitted the Nazis at their own deadly game. And, true to his word, it was noted in his obituary three years after the interview at age seventy-two, "He survived the Nazis but never stopped working until about a year ago when he was diagnosed with brain cancer" (Oliver, 2000, p. 20). His resilient, masculine self was tireless and his victory over his enemies and oppressors was effected through his education and enormous success in his work. His capacity for such sublimation reflected great ego strength in order to channel his aggression, his massive losses, and his long-suppressed affect.

From another perspective, the development of resilience seen in the masculine self may be viewed through Anthony's model of the buffering system, drawn from his work with the so-called invulnerable child (Anthony and Cohler, 1987). In his schematic diagram, there are six concentric circles representing different layers and different levels of protection. The innermost circle is neonatal cortical sleepiness. The next circle is the protective shield or stimulus barrier. The next layer of defense is maternal protection. The next circle is ego resilience, then family safeguards and, finally, community bulwark. We can see that the malignant assault on victims in the death camps could destroy this buffering system and render human beings into zombie-like robots. Such dissociative functioning could be seen to be initially derived from that innermost layer of neonatal cortical sleepiness. To survive such horror—and to reenter the world of the living is truly a miracle of human resilience. Further understanding of this "miracle" would require a narrowing of the chasm between what we do understand clinically and the accompanying changes which occur in the brain. Psychic trauma and resilience might thus be the starting point of a long overdue updating of Freud's 1895 attempt to provide a neurologic basis of psychology (Freud, 1895).

NEUROBIOLOGICAL PERSPECTIVES ON RESILIENCE

According to the contemporary neurobiological approach to understanding behavior, character traits associated with resilience are mediated by three systems and eleven possible neurochemicals or hormones (Charney, 2004). The well-known male hormone, testosterone, is an important part of this exceedingly complex arrangement and contributes to energy, activity, at times aggressivity, and may offer some protection against PTSD. However, it is not exclusive to males and in no way can be simply equated with masculinity or the masculine self. The reward and motivation system, fear responsiveness, and an adaptive social behavior mechanism all operate in a complex and interdependent way resulting in such traits as learned helplessness, optimism, pleasure-seeking, the ability to respond effectively despite fear, social bonding, teamwork, and altruism. The key to resilience, according to this model, is an effective, life-preserving, physiological response to acute stress, known as allostasis, and a rapid return to an internal resting state, homeostasis. The continued outpouring of powerful stress hormones can be damaging to the brain and lead to the well-known psychophysiological signs and symptoms of acute and chronic stress-related syndromes.

In addition to the well-known stress response hormone, cortisol, a second hormone secreted by the adrenal glands is emerging as a modulating influence that appears to be related to psychological resilience. The release of this substance, known as DHEA-S, or dehydroxyepiandrosterone sulfate, is triggered by ACTH in the pituitary. It has memory-enhancing, antidepressant, antianxiety, and antiaggression effects. It also counteracts nerve cell destruction in the hippocampus induced by steroids like cortisol. In a study (Morgan et al., 2004) of twenty-five military personnel enduring the acute stress of a highly selective survival school, the levels of DHEA-S were especially increased in those who performed in a superior range and who reported less dissociative symptoms. These results suggest that higher ratios of DHEA-S to cortisol are associated with a buffering effect against traumatic stress and that these subjects "came to survival training with brain structures and functional capacities that protected them . . ." (Morgan et al., 2004, p. 823). Unfortunately, in this report, there is no correlation with personality traits or developmental history, let alone unconscious mental lives, so we can only speculate on these matters here.

It is thought that in resilient people their reward systems are resistant to change in the face of chronic neglect and abuse or that they are very sensitive to rewards. In the brain, the mesolimbic dopamine pathways are thought to be centrally involved, especially the subcortical nucleus accumbens, the amygdala, and the medial prefrontal cortex. Neural networks determine the valence of a memory of a reward which includes its emotional value, strength and persistence. The cyclic adenosine monophosphate (cAMP) pathway facilitates both rewarding and aversive associations, the plasticity of which is crucial to psychotherapeutic strategies. In other words, new experiences like therapy may alter these associative networks.

THE FEAR RESPONSE SYSTEM AND PSYCHOANALYSIS

The mechanism for fear and anxiety is organized around conditioning, reconsolidation of memories, and extinction. We know that people with PTSD suffer from reexperiencing through memories, flashbacks, and nightmares as well as avoidance/numbing/forgetting, and autonomic hyperarousal. From a strictly behavioral standpoint, resilience could be defined as not overgeneralizing specific fear-inducing stimuli, having emotional memories that are reversible, and being able to easily experience extinction. Potentially traumatic stimulation reaches the thalamus which sends signals to the lateral amygdala, both directly and indirectly, via several areas in the cerebral cortex and the hippocampus allowing higher mental functioning (Le Doux, 1989, 1995). It is, therefore, this latter, slower circuit, involving the ego (Freud, 1923) which is more amenable to psychotherapeutic intervention, whereas the direct route is almost reflexive and unconscious, challenging our classical notions about affects not being unconscious (Weston, 1999). The basal lateral amygdala is a crucial structure in which both glucocorticoids and norepinephrine may interact, and excessive release of both substances results in the creation of indelible traumatic memories and reexperiencing phenomena. Researchers are looking for pharmacologic ways to prevent these symptoms from occurring through, for example, giving calcium channel blockers or antagonists of corticotropin-releasing hormone (CRH), glucocorticoid receptors, and beta-adrenergic receptors. Psychoanalysts, on the other hand, try to ameliorate such memories once they have developed, as a result of this pathological cathexis of the amygdala, as it were.

Of great clinical interest also is the reconsolidation process in which traumatic memories are reactivated, strengthened, and integrated into a new memory by incorporating here-and-now emotional/perceptual experience. Here, too, analytic theory intersects with new findings. Freud's 1895 controversial notion of nachträglichkeit, loosely translated by Strachey as "deferred action," has been invoked to explain being frozen in time and becoming traumatized only after a triggering stimulus. Freud ambiguously contended that "a memory is repressed which has only become a trauma after the event" (Freud, 1895, p. 356). However, some writers, such as Blum, find this concept which focuses on traumatic events and memory antiquated, obscuring the importance of cumulative preoedipal trauma and disturbed object relations. He charitably sees it as "an unrecognized precursor to the contemporary concept of developmental transformation" (Blum, 1996, p. 1155). Yet, others prefer to embrace it and elaborate upon it. For example, Baranger et al. commend Freud for his departure from "the model of mechanical causality and a linear temporality on the past and present vector for a dialectic concept of causality and a 'spiral' model of temporality where future and past condition signify each other reciprocally in structuring the present" (Baranger et al., 1988, pp. 115–116). Similarly, Modell sees nachträglichkeit as reflecting "that the ego is a structure engaged in the processing and reorganizing of time" (Modell, 1990, p. 4). Regardless of this theoretical controversy, if, however, psychic trauma damages the ego's synthetic functioning and prevents an experience from ever becoming "in the past," one would be thrust into a state of timelessness (Bromberg, 1991) and a perpetual living of the trauma. Therefore, it could not become a memory to be repressed because it never stopped happening in the first place intrapsychically. So, instead of a benign event becoming traumatic after a future experience augmented by development, the opposite would be true. A traumatic event could only hope to become detoxified after it becomes part of one's past as a result of some experience in the future. The importance of the therapeutic relationship and the therapist as a "new object" (Loewald, 1960) capitalizes on these phenomena also. The memory traces stored in the amygdala and hippocampus become labile after reactivation, so they may be disrupted by the experimental administration of a protein synthesis inhibitor. Unless they are reconsolidated, they will not return to long-term storage. The opportunities to clinically alter the fate of such memories after their activation has long been known by psychoanalysts who have witnessed abreactions in which the affect laden emergence of forgotten memories woven into the transference could have a therapeutic effect on the patient. Now, with our advanced knowledge of memory pathways, it is thought that giving beta receptor and NMDA (N-methyl-D-aspartate) receptor antagonists shortly after reviving a traumatic memory may also attenuate its intensity and lower the chances of developing PTSD. Here is another crossroads of basic science and psychoanalysis.

The behavioral process of extinction occurs when there is a reduction of learned fear after repeated contact with a conditioned stimulus which is delinked from the unconditioned stimulus. It forms a theoretical basis for "exposure-based psychotherapies," of which psychoanalysis, in my view, is the unlikely ultimate in "exposure" therapy. In the analytic situation, it is crucial to create an atmosphere of safety which defies the patient's daily unconscious expectation of danger, often requiring him/her to repeatedly test the limits of the analyst's composure, tolerance, and boundaries. Through the development and working through of the transference neurosis, the analyst is eventually seen as a benign figure who is empathically working on behalf of the patient, to help neutralize his/her mental representations imbued with fear, rage, dread, sadness, guilt, and shame. Often functioning silently and unobtrusively like the human liver which silently promotes absorption of nutrients and excretion of toxins, so too, the analyst promotes the internalization of good new objects and the detoxification of overwhelming, already internalized bad objects. Fear seems to be ubiquitous in trauma, and from a neurobiological perspective, patients with PTSD have been shown to have increased activity in the left amygdala while experiencing such fear, but during extinction have decreased activity in the medial prefrontal cortex and anterior cingulate gyrus. Therefore, it has been suggested that strengthening the involved NMDA receptors with a glycine agonist like D-cycloserine might enhance extinction and resilience, also.

GROUP SURVIVAL AND THE MIND-BRAIN CONNECTION

The Nazis tried to deprive their victims of their dignity, their spirit, and their pervasive will to live and learn. They deprived them of vital objects, such as air, warmth, food, and life-sustaining people like parents, spouses, and children. Under these circumstances, the libidinization of the self as a valuable, dignified person who is loved and cherished by his or her own people, the libidinization of sensory experiences and satisfactions of the past contributed to raising the self-esteem and the will to survive. These mechanisms prompted not only actions that would save the individual but also enhance the desire of others to save the individual too. A survival that led to the continuation of the heritage and the perpetuation of one's genes through his or her children was also experienced as a triumph over evil and a further justification for living. In Dr. Krystal's words, "In concentration camps and related experiences, no one survived without some help from others. The preservation of some capacity for social interaction was a great aid in maintaining one's sense of humanity. The ability to form temporary alliances for survival and, when possible, to help someone constituted a rare source of re-fueling, a sense of being a good person and maintaining some self-respect. When people were able to stay together with a group from 'home,' they acquired a source of support to their humanity" (p. 17).

The social behaviors associated with resilience are altruism and the capacity to draw new social supports from others. The hormones, oxytocin and vasopressin, appear to mediate social behavior using some of the same brain circuitry as the dopamine-mediated reward systems, that is, the nucleus accumbens, the caudate nucleus and the medial prefrontal cortex. This dual activation suggests that social cooperativeness may be rewarded and that failure to reciprocate may be inhibited. Such a pattern has evolutionary significance in that altruism, acts of courage, strong social attachments, and individual resilience has a survival value for the group as a whole. The anecdote of the child survivors in the smoke-filled room illustrates these features.

CONCLUSION

To summarize these neurobiological findings, it is striking that several brain structures are prominent in the three crucial neural circuits of social behavior, reward, and fear conditioning, namely, the nucleus accumbens, the medial prefrontal cortex, and the amygdala. Therefore, Charney (2004) suggests that a deeper understanding of psychic vulnerability and resilience may be obtained through studying the interdependence of these circuits and their respective neurochemical mediators. They would inform us of the neurobiological substrate of the masculine self. He also reminds us that genetic factors must not be overlooked as, for example, one born with a smaller hippocampus may be more vulnerable to stress, since a smaller sized hippocampus has been associated with PTSD (Gurvits et al., 1996; Gilbertson et al., 2002).

Another question regarding resilience pertains to the neurobiology of those circumstances in which prior experience may "inoculate" or "immunize" someone against future vulnerability to traumatic stress. Extrapolating the data from primate research supports the notion that the hypothalamic-pituitary-adrenal (HPA) axis may provide a neural basis for programming stress resistance in the developing child" (Parker et al., 2004, p. 940). However, the applicability of these findings to survivors of the horrors of genocidal persecution remains a huge question. For example, Yehuda and colleagues reported that cortisol levels in survivors with PTSD were lower than in those without PTSD (1995), suggesting an enhanced negative feedback loop in PTSD survivors relative to their more resilient counterparts. So what is clear is that it appears that their receptors have become supersensitive to the effects of the circulating hormones (Yehuda et al., 2004). Integrating such findings with the developmental line from infantile omnipotence to resilience presents us a challenge which has enormous implications for both the masculine self and the overall human race.

NOTES

This chapter is a revised and expanded version of a paper presented at Center for Mind and Human Interaction, University of Virginia, Charlottesville, VA, October 2004, and published in *The Unbroken Soul: Tragedy, Trauma and Resilience*, 2008, pp. 65–83.

1. In case 2 in chapter 1, Cindy was extremely nearsighted and in different dissociated self states she had different refractions requiring several sets of eyeglasses. Interestingly, her dissociated masculine self did not need glasses as he was convinced that he "saw" things most clearly.

8

Healing

The doctor has nothing else to do than to wait and let things take their
course, a course that cannot be avoided nor always hastened. If he holds
fast to this conviction, he will often be spared the illusion of having failed
when, in fact, he is conducting treatment on the right lines.

—Sigmund Freud, 1914a

Many years ago, I worked with a patient with a history of severe trauma
whose treatment needed to be interrupted due to nonpayment of her
mounting fees. Over time, I found evidence of unreliability and major
inconsistencies in some of her accounts which brought her credibility into
question. Despite these growing signs of her tendency to exaggerate and
fabricate certain elements of her current life, I nevertheless sensed that she
was genuinely suffering even though she had a need to lie to herself as well
as me. I persisted with her for several years until she tried to induce me to
help her inflate an insurance claim for psychological injuries from a "fender
bender" in order to pay me and her other bills. I refused. Enraged, feeling
misunderstood, and falsely accused of having dishonest tendencies, we
brought our three-times-a-week sessions to a close. On the last session, she
tearfully brought me a present, a peace offering and a sign of her thwarted
good intentions. Fearing I would not accept it, she told me it was a bit of
a family heirloom that while having little extrinsic value would mean very
much to her if in her efforts at redemption she could leave it for me. She
also pledged to pay the bill as soon as possible and wondered if we could
resume at that time. My curiosity piqued, and wanting to believe her sincerity on this emotional farewell session, I wondered if my refusal of such an

offer under the circumstances would be more in the service of angry revenge masked by a statement of technical purity, so I decided that affirming her healthy wish to leave on a good note would be in her best interest and accepted it.

Much to my surprise, the box she left behind contained a crystal ball, its metal stand and a brief note of thanks for my tolerance of her behavior which was histrionically characterized by chaos, tantrums, and suicidal regressions. As I examined the ornate and seemingly old metal frame, I noticed a very tiny piece of paper loosely glued to the bottom of it which clearly read "Made in Japan." Apparently in her haste to give me this item with such allegedly great sentimental value, she overlooked the telltale sign that, in fact, it must have been a recent purchase from a gift shop.

I mused over the possible meanings of this rather unusual subterfuge, feeling duped again by her and wondering if she even thought that I would have seen through this clumsy ruse. Did she think I was that gullible? Did she even care? Could she even imagine someone else's capacity to think and react to her outrageousness? And why a crystal ball? Was it to help me see more clearly into the future and into the past? Was it to help me see more clearly into the nature of her character? How much more of a mockery could she have made of me, the profession, and my largely unsuccessful efforts to help her?

By giving me an imitation of the tool of the trade of a medium, a vocation typically thought of as shady at best and downright fraudulent at worst, she was projecting her own fraudulence onto me, reducing me to a storefront fortune-teller who tells clients what they want to hear and purports to communicate with spirits in the afterlife. As Freud described them, "'mediums'— [are] individuals to whom peculiarly 'sensitive' faculties are ascribed but who are by no means distinguished by outstanding qualities of intellect or character and who are not, like the miracle worker of the past, inspired by any great idea or serious purpose. On the contrary, they are looked upon, even by those who believe in their powers, as particularly untrustworthy; most of them have already been detected as cheats and as we may reasonably expect, the same fate awaits the remainder (Freud, 1933, p. 35).

Interestingly, however, he interjects some doubt about his doubt:

> There is a real core of yet unrecognized facts in occultism around which cheating and fantasy have spun a veil which is hard to pierce . . . it is here, I think, that dreams come to our help by giving us a hint that from out of this chaos we should pick the subject of telepathy . . . [because] the state of sleep seems particularly suited for receiving telepathic messages (Freud, 1933, pp. 36–37).

There is a limited but significant body of analytic literature on this topic (Brenner, 2001) and a number of prominent analysts like Bion and Winnicott who take mysticism and mystical union very seriously (Sayers, 2002).

In fact, my new crystal ball did give me powers and enabled me to see into the future but only about one thing. I could see very clearly that I would never get fully paid by this patient without taking legal action! Over the years, I have reflected upon this experience quite often and have come to consider that, in a manner of speaking, all analysts are mediums. Especially for those patients who have sustained losses and have insufficiently mourned, they are consciously and unconsciously plagued by the ghosts of the dearly departed and need help communicating with their internalized representations (Volkan, 1981). Since the medium allegedly functions as a channel, allowing herself to become temporarily possessed by these spirits, when the analyst allows for the temporary projection or depositing of the patient's unconscious world into his or her psyche, there is an analogy here. Included in the patient's world are lost objects, unacceptable wishes, and an elaborate set of mental mechanisms to keep them out of mind. The analyst then helps the patient become aware of these contents through a series of specialized interventions, i.e., interpretations, which, when successful, allow the past to become freed up from the psychological bondage of unresolved mourning and neurotic conflict.

I became fascinated when I realized that the word itself—medium—has several other definitions which also could apply to the role of the analyst. The word "medium" itself might therefore be a useful condensed formula for how treatment works. For example, another definition is that of a substance or environment that promotes growth, like in a laboratory where bacteria or cells multiply in a nutrient-enriched test tube which contains the culture. In cases where the analyst functions as a new object as described by Loewald (1960), the patient's psychological growth, altered by traumatic and/or neurotic factors, is stimulated to resume its path of development. By providing a safe holding environment (Winnicott, 1953), the analyst may be experienced as, for example, a nurturing mother or a father of individuation (Mahler et al., 1975). Most evident in working with fixations of children and adolescents, this phenomenon occurs in the analysis of adults as well.

"Medium" may also be defined as being a means by which things are transmitted, like the visual medium of television or the auditory medium of radio. It was popularized in the sixties by the visionary Marshall McLuhan (1964) whose immortal phrase, "The medium is the message," expanded our social consciousness that there was enormous power and influence not only in "the message" but also in how it was communicated. This "high priest of pop culture" essentially made a societal interpretation that the nature of the messenger is at least as important as the message itself, anticipating many of the ills in our technological society today. This duality between medium and message is echoed in the current debate in psychoanalysis over the importance of the therapeutic relationship, i.e., the medium, relative to what the analyst actually says in his or her interpretations, i.e., the message.

And, finally, perhaps the most commonly thought of definition of medium is a quality of being somewhere in the middle of whatever is being calibrated, be it speed, temperature, or light. This being not too much and not too little but "just right" is beautifully depicted in the story of Goldilocks and the Three Bears. As Bettleheim pointed out, the appeal of fairy tales is in their addressing universal unconscious themes (Bettleheim, 1977). In the Goldilocks story, a young girl who is hungry and tired comes into an empty house. She finds three bowls of porridge—one is too hot, one is too cold, and one is just right. Then she finds three beds—one is too hard, one is too soft, and one is just right. Just as Goldilocks is looking for the right conditions for her comfort so, too, the analyst, in his or her striving for neutrality, is trying to be just right for the patient—not too absent and not too overwhelming, but certainly interested, curious, and empathic. But not too much. Therefore, the analytic stance, the analytic position, or the analytic attitude (Schafer, 1983) requires the analyst to be somewhere in the middle, or "medium."

CONTEMPORARY VIEWS OF THERAPEUTIC ACTION

To see if the multiple meanings of "medium" do indeed capture the essence of therapeutic action, it is necessary to review what the major schools have to say about how analysis works.

Fortunately, contemporary writers representing the prevailing ideologies have a lot to say about both the goals of analysis as well as how one achieves them. In a recent issue of *The Psychoanalytic Quarterly* (2007 Supplement), notable experts from North America, South America, and Europe grapple with this topic (Smith, 2007).

Here is a synopsis of their findings: The classical point of view which derived from Freud's original ideas has evolved into what is now considered "modern conflict theory"; it basically maintains the traditional viewpoint. As Abend states, "Insight is still regarded as the essential element in bringing about change and the study of the transference/countertransference relationship becomes an additional vehicle with which the understanding of the patient's mental activity—leading to interpretation and then to insight—is to be achieved" (Abend, 2007, p. 1431). Although there may be uncertainty over exactly how analysis works, he cautions us not to mistake this tentativeness for any doubt over its great efficacy in improving mental functioning and the quality of life. Expressed in technical terms, analysis aims "to alter the composition of certain compromise formations that account for symptoms or disadvantageous aspects of character in favor of new compromise formations that afford more satisfactions of wishes and entail a lesser degree, if not total relief, of the associated discomfort" (Abend,

2007, pp. 1436–1437). As mentioned above, here the analyst is a medium who interprets and helps the patient communicate between the worlds of the unconscious and the conscious.

From another perspective, proponents of self-psychology who have promulgated Kohut's ideas strive to help the patient achieve better cohesion of the self. Through the mobilization of self-object transferences which reactivate earlier relationships with less than perfect caretakers of infancy and childhood, repair of the self may then occur through the reorganization and building of new psychical structures. Narcissistic configurations of mirroring, alter ego, twinship, and idealized self-objects which help with the earliest affect and tension regulation of the developing child then come to life in treatment so they can be reexperienced and understood in a climate of empathy and optimal frustration. Interpretations are seen as a two-step process of understanding and explanation resulting in transmuting internalization. As concluded by Newman, "The intent is to provide an intense facilitating atmosphere that is still secure enough to affect every working of archaic affects" (Newman, 2007, p. 1543). Here the analyst is both a medium who interprets and connects to two worlds, as well as one who is a growth medium, along with one who creates an atmosphere—or medium—which is safe and solid enough to withstand the unleashed forces of early traumata so that they may be healed.

The followers of Melanie Klein who have refined object relations theory have their own perspective on how therapeutic action despite areas of overlap with others. From her point of departure from Freud's Viennese disciples who emphasize reorganization of the ego's defenses, softening of the superego and enhanced sublimation, Klein elaborated upon the identification with objects which Freud described in *Mourning and Melancholia* (Freud, 1917c). As such, change is thought to be as a result of "a deeper understanding and *insight* into the specific roles and relations exhibited and enacted in the transference" (Hinshelwood, 2007, p. 1483). Therefore, the aim of insight here is to enhance ego strength through self-understanding in the here and now as opposed to improving defenses from the classical perspective or in contrast to self-psychology which promotes self-cohesion and a better self-image. As a result, the validity of a Kleinian "deep interpretation" of, for example, Oedipal or primal scene material is determined by the nature of the patient's associations afterwards in which the lessening of an inhibition is seen as evidence of its accuracy. This principle, based upon empirical observation, now appears to be embraced by all schools that value interpretation.

The evolution of this approach has resulted in increasing awareness of the importance of the analyst's mind to take in and detoxify the patient's intolerable, disowned, and destructive tendencies. As Bion described it in his work with a psychotic patient, "fears of death . . . too powerful for his personality to contain [were] . . . split off . . . and put into me, the idea apparently being that if they were allowed to repose there long enough they would undergo modification by my psyche and could be safely introjected" (Bion, 1959, p. 312). Thus, the internalization of a good, understanding, maternal object in the transference becomes the nucleus of a stronger, healthier ego characterized by self-respect and self-love. It then followed that the analyst's mind as a container became so basic to this therapeutic approach that interpretations tended to be focused on the patient's fantasies of how the analyst's mind works, especially its capacity to bear the patient's unbearable affects associated with aggression and grief. In so doing, here, too, the analyst serves as a medium by allowing himself or herself to become temporarily "possessed" by the patient through the mechanism of projective identification.

Elaborating upon the importance of the analyst's mind from a relational perspective, Spezzano contends that "therapeutic action also involves the patient's getting inside psychoanalysis through a subjective experience of the mind of the analyst as a certain type of psychic environment (or home) as well as through an emotional experience and image of him/herself as a person in that mind" (Spezzano, 2007, p. 1563). Here, the analytic goal of having a freer mind is achieved through not only an identification with the analyst's freedom of mind and functions as an interpreter, but also through the progressive belief that he or she is an autonomous object within the analyst's mind itself. This latter quality is distinct from the Kleinian containment function described above. It adds an additional dimension of the importance of the phantasy (with a "p"), i.e., unconscious infantile fantasy, of the whereabouts of pieces of selves and objects in mental space.

How patients imagine how their analysts imagine them is crucial to the development of their internal freedom and the lessening of resistance. Such freedom lends itself to receptivity which is necessary because, as Spezzano muses, "In granting us the privilege of interpreting to them, patients allow us to tell them that they don't know what they're talking about, don't mean what they think they mean, are revealing aspects of the workings of their minds that they don't know they're revealing, that they want what they don't know they want, are afraid of things they don't know they're afraid of or that they engage in certain forms of mental activity over and over—not for the reasons they think they do but because doing so helps regulate their anxiety" (Spezzano, 2007, p. 1574). In this model of therapeutic action, here, too, the analyst is a medium who interprets and is also a medium who allows the patient to inhabit his/her mind. In this form of possession, the analyst allows the patient's psychical spirit total freedom which is independent of the body and ultimately liberating.

From an intersubjective viewpoint, Renik contends that since most people look to analysis because "they want to feel more satisfaction and less distress in their lives" (Renik, 2007, p. 1547), the patient is the ultimate judge of its success if they feel better. He maintains that while different theories may emphasize different technical approaches, goals, and use different vocabularies, the nature of therapeutic action and benefit is ultimately the same: Regardless of approach, there is "a review and revision of the patient's expectations, assumptions and decision-making, the way the patient constructs his/her reality—seen from different angles of view" (Renik, 2007, p. 1548). It is achieved optimally through collaboration, partnership, and cocreation of a new truth by means of verbal and nonverbal dialogue in which conscious and unconscious conversation takes place. Despite claims that this approach is hermeneutic and has no predictive value, it is argued that, in fact, the traditional "analyst knows best" model lends itself to circularity in goals and research, and is therefore actually less scientific. Because the analyst is both an observer and a participant in the clinical process, it is not possible to completely remove him/herself from the equation to clearly see the risk of a self-fulfilling prophecy by "proving" our favorite theories over and over again. Therefore, the only meaningful measure of outcome is the patient's experience of benefiting or not. Consequently, such cherished theoretical beliefs, such as the importance of the analyst's anonymity or neutrality, must come into question. From this perspective, the analyst is not a medium who is privileged to give interpretations and is not necessarily medium in his or her therapeutic stance but rather a pliable artistic medium through which the patient comes to express and realize his or her own new truth. Through this new cocreation, the analysand's new narrative might provide a great sense of satisfaction and hope for the future. As such, it could also have predictive value in measuring the outcome of treatment scientifically.

Such diversity of viewpoints cannot be easily reconciled and we are cautioned not to rush to assimilate them lest we fail to appreciate the significance of pluralism in contemporary analytic thought. As Goldberg observes, " . . . an improvement in the patient's well-being as a result of psychoanalysis can be explained as a by-product, a reaction to the warmth of the patient's personality, a developmental achievement, an example of the efficiency of insight, learning how to handle discouragement or all other means of explanatory devices" (Goldberg, 2007, pp. 1667–1668. He therefore concludes that "Psychoanalysis must be seen as an evolving set of concepts with variable applicability and not as a 'one-size-fits-all' program" (Goldberg, 2007, p. 1673). With these ideas in mind, I would like to present the following annotated vignette to illustrate this plurality at work in a patient with a very disturbed masculine self.

THE BEGINNING OF AN HOUR, ANNOTATED

Mr. J. (see chapter 2) well into his sixth year of a five-time-a-week widening scope analysis (Stone, 1954), sees me greet him in the waiting room while he is in the middle of an animated conversation on his cell phone with a business associate. He hangs up after declaring, "I'll call you back when I'm *out* of the doctor" (he has perversely sexualized everything in the past so that even prepositions such as "out" or "in" are highly charged. I make note of his aggressive tone and choose not to interpret his preconscious wish to "stick it to me again" until later in the hour). He gets up and rushes past me, quickly glances on the floor in the foyer where an envelope was lying, and seeing it is now gone smirks at me, probably assuming I had picked it up on the way to retrieve him. Entering the office, I close the door and he sits down in the chair. (He stopped using the couch a number of months ago when he became embarrassed and inhibited after realizing that while in a trance-like state he had turned over on his abdomen, got on all fours and began talking about being sodomized by his father when he was a boy. In his secret sexual life, which his wife "knows and doesn't know" about, he proves his manhood over and over again by enduring painful anal penetration by young men who insert the longest and widest dildos he can tolerate. Although he has emphasized repeatedly that I am not his type, a sadomasochistic flavor pervades our relatedness.)

As though he were responding to a silent interrogator asking why he did not pick up the envelope, he blurts out that he did notice an envelope on the floor but decided not to pick it up because it wasn't his business. Instead, he walked around it to get the key to the men's room, went to the men's room, came back, side-stepped the letter again, returned the key, and waited for me in the waiting room. (I sensed a mixture of subtle, disowned guilt, dutiful pseudo-respect for my privacy from a faulty reaction formation, and a playful provocation in his demeanor. Having grossly invaded my privacy in the past by means of Internet research and then impersonating others in order to get information about me by telephone and mail, we both recognize the disingenuous nature of this gesture. Containing the affects of shock, helplessness, and rage over discovering this egregious violation was extremely challenging to me and jeopardized the treatment. Over time, he has recognized that these intolerable feelings actually derive from his own dissociated experience from his traumatic childhood and were induced in me by his identification with the perpetrator. In so doing, he was unconsciously testing me to see how much forceful penetration I could take. The envelope drama is a continuation of this enactment and an allusion to his ongoing efforts to metabolize our relationship and integrate his disowned self states.)

Masking his eagerness for my reply as we begin our daily mental chess match, I wait a moment and say that, of course, it is not his responsibility to bend down (or bend over) and pick up my mail. I also gently confront him, noting that despite his avowed efforts to respect my privacy, he could not not notice who had sent me the letter since we both know that he routinely comments on any mail he sees in the foyer or on my desk and that he can spot any minute change in my office décor. He feigns being insulted by veiled accusations about his excessive intrusiveness and becomes sarcastic. (Out of his deep fear of being raped again and needing to know everything about everyone he has dealings with in order to anticipate their aggression and take preemptive measures, he is just beginning to recognize his own capacity to violate others.) He then tells me that he will make allowances for my tone of voice and forgive me, knowing that it is the end of a work-week. He typically mocks me on Friday, saying that I look "ripe for a nap," thinking that I like to wear sports coats instead of suits as I prefer the less formal look in preparation of leaving him for the weekend. He then notices that I am in fact wearing a suit and wonders if I decided to do so merely to defy him and his prediction since I would know he would chide me if I did otherwise. Knowing from experience that once he dons his sarcasm character armor, his efforts to outwit me could continue indefinitely if I take the "bait" and try to interpret his need for omnipotent control, so I adopt a different strategy. Instead, I decide to comment on his having found "a home in my mind" (Spezzano, 2007) and empathically interpret to him that it must feel very good for him to imagine that I carry him around in my mind all the time and that he would have such an influence on me that it would even affect what I decide to wear. He looks surprised and very pleased. Interestingly, his sarcastic tone evaporates immediately and he then eagerly shows me a document. (I make no comment on the reversal from his voyeuristic wish to look to his exhibitionistic wish that I now look at his letter.)

It is a business letter dated last September 8th to a man of Middle East-ern background and he implores me to make a special note of the date and imagine what an impact it would have had on his negotiations if he had waited just another day to send it. I am puzzled by his reference to September 9th. He looks very disappointed at my uncomprehending ex-pression. He becomes impatient and irritated at how dimwitted I appear since I could not collude with him nor give him the mirroring he needed about how clever and how shrewd he is. Just as he is about to yell at me for my being such an idiot, he gives me one last chance to redeem myself and gives me a clue: he asks me what happened in America on that day, and I then realize that he was alluding to September 11. He felt that he lost an-other chance for revenge by not launching his own surprise attack on that infamous day in his effort to intimidate the foreigner and force a hostile takeover of the man's business. Suddenly, the patient looks startled and starts to laugh uncontrollably as he realizes that the joke is on him. (Having learned about his unconscious mind through analysis and his internaliza-tion of the analytic function of interpretation, his capacity for self-analysis has developed. Some of his motivation is in the service of competition and "one-upmanship" to keep me from knowing about his mind before he does. He, nonetheless, has become rather thoughtful and introspective.) He then recognizes that he has been the victim of his own machinations and analyzes his mistake on the spot. He, indeed, confused September 9th with September 11th. (September 9th has always been an infamous day for him because he might be personally attacked, as it happens to be his mother's birthday. Vain, manipulative, neglectful, insatiable, jealous, and vindictive, he felt totally unwanted as a child and undermined by her in every phase of his development especially with regard to his relationship with females. She would complain bitterly on September 9th because he could never please her on her birthday with any birthday present. Furthermore, he hated her for having an affair with a neighbor while he was being abused by the father.) He was in awe of the power of his unconscious mind to trick him and appreciatively gave me a lot of credit for all that he had been learning. (He at times would simply be amazed to recognize his greater capacity to think, to tolerate dysphoric affects and better control his impulses through symbolization and verbalization. Perhaps he is not a lost cause and a hopeless case after all, he decides.)

While he was praising me, he was very proud of himself and invited me to use this example of a Freudian slip in my writing. I agreed and playfully took out a pad of paper, wrote a brief note about this particular incident and he looked rather pleased. (We are both aware of his profound narcissistic wounds from childhood, that he was deemed to be a failure and a loser. He would end up either dying young or being in prison. He appears very boyish and desperate for mirroring, which merges with his exhibitionism. He is so incredulous at his personal growth that his exhibitionism becomes sublimated in fantasy by a wish to write his own memoir someday. I serve as his symbolic biographer and coauthor as I jot notes in our playspace [Herzog, 2001] in the session.) Just then he looked very surprised and wondered why he never realized that I was left-handed just like his brother. (His brother was his best friend and biggest rival who had killed himself about two years to the day prior to his starting treatment with me. Given the seriousness of Mr. J.'s own self-destructive tendencies, I had doubts about his treatability until I saw the pain of his unresolved grief. Seeing that authentic affect as an entrée into his tortured psyche, our alliance was forged by my finding a way to help him mourn for his brother, who was resurrected in the transference once again when he saw me write left-handed.) After a period of solemn reverie, I interpreted to the patient that perhaps he did not realize that I was left-handed prior to that moment because he had been in a trance for much of the time and could not let himself always remember what he knew. After an initial insistence that he never saw me write before because he had usually been on the couch, he then acknowledged that, in fact, he had seen me write in my appointment book in the past but it just did not register in his mind before today. His brother was on his mind as the anniversary of his suicide was approaching.

He then told me how much better he was taking care of his health as he was tending to his physical needs and to his body which he was prone to neglect and abuse in myriad ways. He then cautiously told me his income had increased considerably. This revelation was very courageous because of his fear that telling me would make him vulnerable to my financial exploitation were I to raise his fee an exorbitant amount. (The fee and every issue related to payment have been "highly charged" issues. I choose not to interpret the projection of his wish to exploit me and others as it might increase his defensiveness.) His gratitude was genuine but he could not tolerate his love for too long. He regressed and, with a mischievous twinkle in his eye, reminded me that he was "still analyzing" the bill that I had given him two weeks prior to that and could not pay me just yet. I decided not to point out to him that his earlier comment about giving me "credit" was perhaps, on a deeper level, an unconscious allusion to the fact that it was actually I who was giving him credit because he had not paid me yet. (He had told me repeatedly that he has felt out of control, indebted, and vulnerable unless he was all paid up, so it is an ironic show of trust on his part to let me let him owe me money.) I thought doing so at that moment would only perpetuate the mental chess match so instead I simply listened as empathically as I could in realizing the importance of being neutral and "medium" to him.

DISCUSSION

As evidenced in the fragment of the analytic hour offered here, I served as an empathic, neutral object, an interpreter of unconscious conflict, a bridge to the world of dead, lost objects, a holding environment for the patient's developmental growth, a container of disowned, mental contents, and a pliable artistic medium for playing in our spielraum, or playspace (Herzog, 2001). These six forms of medium reflect how I, as the analyst, functioned. Therapeutic action appeared to be a synergistic effect of these various and overlapping modes. As a result, the patient's defenses were modified, his ego was strengthened, there was increased cohesion of the self, more ownership of disowned psychical contents, less impulsivity, increased mental freedom and, ultimately, he started feeling better. In addition, he began to tend to his body and physical health.

It is curious how little is mentioned in the literature on therapeutic action about the fate of the body and the mind-body connection but in cases, for example, where self-destructive behavior, addictions, conversion reactions, bodily neglect, and psychophysiological disturbances are prominent, this realm is very important. It may literally be a matter of life and death.[1] Because "The body ego itself needs a home" (Money-Kyrle, 1968, p. 695), the "psychic base" provided to Mr. J. through analysis seemed to be crucial in order to counteract the disorientation and despair associated with his own psychical homelessness. Once Mr. J. became a teenager, he never spent another night at home so that he was both literally and psychologically homeless ever since. The feeling of being welcomed and his sense of belonging in both the transference and in my mind seemed to underlie a repair in his basic trust and enable attachment to benign objects which, when internalized, perhaps increased his own self-love and respect for his body. This narcissism in the service of survival (Kestenberg and Brenner, 1995) seemed to enhance his sense of self-worth and served as an antidote to feeling so unwanted as a child.

With all of these "curative" factors in place, the question of what the primary active ingredient is in analysis remains a source of great debate. The patient reports a certain moment outside of session but very much a part of the process (Stern et al., 1998) when things crystallize in his mind and he decided he needed to start taking care of himself. His car had broken down in a freak snowstorm as a result of willful neglect and an obsessional/masochistic game to see how long it would run without fixing a certain problem. While he was walking to get help and suffering from exposure with near-frostbite, he realized that his car was an extension of himself and that he was getting tired of behaving foolishly, "like a jerk." His capacity for self-reflection during this dangerous trek and his imagining telling me about his insight were important indicators of his deep involvement in both analysis and the analytic relationship. As Eizirik describes it, "The therapeutic action of psychoanalysis rests in the unique experience of being listened to and understood by another in a new way, while present in what has been described as a psychoanalytic field, which leads to the patient acquiring a new understanding of himself, thus reducing his psychic pain and becoming more free to enjoy his own capabilities. [Therefore], this is the way through which insight might be obtained as a result of the experience of being understood in a new, fuller way than any previous experiences have provided" (Eizirik, 2007, p. 1477). Incorporating this idea of a new experience and emphasizing the centrality of the transference, Kernberg believes that "The systematic interpretation of the transference is the major factor of therapeutic action specific to psychoanalysis and that the unique type of personal relationship achieved . . . centered on the analysis permits the building up of a new, unique type of object relation that gradually becomes an additional, important, therapeutic function as a consequence of the systematic transference analysis" (Kernberg, 2007, p. 1722). Thus, Kernberg also retains a classical position while acknowledging the importance of the relationship. This hybrid viewpoint individually negotiated by each analyst is thought to reflect the preponderance of opinion in contemporary clinicians (Josephs, 1995).

CONCLUSION

While there is as yet no consensus about the nature of therapeutic action, most analysts would probably agree that there is something quite remarkable about the process of analysis itself and that at times it seems to have a life of its own. As Freud optimistically described it, "The doctor has nothing else to do than to wait and let things take their course, a course which cannot be avoided nor always hastened" (Freud, 1914, p. 155). However, contemporary thought considers that there is a "spectrum stretching from the more insight-oriented group . . . to a more relationship-oriented one . . . with . . . an idiosyncratic blending of the two . . . but [unfortunately] examining two terms representative of each group—insight . . . and containment. . . . we find such sharp disagreement about what is meant by each . . . the result is a confusion of tongues" (Smith, 2007, p. 1760). This confusion over the meaning of terms is perhaps compounded by the so-called transferential-countertransferential theoretical-clinical magma described by Aisenstein (Aisenstein, 2007). She alludes to that deep, molten state of influences somewhat beyond our control and influenced by unconscious factors which would have a unique composition for each analyst and his or her analysand. Yet, despite these individual, inchoate differences, there may be more similarities in our daily work than we realize. As illustrated in this brief vignette of my work with a very disturbed, traumatized, and resilient patient, there is evidence of pluralism at work. In this case, it could be thought that a healing of the rifts in the mind as well as a healthier mind-body connection was taking place. As a result, Mr. J.'s very damaged and fragile masculine self began to heal. It seems as though a somatopsychic integration was occurring through interpretation, empathy, mourning, development, containment, therapeutic play, and analysis of the transference in a relationally mediated context. As such, perhaps the importance of the analyst as being "medium" may encapsulate the essence of this most impossible profession.

NOTES

1. It would be a fascinating study to examine the longevity and overall health issues in a controlled study of analyzed individuals. Is, for example, the life expectancy of an analyst significantly different from other mental health professionals or M.D.s?

References

Abend, S. (2007). Therapeutic action in modern conflict theory. *Psychoanalytic Quarterly* 76 (Suppl.):1417–1442.

Abse, D. W. (1974). Hysterical conversion and dissociative syndromes and the hysterical character. In *American Handbook of Psychiatry*, ed. S. Arieti and E. B. Brody. New York: Basic Books, pp. 155–194.

———. (1983). Multiple personality. In *New Psychiatric Syndromes: DSM III and Beyond*, ed. S. Akhtar. New York: Jason Aronson, pp. 339–361.

Aisenstein, M. (2007). On therapeutic action. *Psychoanalytic Quarterly* 76 (Suppl.):1443–1461.

Akhtar, S. (1992). *Broken Structures: Severe Personality Disorders and Their Treatment.* New York: Jason Aronson.

———. (1999). *Inner Torment: Living between Conflict and Fragmentation.* Northvale, NJ: Jason Aronson.

———. (2003). Things: developmental, psychopathological, and technical aspects of inanimate objects. *Canadian Journal of Psychoanalysis* 11:1–44.

Alexander, F. A. (1940). Psychoanalysis revised. *Psychoanalytic Quarterly* 9:1–36.

Alexander, F. A., and French, T. M. (1946). *Psychoanalytic Therapy: Principles and Application.* New York: Ronald Press Company.

Almond, R. (1997). Omnipotence and power. In *Omnipotent Fantasies and the Vulnerable Self*, ed. C. Ellman and J. Reppen. Northvale, NJ: Jason Aronson, pp. 1–37.

Amati-Mehler, J., and Argentieri, S. (1989). Hope and hopelessness: A technical problem? *International Journal of Psychoanalysis* 70:295–304.

American Psychiatric Association (APA). (2000). *Diagnostic Criteria from DSM-IV-TR.* Arlington, VA: American Psychiatric Press.

Andreasen, N. C., Olsen, S. A., Dennert, J. W., and Smith, M. R. (1982). Ventricular enlargement in schizophrenia: Relationship to positive and negative symptoms. *American Journal of Psychiatry* 139:297–302.

Anthony, E. J., and Cohler, B. J. (1987). *The Invulnerable Child*. New York: Guilford Press.

Apprey, M. (1993). The African-American experience: Forced migration and transgenerational trauma. *Mind and Human Interaction* 4:70–75.

Arlow, J. A. (1959). The structure of the déjà vu experience. *Journal of the American Psychoanalytic Association* 7:611–631.

———. (1966). Depersonalization and derealization. In *Psychoanalysis—A General Psychology*, ed. R. M. Loewenstein, L. M. Newman, M. Schur, and A. J. Solnit. New York: International Universities Press, pp. 456–478.

———. (1984). Disturbances of the sense of time. *Psychoanalytic Quarterly* 53:13–37.

———. (1986). Psychoanalysis and time. *Journal of the American Psychoanalytic Association* 34:507–528.

———. (1988). Summary comments: Panels on psychic structure. *Journal of the American Psychoanalytic Association* 36S:283–294.

———. (1992). Altered ego states. *Israel Journal of Psychiatry and Related Sciences* 29:65–76.

Aron, L. (2000). Ethical considerations in the writing of psychoanalytic case histories. *Psychoanalytic Dialogues* 10:231–245.

Bach, S. (1986). Self-constancy and alternate states of consciousness. In *Self and Object Constancy: Clinical and Theoretical Perspectives*, ed. E., Lax, S. Bach, and J. A. Borland. New York: Guildford Press, pp. 135–152.

———. (2001). On being forgotten and forgetting one's self. *Psychoanalytic Quarterly* 70:739–756.

Bak, R. C. (1968). The phallic woman: The ubiquitous fantasy in perversions. *Psychoanalytic Study of the Child* 23:15–36. New York: International Universities Press.

Balint, M. (1955). Friendly expanses—horrid empty spaces. *International Journal of Psychoanalysis* 36:225–241.

———. (1968). *The Basic Fault: Therapeutic Acts of Regression*. London: Tavistock Publications.

Baranger, M., Baranger, W., and Moms, J. M. (1988). The infantile psychic trauma from us to Freud: Pure trauma, retroactivity, and reconstruction. *International Journal of Psycho-Analysis* 69:113–128.

Barocas, H., and Barocas, G. (1983). Wounds of the fathers: The next generation of Holocaust victims. *International Review of Psycho-Analysis* 5:331–341.

Bass, A. (1997). The problem of concreteness. *Psychoanalytic Quarterly* 66:642–682.

Beebe, B. (2005). Personal communication.

Beebe, B., and Lachman, F. (2002). *Infant Research and Adult Treatment: Co-Constructing Interactions*. Hillsdale, NJ: Analytic Press.

Beebe, B., Lachman, F., and Jaffe, J. (1997). Mother-infant interactions, structures and presymbolic self and object representations. *Psychoanalytic Dialogues* 7:133–182.

Bergmann, M. S., and Jucovy, M. E. (eds.) (1982). *Generations of the Holocaust*. New York: Basic Books.

Berman, E. (1981). Multiple personality: *Psychoanalytic Perspectives*. *International Journal of Psycho-Analysis* 62:283–300.

Bernardi, R. (2007). The concept of therapeutic action today: Light and shadows of pluralism. *Psychoanalytic Quarterly* 76 (Suppl.):1585–1599.

Bettelheim, B. (1977). *The Uses of Enchantment: The Meaning and Importance of Fairy Tales.* New York: Random House.

Bick, E. (1968). The experience of the skin in early object relations. *International Journal of Psychoanalysis,* 49:484–486.

Bion, W. (1959). Attacks on linking. *International Journal of Psycho-Analysis* 40:308–315.

———. (1962). *Learning from Experience.* New York: Basic Books.

———. (1970). *Attention and Interpretation.* London: Tavistock.

Blanchard, D. C., Sakai, R. R., McEwen, B., Weiss, S. M., and Blanchard, R. J. (1993). Subordination stress: Behavioral, brain and neuroendocrine correlates. *Behavioral Brain Research* 58:113–121.

Blos, P. (1967). The second individuation process of adolescence. *Psychoanalytic Study of the Child* 22:162–186.

———. (1985). *Son and Father: Before and Beyond the Oedipus Complex.* New York: Free Press.

Blum, H. P. (1985). Superego formation, adolescent transformation, and the adult neurosis. *Journal of the American Psychoanalytic Association* 33:887–909.

———. (1987). The role of identification in the resolution of trauma. *Psychoanalysis Quarterly* 56:609–627.

———. (1994). The confusion of tongues and psychic trauma. *International Journal of Psycho-Analysis* 71:871–882.

———. (1996). Seduction trauma: Representation, deferred action, and pathogenic development. *Journal of the American Psychoanalytic Association* 44:1147–1164.

Bollas, C. (1987). *The Shadow of the Object: Psychoanalysis of the Unthought Known.* New York: Columbia University Press.

———. (1989). *Forces of Destiny: Psychoanalysis and Human Idiom.* Northvale, NJ: Jason Aronson.

———. (1992). *Being a Character: Psychoanalysis and Self-Experience.* New York: Hill and Wang.

Borch-Jacobsen, M. (1996). *Remembering Anna O: A Century of Mystification.* New York: Routledge.

Boulanger, G. (2002). The cost of survival: Psychoanalysis and adult onset trauma. *Contemporary Psychoanalysis* 38:17–44.

Bowlby, J. (1969). *Attachment and Loss, vol. I: Attachment.* New York: Basic Books.

Brady, M. J. (2006). Panel report: The riddle of masculinity. *Journal of the American Psychoanalytic Association* 54:1195–1206.

Brenner, C. (1980). Metapsychology and psychoanalytic theory. *Psychoanalytic Quarterly* 49:189–214.

———. (1982). *The Mind in Conflict.* New York: International Universities Press.

Brenner, I. (1988). Multi-sensory bridges in response to object loss during the Holocaust. *Psychoanalytic Review* 75:573–587.

———. (1994). The dissociative character: A reconsideration of multiple personality. *Journal of the American Psychoanalytic Association* 42:819–846.

———. (1996a). On trauma, perversion, and "multiple personality." *Journal of the American Psychoanalytic Association* 44:785–814.

———. (1996b). The characterological basis of "multiple personality." *American Journal of Psychotherapy* 50:154–166.

————. (2000). Stacheldraht in der Seele. In *Das Ende-der Sprachlosigkeit?* ed. L. Opher-Cohn, J. Pfafflin, B. Sontag, B. Klose, and P. Ponagy-Wnendty, pp. 113–139. Giesen: Psychosozial-Verlag.

————. (2001). *Dissociation of Trauma: Theory, Phenomenology and Technique.* Madison, CT: International Universities Press.

————. (2002). Reflections on the Aftermath of Sept. 11. *Philadelphia Interpreter,* Feb. 2002:4.

————. (2004a). *Psychic Trauma: Dynamics, Symptoms, and Treatment.* Lanham, MD: Jason Aronson.

————. (2004b). Panel report: Psychoanalytic treatment of schizophrenic patients. *International Journal of Psycho-Analysis* 85:1231–1234.

————. (2006). Letter to the Editor. "More thoughts on dissociation." *Clinical Psychiatric News,* February 2006, pp. 11–12.

————. (2007). Dissociation and the Enactment-Prone Patient. Presented at International Psychoanalytic Association, Berlin, July 2007.

Breslau, N., Peterson, E. L., and Schultz, L. R. (2008). A second look at prior trauma and the posttraumatic stress disorder effects of subsequent trauma. *Archives of General Psychiatry* 65:431–437.

Breuer, J., and Freud, S. (1893–1895). Studies on hysteria. *Standard Edition* 2.

Bromberg, P. M. (1991). On knowing one's patient inside out: The aesthetics of unconscious communication. *Psychoanalytic Dialogues* 1(4):399–422.

————. (1994). "Speak! that I may see you": Some reflections on dissociation, reality, and psychoanalytic listening. *Psychoanalytic Dialogues* 4:517–547.

————. (1998). *Standing in the Spaces: Essays on Clinical Process, Trauma, and Dissociation.* Hillside, NJ: Analytic Press.

Buck, O. D. (1983). Multiple personality as a borderline state. *Journal of Nervous and Mental Disease* 171:62–65.

Busch, F. (2006). Countertransference in defense enactments. *Journal of the American Psychoanalytic Association* 54:67–86.

Cabaniss, D. L., Forand, N., and Raase, S. P. (2004). Conducting analysis after September 11: Implications for psychoanalytic technique. *Journal of the American Psychoanalytic Association* 2:717–734.

Canestri, J. (2007). Comments on therapeutic action. *Psychoanalytic Quarterly* 76 (Suppl.):1601–1634.

Caper, R. (1999). *A Mind of One's Own: A Kleinian View of Self and Object.* London: Routledge.

Charney, D. (2004). Psychobiological mechanisms of resilience and vulnerability: Implications for successful adaptation to extreme stress. *American Journal of Psychiatry* 161:195–216.

Chassaguet-Smirgel, J. (1974). Perversion, idealization and sublimation. *International Journal of Psycho-Analysis.* 55:349–357.

————. (1978). Reflexions on the connections between perversion and sadism. *International Journal of Psycho-Analysis* 59:27–35.

————. (1981). Loss of reality in perversions—with special reference to fetishism. *Journal of the American Psychoanalytic Association* 29:511–534.

————. (1984). *Creativity and Perversion.* New York: Norton.

Churchill, W. (1941). War-Time Speech, October 29, 1941.

Clarey, W. F., Burstin, K. J., and Carpenter, J. S. (1984). Multiple personality and borderline personality disorder. *Psychiatric Clinics of North America* 7:89–99.

Clifft, M. (1986). Writing about psychiatric patients. *Bulletin of the Menninger Clinic* 50:511–524.

Colarusso, C. (1979). The development of time sense—From birth to object constancy. *International Journal of Psycho-Analysis* 60:243–251.

———. (1998). A developmental line of time sense: In late adulthood and throughout the life cycle. *Psychoanalytic Study of the Child* 53:113–140.

Coons, P., Bowan, E., and Milstein, V. (1988). Multiple personality disorder: A clinical investigation of 50 cases. *Journal of Nervous and Mental Disease* 176:519–527.

Coplan, J., Andrews, M., Rosenblum, L., Owens, M., Friedman, S., Gorman, J., and Nemenoff, C. (1996). Persistent elevations of cerebrospinal fluid concentrations of corticotrophin-releasing factor in adult nonhuman primates exposed to early-life stressors: Implications for the pathophysiology of mood and anxiety disorders. *Proceedings of the National Academy of Sciences* 93:1619–1623.

Crastnopol, N. (1999). The analyst's professional self as a "third" influence on the dyad. *Psychoanalytic Dialogues* 9:445–470.

Davies, J. M. (2002). Erotic overstimulation and the co-construction of sexual meanings in transference-countertransference experience. *Psychoanalytic Quarterly* 70:757–788.

Davies, J. M., and Frawley, M. G. (1991). Dissociative processes and transference-counter-transference paradigms in the psychoanalytically oriented treatment of adult survivors of childhood sexual abuse. *Psychoanalytic Dialogues* 2:5–36.

———. (1994). *Treating the Adult Survivor of Childhood Sexual Abuse.* New York: Basic Books.

DeBellis, M. D. (2001). Developmental traumatology: The psychobiological development of maltreated children and its implications for research, treatment, and policy. *Development and Psychopathology* 13:359–364.

Dewald, P. A. (1982). The clinical importance of the termination phase. *Psychoanalytic Inquiry* 2:441–461.

deWind, E. (1968). The confrontation with death. *International Journal of Psycho-Analysis* 49:302–305.

Diamond, J. (2006). Masculinity unraveled: The roots of male gender identity and the shifting of male ego ideals throughout life. *Journal of the American Psychoanalytic Association* 54:1099–1130.

Dickes, R. (1965). The defensive function of an altered state of consciousness: A hypnoid state. *Journal of the American Psychoanalytic Association* 13:365–403.

Drexel, J. (1980). Rueckkehr Unerwuenscht: Joseph Drexel Reise Mathausen der Widerstand Kreis Ernst Niekisch, ed. W. R. Berger. D TV Dokumente. Muenchen: Deutsch Taschenbuch Verlag. Memoir.

Edelson, J. (1983). Freud's use of metaphor. *Psychoanalytic Study of the Child* 38:17–59.

Eissler, K. R. (1953). The effect of the structure of the ego on psychoanalytic technique. *Journal of the American Psychoanalytic Association* 1:104–143.

Eizirik, C. L. (2007). On the therapeutic action of psychoanalysis. *Psychoanalytic Quarterly* 76 (Suppl.):1463–1478.

Ellenberger, H. F. (1970). *The Discovery of the Unconscious*. New York: Basic Books.

Engel, G. L. (1975). Death of a twin: Mourning and anniversary reactions. Fragments of a 10-year analysis. *International Journal of Psycho-Analysis* 56:23–40.

Erickson, M. H., and Kubie, L. S. (1939). The permanent relief of an obsessional phobia by means of communications with an unsuspected dual personality. *Psychoanalytic Quarterly* 8:471–509.

Eshel, O. (1998). 'Black holes,' deadness and existing analytically. *International Journal of Psychoanalysis* 79:1115–1130.

Estabrooks, G. H. (1945). Hypnotism in warfare. In *Hypnotism*. New York: E. P. Dutton, pp. 185–205.

Faimberg, H. (1988). The telescoping of generations. *Contemporary Psychoanalysis* 23:99–118.

Fairbairn, W. R. D. (1940). Schizoid factors in the personality. In *Psychoanalytic Studies of the Personality*. London: Routledge/KeganPaul, 1952, pp. 3–27.

———. (1952). *An Object-Relations Theory of the Personality*. New York: Basic Books.

Federn, P. (1952). *Ego Psychology and the Psychoses*, ed. E. Weiss. New York: Basic Books.

Fenichel, O. (1945). *The Psychoanalytic Theory of Neurosis*. New York: W. W. Norton.

Ferenczi, S. (1927). The problem of termination of the analysis. In *Final Contributions to the Problems and Methods of Psychoanalysis*, ed. M. Balint. New York: Basic Books, 1955, pp. 77–86.

———. (1929). The unwelcome child and his death instinct. In *Final Contributions to the Problems and Methods of Psychoanalysis*, ed. M. Balint, pp. 102–107. New York: Basic Books, 1955.

———. (1933). Confusion of tongues between the adult and the child. In *Final Contribution to the Problem and Methods of Psychoanalysis*. New York: Basic Books, pp. 155–167.

Firestein, S. K. (1978). *Termination in Psychoanalysis*. New York: International Universities Press.

Fliess, R. (1953). The hypnotic evasion: A clinical observation. *Psychoanalytic Quarterly* 22:497–516.

Fogel, G. I. (2006). Riddles of masculinity: Gender, bisexuality, and thirdness. *Journal of the American Psychoanalytic Association* 54:1139–1163.

Fonagy, P. (1991). Thinking about thinking: Some clinical and theoretical considerations. *International Journal of Psycho-Analysis* 72:1–18.

Fonagy, P., and Target, M. (1996). Playing with reality: Theory of mind and the normal development of psychic reality. *International Journal of Psycho-Analysis* 77:217–233.

Fraiberg, S. (1982). Pathological defenses in infancy. *Psychoanalytic Quarterly* 51:612–635.

Fraser, J. T. (1975). *Of Time, Passion, and Knowledge—Reflections on the Strategy of Existence*. New York: George Braziller.

Frawley-O'Dea, M. G. (2003). When the trauma is terrorism and the therapist is traumatized too: Working as an analyst since 9/11. *Psychoanalytic Perspectives* 1:67–89.

Freud, A. (1936). The ego and the mechanisms of defense. In *Writings*, Vol. 2, New York: International Universities Press, 1966.

————. (1954). Problems of technique in adult analysis. In *Writings*, 4. New York: International Universities Press, 1968, pp. 377–406.

Freud, A. (1966). The Ego and the mechanisms of defence. *The Writings of Anna Freud Vol.II, 1936*. Revised edition. New York: International Universities Press.

————. (1968).

Freud, S. (1891). Hypnosis. *Standard Edition* 1:103–115.

————. (1895). Project for a scientific psychology. *Standard Edition* 1:295–343.

————. (1896). The aetiology of hysteria. *Standard Edition* 2:187–221.

————. (1900). The interpretation of dreams. *Standard Edition* 4–5:1–626.

————. (1901). The psychopathology of everyday life. *Standard Edition* 6:1–310.

————. (1905a). A fragment of an analysis of a case of hysteria. *Standard Edition* 7:1–122.

————. (1905b). Three essays on the theory of sexuality. *Standard Edition* 7:135–243.

————. (1910). Leonardo Da Vinci and a memory of his childhood. *Standard Edition* 11:57–138.

————. (1912a). The dynamics of transference. *Standard Edition* 12:97–108.

————. (1912b). Recommendations to physicians practicing psychoanalysis. *Standard Edition* 12:109–120.

————. (1913a). On beginning the treatment. *Standard Edition* 12:123–144.

————. (1913b). Totem and taboo: Some points of agreement between the mental lives of savages and neurotics. *Standard Edition* 13:vii–162.

————. (1914a). Remembering, repeating and working through. *Standard Edition* 12:145–156.

————. (1914b). On narcissism. *Standard Edition* 14:67–103.

————. (1914c). On the history of psycho-analytic movement. *Standard Edition* 14:7–66.

————. (1915). Thoughts for the times on war and death, *Standard Edition* 14.

————. (1916a). Some character types met with in psycho-analytic work. *Standard Edition* 14:310–333.

————. (1916b). Introductory lectures on psycho-analysis. *Standard Edition* 16:243–263.

————. (1917a). A childhood recollection. *Standard Edition* 17:145–157.

————. (1917b). A metapsychological supplement to the theory of dreams. *Standard Edition* 14:222–235.

————. (1917c). Mourning and melancholia. *Standard Edition* 14:237–260.

————. (1918). From the history of an infantile neurosis. *Standard Edition* 17:65–143.

————. (1920). Beyond the pleasure principle. *Standard Edition* 18:7–64.

————. (1921). Group psychology and the analysis of the ego. *Standard Edition* 18:65–143.

————. (1922). Some neurotic mechanisms in jealousy, paranoia and homosexuality. *Standard Edition* 18:221–233.

————. (1923). The ego and the id. *Standard Edition* 19:3–68.

————. (1924a). Neurosis and psychosis. *Standard Edition* 19:147–154.

————. (1924b). The loss of reality in neurosis and psychosis. *Standard Edition* 19:181–188.

————. (1925). Some psychical consequences of the anatomical differences between the sexes. *Standard Edition* 19, pp. 24–258.

————. (1926). Inhibitions, symptoms and anxiety. *Standard Edition* 20:77–174.

————. (1927). Fetishism. *Standard Edition* 21:149–157.

————. (1933a). New introductory lectures. *Standard Edition* 22:1–182.

————. (1933b). Why war? Standard Edition 22:195–216.

————. (1936). A disturbance of memory on the Acropolis. *Standard Edition* 22: 237–248.

————. (1937). Analysis terminable and interminable. *Standard Edition* 23:211–253.

————. (1939). Moses and Monotheism: Three Essays. *Standard Edition* 23:7–137.

————. (1940a). An outline of psychoanalysis. *Standard Edition* 23:139–207.

————. (1940b). Splitting of the ego in the process of defense. *Standard Edition* 23.

Friedman, L. (2007). Who needs theory of therapeutic action? *Psychoanalytic Quarterly* 76 (Suppl.):1635–1662.

Frischholz, E. J., Lipman, L. S., Braun, B. G., and Sachs, R. G. (1992). Psychopathology, hypnotizability, and dissociation. *American Journal of Clinical Hypnosis* 149: 1521–1525.

Fromm, E., and Nash, M. (1997). *Psychoanalysis and Hypnosis*. Madison, CT: International Universities Press.

Frosch, J. (1983). *The Psychotic Process*. New York: International Universities Press.

Gabbard, G. (2000). Disguise or consent? Problems and recommendations concerning the publication and presentation of clinical material. *International Journal of Psycho-Analysis* 81:1071–1086.

Gabbard, G., and Twemlow, S. W. (1984). The metapsychology of altered mind/body perception. In *With the Eyes of the Mind: An Empirical Analysis of Out-of-Body States*. New York: Praeger, pp. 169–183.

Galea, S., Ahern, J., Kilpatrick, D., Bucuvalas, M., Gold, J., and Vilanov, D. (2002). Psychological sequelae of the September 11 terrorist attacks in New York City. *New England Journal of Medicine* 346:982–987.

Gaskill, H. S. (1980). The closing phase of the psychoanalytic treatment of adults and the goals of psychoanalysis: The myth of perfectibility. *International Journal of Psycho-Analysis*. 61:11–23.

Gensler, D. (2002). In voices from New York. *Contemporary Psychoanalysis* 38:77–81.

Gerson, S. (2000). Therapeutic action of writing about patients: Commentary on papers by Lewis Aron and Stuart A. Pizer. *Psychoanalytic Dialogues* 10:261–266.

Gifford, S. (1960). Sleep, time, and the early ego. *Journal of the American Psychoanalytic Association* 8:5–42.

Gilbertson, M. W., Swenton, M. E., Ciszewski, A., Kasal, K., Laso, M. B., Orr, S. P., and Pitman, R. K. (2002). Smaller hippocampal volume predicts pathological vulnerability to psychological trauma. *Nature Neuroscience* 5:1242–1247.

Glick, B. (1966). Freud, the problem of quality and the "Secretory Neuron." *Psychoanalytic Quarterly* 35:84–97.

Glover, E. (1943). The concept of dissociation. *International Journal of Psycho-Analysis* 24:7–13.

————. (1955). *The Technique of Psychoanalysis*. New York: International Universities Press.

Goldberg, A. (1997). Writing case histories. *International Journal of Psycho-Analysis* 78:435–438.

———. (2007). Pity the poor pluralist. *Psychoanalytic Quarterly* 76 (Suppl.):1663–1674.

Goldberg, A., and Marcus, D. (1985). Natural termination: Ending analysis without setting a date. *Psychoanalytic Quarterly* 54:46–65.

Goldman, D. (2002). In voices from New York. *Contemporary Psychoanalysis* 38:77–81.

Gordon, R. M. (2002). In voices from New York. *Contemporary Psychoanalysis* 38:95–99.

Gottesman, I. I. and Shields, J. (1972). *Schizophrenia and Genetics—A Twin Study Vantage Point.* New York: Academic Press.

Greaves, G. B. (1980). Multiple personality—165 years after Mary Reynolds. *Journal of Nervous and Mental Disease* 168:577–596.

———. (1993). A history of multiple personality disorder. In *Clinical Perspectives on Multiple Personality Disorder,* ed. R. P. Kluft and C. G. Fine. Washington, DC: American Psychiatric Press, pp. 335–380.

Greenberg, J. (2007). Therapeutic action—Convergence without consensus. *Psychoanalytic Quarterly* 76 (Suppl.):1675–1688.

Greene, B. (1999). *The Elegant Universe—Superstrings, Hidden Dimensions and the Quest for the Ultimate Theory.* New York: W. W. Norton.

Greenson, R. R. (1967). *The Technique and Practice of Psychoanalysis.* New York: International Universities Press.

———. (1968). Disidentifying from mother: Its special importance for the boy. *International Journal of Psycho–Analysis* 49:370–374.

———. (1974). The decline and fall of the 50 minute hour. *Journal of the American Psychoanalytic Association* 22:785–791.

Grossman, D. (1995). *On Killing: The Psychological Cost of Learning to Kill in War and Society.* New York: Little, Brown.

Grotstein, J. (1928). Inner space: Its dimensions and coordinates. *International Journal of Psycho-Analysis* 59:55–61.

———. (1984). A proposed revision of the psychoanalytic concept of the death instinct. In *The Yearbook of Psychoanalysis and Psychotherapy.* ed. R. J. Langs. New York: Gardner Press, pp. 299–326.

———. (1990). The "black hole" as the basic psychotic experience. *Journal of the American Academy of Psychoanalysis* 18:29–46.

Grubrich-Simitis, I. (1981). Extreme traumatization as cumulative trauma: Psychoanalytic investigation of the effects of concentration camp experiences on survivors and their children. *Psychoanalytic Study of the Child* 36:415–450.

———. (1984). From concretism to metaphor—Children of Holocaust survivors. *Psychoanalytic Study of the Child* 39:301–319.

Gruenwald, D. (1977). Multiple personality and splitting phenomena: A reconceptualization. *Journal of Nervous and Mental Disease* 164:385–393.

Gullestad, E. S. (2005). Who is "Who" in dissociation? *International Journal of Psycho-Analysis* 86:639–656.

Guntrip, H. (1969). *Schizoid Phenomena, Object Relations, and the Self.* New York: International Universities Press.

Gurvits, T. Y., Swenton, M. E., Hokama, H., Owta, H., Lasko, N. B., Gilbertson, M. W., Orr, S. P., Kikinis, R., Jolescz, F. A., McCanley, R. W., and Pitman, R. K. (1996). Magnetic resonance imaging study of hippocampal volume in chronic, limbat-related post-traumatic stress disorder. *Biological Psychiatry* 40:1091–1099.

Halgren, E., and Marinkovic, K. (1995). Neurophysiological networks integrating human emotion. In *The Cognitive Neurosciences*, ed. M. S. Gazzaniga. Cambridge: MIT Press, pp. 1137–1152.

Harris, A. (2005). *Gender as Soft Assembly*. Hillsdale, NJ: Analytic Press.

Hart, K. (1981). *Return to Auschwitz: The Remarkable Life of a Girl Who Survived the Holocaust*. Saddle Brook, NJ: American Book-Stratford Press.

Hartmann, H. (1939). *Ego Psychology and the Problem of Adaptation*, trans. D. Rapaport. New York: International Universities Press, 1958

Hartocollis, P. (1972). Time as a dimension of affects. *Journal of the American Psychoanalytic Association* 20:92–108.

———. (1976). On the experience of time and its dynamics: Reference to affects. *Journal of the American Psychoanalytic Association* 24:363–375.

———. (1978). Time and affects in borderline disorders. *International Journal of Psycho-Analysis* 59:157–163.

Hawking, S. (1988). *A Brief History of Time*. New York: Bantam Books.

Henry, J. P., Liu, Y. Y., Nadra, W. E., Qian, C. G., Mormede, P., Lemaire, V., Ely, D., and Hendley, E. D. (1993). Psychosocial stress can induce chronic *Hypertension* in normotensive strains of rats. *Hypertension* 21:714–723.

Herman, J. L. (1992). *Trauma and Recovery*. New York: Basic Books.

Hersh, S. M. (2007). Annals of national security—The general's report. *The New Yorker*, June 25, 2007, pp. 58–69.

Herzog, J. M. (1982). World beyond metaphor: Thoughts on the transmission of trauma. In *Generations of the Holocaust*, ed. M. S. Bergmann and M. E. Jucovy, pp. 103–119. New York: Basic Books.

———. (2001). *Father Hunger: Explorations with Adults and Children*. Hillsdale, NJ: Analytic Press.

Hesse, E., and Main, M. (1999). Second generation effects of unresolved trauma in nonmaltreating patients: Dissociated, frightened, and threatening parental behavior. *Psychoanalytic Inquiry* 19:481–540.

Hilgard, E. R. (1986). *Divided Consciousness: Multiple Controls in Human Thought and Action*. New York: Wiley.

Hinshelwood, R. D. (2007). The Kleinian theory of therapeutic action. *Psychoanalytic Quarterly* 76 (Suppl.):1479–1498.

Hitchens, C. (2007). *God Is Not Great: How Religion Poisons Everything*. New York: Twelve.

Hoffman, I. (1995). The patient as interpreter of the analyst's experience. *Psychoanalytic Dialogues* 19:389–422.

Horney, K. (1924). On the genesis of the castration complex in woman. *International Journal of Psycho-Analysis* 5:50–65.

———. (1926). The flight from womanhood. *International Journal of Psycho-Analysis* 7:324–339.

———. (1932). The dread of women: Observations on a specific difference in the dread felt by men and women respectively for the opposite sex. *International Journal of Psycho-Analysis* 13:348–360.

Howell, E. F. (2005). *The Dissociative Mind*. Hillsdale, NJ: Analytic Press, Inc.

Hurvich, M. (1989). Traumatic moment, basic dangers and annihilation anxiety. *Psychoanalytic Psychology* 6:309–323.

————. (2003). The place of annihilation anxieties in psychoanalytic theory. *Journal of the American Psychoanalytic Association* 51:579–616.

Inderbitzin, L., and Levy, S. (1994). External reality as a defense. *Journal of the American Psychoanalytic Association* 42:763–788.

Jacobs, T. (1986). On countertransference enactments. *Journal of the American Psychoanalytic Association* 34:289–307.

Jacobs, T. J. (1990). The corrective emotional experience: Place in current technique. *Psychoanalytic Inquiry* 10:433–454.

Jacobson, E. (1957). Normal and pathological moods. *Psychoanalytic Study of the Child* 12:73–113.

————. (1959). The "exceptions"? An elaboration of Freud's character study. *Psychoanalytic Study of the Child* 14:135–153.

————. (1964). *The Self and the Object World.* New York: International Universities Press.

Jacobovitz, D., Hazen, N., and Riggs, S. (1997). Disorganized mental processes in mothers, frightening/frightened caregiving and disoriented/disorganized behavior in infancy. Paper presented at symposium, Caregiving Correlates and Longitudinal Outcomes of Disorganized Attachments in Infants, Biennial Meeting of the Society for Research in Child Development. Washington, D.C.

James, W. (1890). *The Principles of Psychology.* New York: Dover, 1950.

Janet, P. (1889). *L'Automatisme Psychologique.* Paris: Baillière.

Jones, E. (1907). *The Major Symptoms of Hysteria.* New York: Macmillan.

————. (1927). The early development of female sexuality. In *Papers on Psychoanalysis.* London: Ballière, Tindall, and Cox, 1948, pp. 438–451.

————. (1929). Fear, guilt and hate. *International Journal of Psycho-Analysis* 10: 383–397.

————. (1933). The phallic phase. In *Papers on Psychoanalysis.* London: Ballière, Tindall, and Cox, 1948, pp. 452–484.

————. (1953). *The Life and Work of Sigmund Freud,* vol. 1. New York: Basic Books.

Josephs, L. (1995). *Balancing Empathy and Interpretation: Relational Character Analysis.* Northvale, NJ: Jason Aronson.

Jung, C. G. (1902). *Zur Psychologie und Pathologie sogenannter okkulter Phänomene.* Leipzig: Mutze.

Ka-Tzetnik 135633. (1989). *Shiviti—A Vision.* San Francisco, CA: Harper & Row.

Kafka, J. (1972). The experience of time. *Journal of the American Psychoanalytic Association* 20:650

Kantrowitz, J. L. (2004a). Writing about patients, I: Analysts' ways of protecting confidentiality and analysts' conflicts over choice of method. *Journal of the American Psychoanalytic Association* 52:69–99.

————. (2004b). Writing about patients, II: Patients reading about themselves and their analysts' perceptions of its effect. *Journal of the American Psychoanalytic Association* 52:101–123.

————. (2005a). Patients reading about themselves—A stimulus to psychoanalytic work. *Psychoanalytic Quarterly* 74:365–395.

————. (2005b). Writing about patients, III: Comparisons of attitudes and practices of analysts residing outside of and within the United States. *International Journal of Psycho-Analysis* 85:3–22.

———. (2005c). Writing about patients, IV: Patients' reactions to reading about themselves. *Journal of the American Psychoanalytic Association* 53:103–130.

———. (2005d). Writing about patients, V: Analysts reading about themselves as patients. *Journal of the American Psychoanalytic Association* 53:131–153.

Katan, A. (1961). Some thoughts about the role of verbalization in early childhood. *Psychoanalytic Study of the Child* 16:184–188. New York: International Universities Press.

Kelman, H. (1975). Metapsychological analysis of a parapraxis. *Journal of the American Psychoanalytic Association* 23:555–568.

Kendler, K. S., Gruenberg, A. M., and Strauss, J. S. (1982). An independent analysis of the Copenhagen sample of the Danish adoption study of schizophrenia, V: The relationship between childhood social withdrawal and adult schizophrenia. *Archives of General Psychiatry* 39:1257–1261.

Kernberg, O. F. (1973). Discussion of presentation by F. Coplan and E. Berman In S. Bauer (Chm.). *Multiple Personality—A Reevaluation.* Symposium at the Annual Meeting of the American Psychiatric Association, Honolulu, Hawaii.

———. (1975). *Borderline Conditions and Pathological Narcissism.* New York: Aronson.

———. (1991). Transference regression and psychoanalytic technique with infantile personalities. *International Journal of Psycho-Analysis* 72:189–200.

———. (2007). The therapeutic action of psychoanalysis: Controversies and challenges. *Psychoanalytic Quarterly* 76 (Suppl.):1689–1723.

Kestenberg, J. S. (1980). Psychoanalyses of children of survivors from the Holocaust—Case presentations and assessment. *Journal of the American Psychoanalytic Association* 28:775–804.

———. (1982). A metapsychological assessment based on an analysis of a survivor's child. In *Generations of the Holocaust.* eds. M. S. Bergmann and M. E. Jucovy. New York: Basic Books, Inc., pp. 137–158.

Kestenberg, J., and Brenner, I. (1986). Children who survived the Holocaust. *International Journal of Psycho-Analysis* 67:309–316.

———. (1995). Narcissism in the service of survival. In *The Vulnerable Child,* Vol. 2, eds. T. Cohen, M. H. Etezady, and B. Pacella. Madison, CT: International Universities Press, pp. 35–50.

———. (1996). *The Last Witness: The Child Survivor of the Holocaust.* Washington, DC: American Psychiatric Publishing, Inc.

Kestenberg, J., and Gampel, Y. (1983). Growing up in the Holocaust culture. *Israel Journal of Psychiatry and Related Sciences* 29:129–146.

Kestenberg, M., and Kestenberg, J. S. (1988). The sense of belonging and altruism in children who survived the Holocaust. *Psychoanalytic Review* 75:533–560.

Khan, M. M. (1963). The concept of cumulative trauma. *Psychoanalytic Study of the Child* 18:286–306.

Kinston, W., and Cohen J. (1986). Primal repression: Clinical and theoretical aspects. *International Journal of Psycho-Analysis* 67:337–355.

Kirschner, L. (2005). Rethinking desire: The "object petit A" in Lacanian theory. *Journal of the American Psychoanalytic Association* 53:83.

Klauber, J. (1972). On the relationship of transference and interpretation in psychoanalytic therapy. *International Journal of Psycho-Analysis* 53:385–392.

Klein, M. (1921). The development of a child. In *Love, Guilt and Reparation: And*

Other Works, 1921–1945. New York: Delacorte Press, 1975, pp. 1–53.

————. (1928). Early stages: The Oedipus complex. *International Journal of Psycho-Analysis* 9:168–180.

————. (1935). A contribution to the psychogenesis of manic-depressive states. In *Love, Guilt and Reparation: And Other Works, 1921–1945.* New York: Delacorte Press, 1975, pp. 262–289.

————. (1940). Mourning and its relation to the manic-depressive states. In *Love, Guilt and Reparation: And Other Works, 1921–1945.* New York: Free Press, 1975, pp. 344–369.

Kluft, R. P. (1984). Treatment of multiple personality: A study of 33 cases. *Psychiatric Clinics of North America* 7:9–29.

————. (1986a). Personality unification in multiple personality disorder: A follow-up study. In *Treatment of Multiple Personality Disorder,* ed. B. G. Braun. Washington, DC: American Psychiatric Press, pp. 29–60.

————. (1986b). High-functioning multiple personality patients: Three cases. *Journal of Nervous and Mental Disease* 174:722–726.

————. (1987). First rank symptoms as a diagnostic clue to multiple personality disorder. *American Journal of Psychiatry* 144:293–298.

Kogan, I. (1995). *The Cry of Mute Children.* London: Free Association Books.

Kohut, H. (1971). *The Analysis of the Self.* New York: International Universities Press.

————. (1977). *The Restoration of the Self.* New York: International Universities Press.

Kraemer, F. W. (1992). A psychobiological theory of attachment. *Brain and Behavioral Sciences* 15:493–541.

Kramer, S. (1987). A contribution to the concept "the exception" as a developmental phenomenon. *Child Abuse and Neglect* 11:367–370.

————. (1993). Personal communication.

Kris, A. O. (1976). On wanting too much: the "exceptions" revisited. *International Journal of Psycho-Analysis* 57:85–95.

Kris, E. (1956). The recovery of childhood memories in psychoanalysis. *Psychoanalytic Study of the Child* 11:54–88.

Krystal, H. (1968). *Massive Psychic Trauma.* New York: International Universities Press.

————. (1988). *Integration and Self Healing.* Hillsdale, NJ: Analytic Press.

————. (1997). The trauma of confronting one's vulnerability and death. In *Omnipotent Fantasies and the Vulnerable Self,* ed. C. Ellman and J. Reppen. Northvale, NJ: Jason Aronson, pp. 117–138.

————. (2003). Resilience. Presented at the Margaret Mahler Symposium, Philadelphia, PA, May 3, 2003.

Kumin, I. (1997). *Preobject Relatedness: Early Attachment and the Psychodynamic Situation.* New York: Guilford Press.

Kurtz, S. A. (1988). The psychoanalysis of time. *Journal of the American Psychoanalytic Association* 36:985–1004.

LaFarge, L. (2000). Interpretation and containment. *International Journal of Psycho-Analysis* 81:67–84.

Lander, R. (2007). The mechanisms of cure in psychoanalysis. *Psychoanalytic Quarterly* 76 (Suppl.):1499–1512.

Laplanche, J. (1976). *Life and Death in Psychoanalysis.* Baltimore: Johns Hopkins University Press.

Laskey, R. (1978). The psychoanalytic treatment of a case of multiple personality. *Psychoanalytic Review* 65:353–380.

Laub, D. (2002). Personal communication.

Laub, D., and Auerhahn, N. (1993). Knowing and not knowing massive psychic trauma: Forms of traumatic memory. *International Journal of Psycho-Analysis* 74: 287–302.

Le Doux, J. (1989). Cognitive-emotional interactions in the brain. *Cognition and Emotion* 3:267–289.

———. (1995). Emotion: Clues from the brain. *Annual Review of Psychology* 46:209–235.

Levine, H. B. (1982). Toward a psychoanalytic understanding of children of survivors of the holocaust. *Psychoanalysis Quarterly* 51:70–92.

Levine, H. B. (ed.) (1990). *Adult Analysis and Childhood Sexual Abuse.* Hillsdale, NJ: Analytic Press.

Lichtenstein, H. (1964). The malignant no: Instinctual drives and the sense of self. In *The Dilemma of Human Identity.* New York: Aronson, 1977, pp. 293–322.

Lifton, R. J. (1986). *The Nazi Doctors.* New York: Basic Books.

Lim, K. O. (2007). Connections in schizophrenia. *American Journal of Psychiatry* 164: 7, pp. 995–998.

Liotti, G. (1992). Disorganized/disoriented attachment in the etiology of the dissociative disorders. *Dissociation* 4:196–204.

Lipton, E. L. (1991). The analyst's use of clinical data and other issues of confidentiality. *Journal of the American Psychoanalytic Association* 39:967–985.

Lipton, S. (1961). The last hour. *Journal of the American Psychoanalytic Association* 9:325–330.

Little, M. (1960). On basic unity (primary total undifferentiatedness). In *Transference Neurosis and Transference Psychosis: Toward Basic Unity.* New York: Aronson, 1981, pp. 88–91.

Loewald, E. L. (1987). Therapeutic play in space and time. *Psychoanalytic Study of the Child* 42:173–192.

Loewald, H. W. (1960). On the therapeutic action of psycho-analysis. *International Journal of Psycho-Analysis* 41:16–33.

———. (1962). The superego and the ego-ideal. *International Journal of Psycho-Analysis* 43:264–268.

———. (1972). The experience of time. *Psychoanalytic Study of the Child* 27:401–410.

Loomis, C. J. (1998). Everything in history was against them. *Fortune,* April 13, pp. 66–84.

Lyons-Ruth, K. (1999). The two-person unconscious: Intersubjective dialogue, enactive relational representation and the emergence of new forms of relational organization. *Psychoanalytic Inquiry* 19:576–617.

———. (2003). Dissociation and the parent-infant dialogue: A longitudinal perspective from attachment research. *Journal of the American Psychoanalytic Association* 51:883–911.

Lyons-Ruth, K., Bronfman, E., and Parsons, E. (1999). Maternal disrupted affective communication, maternal frightened or frightening behavior, and disorganized infant attachment strategies. In *Atypical Patterns of Infant Attachment: Theory, Research, and Current Directions*, ed. J. Vondra and D. Barnett. Monographs of the Society for Research in Child Development (Serial No. 258), pp. 67–96.

Lyons-Ruth, K., and Jacobovitz, D. (1999). Attachment disorganization: Unresolved loss, relational violence, and lapses in behavioral and attentional strategies. In *Handbook of Attachment: Theory, Research, and Clinical Applications*, ed. J. Cassidy and P. Shaver. New York: Guilford Press, pp. 520–544.

Mahler, M. (1952). On child psychosis and schizophrenic-autistic and symbiotic infantile psychoses. *Psychoanalytic Study of the Child* 7:286–305.

Mahler, M., Bergman, A., and Pine, F. (1975). *The Psychological Birth of the Human Infant*. New York: Basic Books.

Mahler, M., and Furer, M. (1968). *On Human Symbiosis and the Vicissitudes of Individuation*. New York: International Universities Press.

Main, M. (1993). Discourse, prediction and recent studies in attachment: Implications for psychoanalysis. *Journal of the American Psychoanalytic Association* 41 (Suppl.):209–243.

Main, M., and Hesse, E. (1990). Parents' unresolved traumatic experiences are related to infant disorganized status: Is parental frightened or frightening behavior in the linking mechanism? In *Attachment in the Preschool Years: Theory, Research, and Intervention*, ed. M. Greenberg, D. Cicchetti, and E. M. Cummings. Chicago: University of Chicago Press, pp. 161–184.

Main, M., and Solomon, J. (1990). Procedures for identifying infants as disorganized/disoriented during the Ainsworth Stranger Situation. In *Attachment in the Pre-School Years: Theory, Research, and Intervention*, ed. M. Greenberg, D. Cicchetti, and E. M. Cummings. Chicago: University of Chicago Press, pp. 121–160.

Marmer, S. S. (1980). Psychoanalysis of multiple personality. *International Journal of Psycho-Analysis* 61:439–459.

Marrus, M. R. (1987). *The Holocaust in History*. New York: Meridian.

Matte-Blanco, I. (1988). *Thinking, Feeling and Being*. London: Routledge.

McDougall, J. (1972). Primal scene and sexual perversion. *International Journal of Psycho-Analysis* 53:371–384.

———. (1982). *Plea for a Measure of Abnormality*. New York: International Universities Press.

———. (1995). *The Many Faces of Eros*. New York: Norton.

McDougall, W. (1926). *An Outline of Abnormal Psychology*. London: Methuen.

McLuhan, M. (1964). *Understanding Media: The Extension of Man*. New York: McGraw-Hill.

McWilliams, N. (1994). Dissociative personalities. In *Psychoanalytic Diagnoses*. New York: Guilford Press, pp. 502–540.

Meissner, S. J. (2005). Gender identity and the self: I. Gender formation in general and in masculinity. *Psychoanalytic Review* 92:1–29.

Meissner, W. W. (1985). Psychoanalysis: The dilemma of science and humanism. *Psychoanalytic Inquiry* 5:471–498.

Meltzer, D. (1975). Adhesive identification. *Contemporary Psychoanalysis* 11:289–310.

Michels, R. (2007). The theory of therapeutic action. *Psychoanalytic Quarterly* 76 (Suppl.):1725–1733.

Miczeck, K. A., Thompson, M. L., and Tornatzky, W. (1990). Subordinate animals: Behavioral and physiological adaptation and opioid tolerance. In *Stress: Neurobiology and Neuroendocrinology*, ed. M. R. Brown, G. F. Koob, and C. Rivier. New York: Marcel Dekker, pp. 323–357.

Miller, J. P. (1990). The corrective emotional experience: Reflections in retrospect. *Psychoanalytic Inquiry* 10:373–388.

Mintz, I. (1971). The anniversary reaction: A response to unconscious sense of time. *Journal of the American Psychoanalytic Association* 19:720–735.

———. (1975). Parapraxis and the mother-child relationship. *Psychoanalytic Quarterly* 44:460–461.

Mitchell, S. (1993). *Hope and Dread in Psychoanalysis*. New York: Basic Books.

Modell, A. H. (1990). *Other Times, Other Realities: Toward a Theory of Psychoanalytic Treatment*. Cambridge, MA: Harvard University Press.

Money-Kyrle, R. E. (1968). Cognitive development. *International Journal of Psycho-Analysis* 49:691–698.

Moran, M. (2008). Independent report spotlights war's MH devastation. *Philadelphia News*, 43, #10, May 16, 2008, pp. 1, 24.

Morgan, C. A., Southwick, G., Hazlett, G., Rasmussen, A., Hoyt, G., Zimolo, Z., and Charney, D. (2004). Dissociation in military training. *Archives of General Psychiatry* 820–825.

Moss, D. (2006). Masculinity as masquerade. *Journal of the American Psychoanalytic Association* 54:1187–1194.

Newman, K. (2007). Therapeutic action in self psychology. *Psychoanalytic Quarterly* 76 (Suppl.):1513–1546.

Nunberg, H. (1955). *Principles of Psychoanalysis*. New York: International Universities Press.

Ogawa, J. R., Srolfe, L., Weinfield, N. S., Carlson, E. A., and Egeland, B. (1997). Development and the fragmented self: Longitudinal study of dissociative symptomatology in a nonclinical sample. *Development and Psychopathology* 9: 855–879.

Ogden, T. H. (1985). On potential space. *International Journal of Psycho-Analysis* 66:129–141.

———. (1986). *The Matrix of the Mind*. Northvale, NJ/London: Aronson.

———. (1989). *The Primitive Edge of Experience*. New York: Aronson.

———. (1994). The analytic third: Working with intersubjective clinical facts. *International Journal of Psycho-Analysis* 75:3–20.

Oliver, M. (2000). In memoriam—Sigi Ziering: survived Nazi camps. *American Gathering of Jewish Holocaust Survivors* 15:20.

Orgel, S. (1965). On time and timelessness. *Journal of the American Psychoanalytic Association* 13:102–121.

Orne, M. T., Dinges, D. F., and Orne, E. C. (1984). The differential diagnosis of multiple personality disorder in the forensic context. *International Journal of Clinical Experimental Hypnosis* 32:118–167.

Ornstein, P. W. (1997). Omnipotence in health and illness. In *Omnipotent Fantasies and the Vulnerable Self*, ed. C. Ellman and J. Reppen. Northvale, NJ: Jason Aronson, Inc., pp. 117–138.

Oxnam, R. B. (2005). *A Fractured Mind: My Life with Multiple Personality*. New York: Hyperion.

Paniagua, C. (2002). A terminating case. *International Journal of Psycho-Analysis* 83:179–187.

Pao, P.-N. (1979). *Schizophrenic Disorders.* New York: International Universities Press.

Parens, H. (2004). *Renewal of Life: Healing from the Holocaust.* Rockville, MD: Schreiber Publishing.

———. (2005). Personal communication.

Parker, K. J., Buckmaster, C. L., Schatzberg, A. F., and Lyons, D. M. (2004). Prospective investigation of stress inoculation in young monkeys. *Archives of General Psychiatry* 61:933–941.

PDM Task Force (2006). *Psychodynamic Diagnostic Manual.* Silver Spring, MD: Alliance of Psychoanalytic Organizations.

Perry, B. D. (2001). The neurodevelopmental impact of violence in childhood. In *Textbook of Child and Adolescent Forensic Psychiatry,* ed. D. Schetky and E. P. Benedek. Washington, DC: American Psychiatric Press, Inc., pp. 221–238.

Person, E. S. (2006). Masculinities, plural. *Journal of the American Psychoanalytic Association* 54:1165–1186.

Piaget, J. (1955). *The Child's Construction of Reality,* trans. M. Cooke. London: Routledge and Kegan Paul.

Piccioli, E. (ed.) (1996). *Writing in Psychoanalysis.* Hillsdale, NJ: Analytic Press.

Pine, F. (1992). Some refinements of the separation individuation concept in light of research on infants. *Psychoanalytic Study of the Child* 47:103–116.

Pizer, S. A. (2000). A gift in return: The clinical use of writing about a patient. *Psychoanalytic Dialogues* 10:247–259.

Poland, W. S. (1992). Non analytic surface to analytic space. *Journal of the American Psychoanalytic Association.* 40:381-404.

Pollin, W., and Stabenau, J. R. (1968). Biological, psychological, and historical differences in a series of monozygotic twins discordant for schizophrenia. In *The Transmission of Schizophrenia,* ed. D. Rosenthal and S. S. Kety. New York: Pergamon Press, pp. 317–322.

Pollock, G. H. (1970). Anniversary reactions, trauma, and mourning. *Psychoanalytic Quarterly* 39:347–371.

Prince, R. (2002). In voices from New York. *Contemporary Psychoanalysis* 38:89–95.

Purcell, S. D. (2006). The analyst's excitement in the analysis of perversion. *International Journal of Psycho-Analysis* 87:105–124.

Putnam, F. (1989). *Diagnosis and Treatment of Multiple Personality Disorder.* New York: Guilford.

Quinodoz, D. (1998). A female transsexual patient in psychoanalysis. *International Journal of Psycho-Analysis* 79:95–111.

Rachman, A. W. (1997). The suppression and censorship of Ferenczi's "Confusion of Tongues" paper. *Psychoanalytic Inquiry* 17:459–485.

Reis, B. (1995). Time as the missing dimension in traumatic memory and dissociation subjectivity. In *Sexual Abuse Recalled—Treating Trauma in the Era of the Recovered Memory Debate,* ed. J. L. Alpert. Northvale, NJ: Jason Aronson, Inc., pp. 215–233.

Renik, O. (2007). Intersubjectivity, therapeutic action and analytic technique. *Psychoanalytic Quarterly* 76 (Suppl.):1547–1562.

Resnik, S. (1995). *Mental Space.* London: Karnac Books.

Rizzuto, A. (2001). Metaphors of a bodily mind. *Journal of the American Psychoanalytic Association* 49:535–568.

Rosenbach, N. (2002). In voices from New York. *Contemporary Psychoanalysis* 38:81–83.

Rosenbaum, M. (1980). The role of the term schizophrenia in the decline of the diagnosis of multiple personality. *Archives of General Psychiatry* 37:1383–1385.

Rosenberg, D. (2007). Rethinking Gender. *Newsweek*, May 21, 2007, pp. 50–57.

Rosenfeld, D. (1992). *The Psychotic Aspects of Personality.* London: Karnac Books.

Rosenfeld, H. A. (1965). *Psychotic States: A Psychoanalytic Approach.* London: Hogarth Press.

Ross, C. (1989). *Multiple Personality Disorder, Diagnosis, Clinical Features, and Treatment.* New York: Wiley.

Ross, D. R., and Loewenstein, R. J. (1992). Multiple personality and psychoanalysis: An introduction. Perspectives on multiple personality. *Psychoanalytic Inquiry* 12: 3–48.

Ross, J. M. (1992). *The Male Paradox.* New York: Simon & Schuster.

Salisbury, D. F., Kuroki, N., Kasai, K., Shenton, M. E., and McCarley, R. W. (2007). Progressive and interrelated functional and structural evidence of post-onset brain recovery in schizophrenia. *Archives of General Psychiatry*, 64:5, pp. 521–529.

Sandler, J. (1960). The background of safety. In *From Safety to Superego: Selected Papers.* New York: Guildford Press, 1987, pp. 1–8.

————. (1986). Comments on the self and its objects. In *Self and Object Constancy: Clinical and Theoretical Perspectives*, ed. R. F. Lax, S. Bach, and J. A. Burland. NY: Guilford Press, pp. 97–106.

Sass, L. A. (1985). Time, space, symbol: Narrative form, representational structure. *Psychoanalytic Contemporary Thought* 8:45–85.

Sayers, J. (2002). Mysticism and psychoanalysis: The case of Marian Milner. *International Journal of Psycho-Analysis* 83:105–120.

Schafer, R. (1983). *The Analytic Aptitude.* New York: Basic Books.

Schiffer, I. (1978). *The Trauma of Time—A Psychoanalytic Investigation.* New York: International Universities Press.

Schilder, P. (1935). The psychoanalysis of space. *International Journal of Psycho-Analysis* 59:55.

Schore, A. N. (1994). *Affect Regulation and the Origin of the Self: Neurobiology of Emotional Development.* Hillsdale, NJ: Erlbaum.

Schur, M. (1953). The ego in anxiety. In *Drives, Affects and Behavior*, ed. R. M. Loewenstein. New York: International Universities Press, pp. 67–103.

Schuster, M. (2001). A national survey of stress reactions after September 11, 2001, terrorist attacks. *New England Journal of Medicine* 345:1507–1512.

Schwengel, C., Bakermans-Kronenberg, M., and Van Ijzendoorn, M. (1999). Frightening maternal behavior linking unresolved loss and disorganized infant attachment. *Journal of Consulting and Clinical Psychology* 67:54–63.

Shay, J. (1994). *Achilles in Vietnam: Combat Trauma and the Undoing of Character.* New York: Scribner.

Shay, J., Cleland, M., and McCain, J. (2002). *Odysseus in America: Combat Trauma and the Trials of Homecoming.* New York: Scribner.

Shengold, L. (1989). *Soul Murder: The Effect of Childhood Abuse and Deprivation.* New

Haven, CT: Yale University Press.

Silberer, H. (1909). Report on the method of eliciting and observing certain symbolic hallucination-phenomena. In *Organization and Pathology of Thought*, ed. D. Rappaport. New York: Columbia University Press, 1957, pp. 195–207.

Smith, H. F. (1995). Analytic listening and the experience of surprise. *International Journal of Psycho-Analysis* 76:76–78.

———. (2007). In search of a theory of therapeutic action. *Psychoanalytic Quarterly* 76 (Suppl.):1735–1761.

Solomon, Z., Kotler, M., and Mikulincer, M. (1988). Combat-related posttraumatic stress disorder among second generation Holocaust survivors: Preliminary findings. *American Journal of Psychiatry* 145:865–868.

Spangler, G., and Grossman, K. E. (1993). Biobehavioral organization in securely and insecurely attached infants. *Child Development* 64:1439–1450.

Spezzano, C. (2007). A home for the mind. *Psychoanalytic Quarterly* 76 (Suppl.): 1563–1583.

Spruiell, V. (1989). The future of psychoanalysis. *Psychoanalytic Quarterly* 58:1–28.

Stein, M. (1988). Writing about psychoanalysis. II. Analysts who write, patients who read. *Journal of the American Psychoanalytic Association* 36:393–428.

Stein, R. (1998). The poignant, the excessive and the enigmatic in sexuality. *International Journal of Psycho-Analysis* 79:259–268.

Stern, D. B. (1997). *Unformulated Experience: From Dissociation to Imagination in Psychoanalysis*. Hillsdale, NJ: Analytic Press.

Stern, D. N. (1985). *The Interpersonal World of the Infant: A View From Psychoanalysis and Developmental Psychology*. New York: International Universities Press.

Stern, D. N., Sander, L. W., Nahum, J. P., Harrison, A. M., Lyons-Ruth, K., Morgan, A. C., Bruschweiler-Stern, N., and Tronick, E. Z. (1998). Noninterpretive mechanisms in psychoanalytic therapy: The "something more" than interpretation. *International Journal of Psycho-Analysis* 79:903–921.

Stern, M. (1951). Anxiety, trauma and shock. *Psychoanalytic Quarterly* 20:179–203.

Stoller, R. J. (1965). The sense of maleness. *Psychoanalytic Quarterly* 34:207–218.

———. (1968). A further contribution to the study of gender identity. *International Journal of Psycho-Analysis* 49:364–368.

———. (1973a). *Splitting: A Case of Female Masculinity*. New York: Quadrangle.

———. (1973b). The male transsexual as "experiment." *International Journal of Psycho-Analysis* 54:215–225.

———. (1976). Primary femininity. *Journal of the American Psychoanalytic Association* 24 (Suppl.):59–78.

———. (1988). Patients' responses to their own case reports. *Journal of the American Psychoanalytic Association* 36:371–391.

Stone, L. (1954). The widening scope of indications for psychoanalysis. *Journal of the American Psychoanalytic Association* 2:567–594.

Strachey, J. (1934). The nature of the therapeutic action in psychoanalysis. *International Journal of Psycho-Analysis* 15:127–159.

Sullivan, H. S. (1953). *The Interpersonal Theory of Personality*. New York: Norton.

———. (1962). *Schizophrenia as a Human Process*. New York: W.W. Norton.

Szalai, A. (1934). "Infectious" parapraxes. *International Journal of Psycho-Analysis* 15:187–190.

Taniello, T. (2008). *Invisible Wounds of War: Psychological and Cognitive Injuries, Their Consequences and Services to Assist Recovery.* Santa Monica, CA: Rand Corp.

Taxman, J. (2004). Concurrent intervention during massive community trauma: An analyst's experience at Ground Zero. In *Analysts in the Trenches,* ed. B. Sklaren, S. W. Twemlow, and S. Wilkinson. Mahwah, NJ: Analytic Press.

Taylor, W. S., and Martin, M. F. (1944). Multiple personality. *Journal of Abnormal Social Psychology* 49:135–151.

Terr, L. L. (1984). Time and trauma. *Psychoanalytic Study of the Child* 39:633–665.

The New Shorter Oxford English Dictionary. (1993). ed. Lesley Brown. Oxford: Clarendon Press.

Ticho, E. (1972). Termination of psychoanalysis: Treatment goals, life goals. *Psychoanalytic Quarterly* 41:315–333.

Tuckett, D. (2000). Commentary on Robert Michel's "The Case History." *Journal of the American Psychoanalytic Association* 48:403–411.

Tustin, F. (1972). *Autism and Childhood Psychosis.* London: Hogarth Press.

———. (1981). Psychological birth and psychological catastrophe. In *Do I Dare Disturb the Universe? A Memorial to W. R. Bion,* ed. J. S. Grotstein. London: Karnac Books, pp. 181–196.

———. (1996). *Autistic Barriers in Neurotic Patients.* London: Karnac Books.

Tutte, J. L. (2004). The concept of psychical trauma: A bridge in interdisciplinary space. *International Journal of Psycho-Analysis* 85:897–922.

Twemlow, S. W. (1995). Traumatic object relations configurations seen in victim/victimizer relationships. *Journal of the American Academy of Psychoanalysis* 23:563–580.

———. (2000). The roots of violence: Converging psychoanalytic explanatory models for power struggles and violence in schools. *Psychoanalytic Quarterly* 69:741–785.

———. (2003). A crucible for murder: The social context of violent children and adolescents. *Psychoanalytic Quarterly* 72:659–698.

Viderman, S. (1974). Interpretation in the analytical space. *International Review of Psychoanalysis* 1:467–480.

Volkan, V. D. (1976). *Primitive Internalized Object Relations: A Clinical Study of Schizophrenic, Borderline and Narcissistic Patients.* New York: International Universities Press.

———. (1979). Transsexualism. In *On Sexuality: Psychoanalytic Observations,* ed. T. B. Karasu and C. W. Socarides. New York: International Universities Press.

———. (1981). *Linking Objects and Linking Phenomena.* New York: International Universities Press.

———. (1995a). *The Infantile Psychotic Self and Its Fates: Understanding and Treating Schizophrenic and Other Difficult Patients.* Northvale, NJ: Jason Aronson.

———. (1995b). Intergenerational transmission and "chosen" traumas: A link between the psychology of the individual and that of an ethnic group. In *Psychoanalysis at the Political Border: Essays in Honor of Rafael Moses,* ed. L. Rangull and R. Moses, pp. 251–276. Madison, CT: International Universities Press.

———. (1996). Bosnia-Herzegovina: Ancient fuel of a modern inferno. *Mind and Human Interaction* 7:116–127.

———. (2004). Cat people revisited. In *Mental Zoo: Animals in the Human Mind and Its Pathology*. Madison, CT: International Universities Press.

Volkan, V. D., and Akhtar, S. (eds.) (1997). *The Seed of Madness: Constitution, Environment and Fantasy in the Organization of the Psychotic Core*. Madison, CT: International Universities Press.

Volkan, V. D., and Ast, G. (2001). Curing Gitta's "leaking body": Actualized unconscious fantasies and therapeutic play. *Journal of Clinical Psychoanalysis* 10: 567–606.

Volkan, V. D., Ast, G., and Greer, W. F. (2002). *The Third Reich in the Unconscious*. New York: Brunner-Routledge.

Waelder, R. (1960). *Basic Theory of Psychoanalysis*. New York: International Universities Press.

Wallerstein, R. S. (1990). The corrective emotional experience: Is reconsideration due? *Psychoanalytic Inquiry* 10:288–324.

Watkins, J. G. (1992). *Hypnoanalytic Techniques: The Practice of Clinical Hypnosis*, vol. 2. New York: Irvington.

Watkins, J. G., and Watkins, W. H. (1979–1980). Ego states—hidden observers. *Journal of Altered States of Consciousness* 5:3–18.

———. (1997). *Ego States: Theory and Therapy*. New York: W. W. Norton & Co.

Weil, A. P. (1970). The basic core. *Psychoanalytic Study of the Child* 25:442

Weston, D. (1999). The scientific status of unconscious processes. *Journal of the American Psychoanalytic Association* 47:1061–1106.

White, M. T. (1986). Self constancy: The elusive concept. In *Self and Object Constancy: Clinical and Theoretical Perspectives*, ed. R. F. Lax, S. Bach, and J. A. Burland. New York: Guilford Press, pp. 73–94.

Whitmer, G. (2001). On the nature of dissociation. *Psychoanalytic Quarterly* 70:807–837.

Wholley, C. (1925). A case of multiple personality. *Psychoanalytic Review* 13:344–345.

Winnicott, D. W. (1935). The manic defense. In *Through Pediatrics to Psychoanalysis: Collected Papers*. London: Routledge, pp. 129–144.

———. (1945). Primitive emotional development. *International Journal of Psycho-Analysis* 26:137–150.

———. (1953). Transitional objects and transitional phenomena. *International Journal of Psycho-Analysis* 34:89–97.

———. (1960a). Ego distortion in terms of true and false self. In *The Maturational Processes and the Facilitating Environment*. New York: International Universities Press, 1965, pp. 140–152.

———. (1960b). The theory of the parent-infant relationship. *International Journal of Psycho-Analysis* 41:585–595.

———. (1965a) The theory of the infant-parent relationship. In *The Maturational Processes and the Facilitating Environment*. London: Hogarth Press, pp. 37–55.

———. (1965b). *The Maturational Processes and the Facilitating Environment*. New York: International Universities Press.

———. (1971). *Playing and Reality*. New York: Basic Books, Inc.

———. (1974). Fear of Breakdown. *International Review of Psycho-Analysis* 1(1,2): 103–107.

Wolfenstein, M. (1966). How is mourning possible? *Psychoanalytic Study of the Child* 21:92–126.

Yates, S. (1935). Some aspects of time difficulties and their relation to music. *International Journal of Psycho-Analysis* 16:341–354.

Yehuda, R. (1999). Parental PTSD as a risk factor for PTSD. In *Risk Factors for Posttraumatic Stress Disorder*, ed. R. Yehuda. Washington, DC: American Psychiatric Press, Inc., pp. 93–123.

Yehuda, R., Grolier, J. A., Halligan, S. L., Meaney, M., and Bierer, L. M. (2004). The ACTH response to dexamethasone in PTSD. *American Journal of Psychiatry* 161:1397–1403.

Yehuda, R., Kahana, B. K., Binder-Brynes, K., Southwick, S. M., Mason, J. W., and Giller, E. L. (1995). Low urinary cortisol in Holocaust survivors with posttraumatic stress disorder. *American Journal of Psychiatry* 152:982–986.

Zetzel, E. R. (1949). Anxiety and the capacity to bear it. In *The Capacity for Emotional Growth*. New York: International Universities Press, 1970, pp. 33–52.

———. (1965). Depression and the incapacity to bear it. In *Drives, Affects, Behavior*, ed. M. Schur. New York: International Universities Press, pp. 243–274.

Index

About the Author

Ira Brenner, M.D. is a clinical professor of psychiatry at Jefferson Medical College and a training and supervising analyst at the Psychoanalytic Center of Philadelphia. He is also director of the adult psychotherapy training program at the center, where he teaches courses on trauma to students in both the analytic and psychotherapy curricula. He has lectured nationally and internationally and has written extensively on the topic of psychological trauma. Brenner's works include three books: *The Last Witness: The Child Survivor of the Holocaust* (1996), coauthored with Judith Kestenberg, M.D.; *Dissociation of Trauma: Theory, Phenomenology and Technique* (2001); and *Psychic Trauma: Dynamics, Symptoms and Treatment* (2004). He was awarded the Pierre Janet Writing Prize from the International Society for the Study of Dissociation for his 2001 book and the Gradiva Award Honorable Mention for his 2004 book. He maintains a private practice in suburban Philadelphia.